ROUTLEDGE LIBRARY EDITIONS: THE ADOLESCENT

Volume 2

ADOLESCENT GIRLHOOD

ADOLESCENT GIRLHOOD

MARY CHADWICK

Routledge
Taylor & Francis Group

LONDON AND NEW YORK

First published in 1932 by George Allen & Unwin Ltd

This edition first published in 2023
by Routledge
4 Park Square, Milton Park, Abingdon, Oxon OX14 4RN

and by Routledge
605 Third Avenue, New York, NY 10158

Routledge is an imprint of the Taylor & Francis Group, an informa business

ISBN: 978-1-032-37655-4 (Set)
ISBN: 978-1-032-38458-0 (Volume 2) (hbk)
ISBN: 978-1-032-38532-7 (Volume 2) (pbk)
ISBN: 978-1-003-34547-3 (Volume 2) (ebk)

DOI: 10.4324/9781003345473

Publisher's Note
The publisher has gone to great lengths to ensure the quality of this reprint but points out that some imperfections in the original copies may be apparent.

Disclaimer
The publisher has made every effort to trace copyright holders and would welcome correspondence from those they have been unable to trace.

ADOLESCENT GIRLHOOD

by

MARY CHADWICK

LONDON
GEORGE ALLEN & UNWIN LTD
MUSEUM STREET

FIRST PUBLISHED IN 1932

PREFACE

It may perhaps be an unwise policy to start a book with an explanation or an apology. But, nevertheless, upon reading through this book, one cannot help feeling that many subjects have of necessity been omitted altogether, or mentioned briefly, that one would have liked to include or to treat with more detail.

When one comes to consider the subject carefully, it appears to stretch out to an almost boundless horizon; and therefore one does not wish readers to gain an impression that the problems mentioned here are the only ones which the writer believes to be of importance, and that those not specified or only touched upon in passing have not yet been investigated, or are of slight significance only.

It has been taken for granted that all readers of this book will already be well informed concerning the general concepts of psychology and psycho-analysis, because, owing to the prominence given to recent discoveries during the last ten or twenty years, there are few of us who are not, when we are at all interested in these problems related to the development and bringing-up of the young. Therefore a great many of the terms used and elementary conceptions mentioned do not receive explanation, which would have been necessary several years ago.

The reasons for our selection of subjects have been various. In the first place, to have given a detailed description of all the difficulties from which the adolescent girl herself suffers, or through which she provides perplexities for those who have her welfare at heart, would, as may be clearly understood, have swelled the dimensions of the volume to an unwieldy size.

However, references in the Bibliography will enable readers who are especially interested in any problem, referred to briefly in the pages of this book, to follow it up for themselves, or, should their interest have been awakened in several topics, by what they may read about them here.

The aim of the present book is to put before the reader a general view of the more everyday problems of the girl at home and at school, and those which, in spite of their prevalence, do not seem to have gained as much attention or understanding as they merit and require.

A detailed discussion of more specialised matters connected with them, such as the psychological troubles from which adolescent girls may suffer, their delinquency, their preferences in books, art, and music, must be left for the moment, but may perhaps in the future, should the need become apparent, receive attention in a supplementary volume.

MARY CHADWICK

48 Tavistock Square
London

December 5, 1931

CONTENTS

SYNOPSIS OF CONTENTS

PART I. HISTORICAL

CHAPTER I

Why should the problems of adolescence be of such great importance?

Adolescence a time of recapitulation and transition.

Opportunities offered by the recapitulation.

Primitive initiation rites accepted the needs of the adolescent.

Present-day civilisations often fail to recognise them fully.

Reasons for this lack of recognition.

Consequences of the want of understanding.

How we make good our own disappointment in life by helping the adolescent to full development.

CHAPTER II

Among primitive peoples boys and girls may be brought up more or less together until puberty, but they are always separated then, if not before.

They are separated from each other and the community for certain reasons.

The place of the girl in the tribe in various parts of the world among the primitives.

Among certain Indian tribes adolescent girls are supposed to possess supernatural powers, not always malign.

CHAPTER III

PART II. HOME-LIFE

CHAPTER I

CHAPTER II

CHAPTER V

CHAPTER VI

CHAPTER IV

Our realisation of her difficulties necessary, without minimising or exaggerating them.

We should not confuse the problems of the modern adolescent with those of our own day and generation.

The adolescent girl needs all our sympathy and the knowledge that she can get our help when she wants it.

The danger of thrusting unwanted advice upon her. Helping her to find herself instead.

Putting possibilities in her way for sublimation.

"Vocational Guidance" versus Identification.

The psychology of shoe-laces.

What the adolescent girl may think of her elders.

She is often exceedingly critical of her parents, teachers, and older friends. This may annoy them or make them feel "nervous."

She fears criticism for herself, and only uses it upon others.

Impatience of others older than herself, especially of elderly teachers.

Searching for her own ideal in others.

The future before her.

PART I
HISTORICAL

CHAPTER I

INTRODUCTION

In considering the many problems that present themselves for solution during the life of any human being, we come to the conclusion that those which force themselves upon our notice connected with adolescence are some of the most complicated, if not the most important, during life, for the following reasons.

It is now generally accepted by psychologists, following upon the discoveries of psycho-analysis, that our first five years lay down the pattern for subsequent emotional tendencies, reactions, and behaviour. We continue to follow these lines for the rest of our lives, varying the details and adding to the design from time to time, it is true, as new influences increase our experience or teach us to modify the tendencies of original instincts and impulses. The attitude we come to adopt during childhood to those around us—parents, brothers and sisters, nurses and the rest—will be found again repeated not only in the home circle but, as our environment widens, among the families of our friends and the world of school, as well as afterwards in marriage relationships and those of business or profession.

These questions of the construction of character and personality, the psychological development of the child from infancy, have already been explained in a book published in 1928 (*Difficulties in Child Development*) where we attempted to show the foundation upon which human patterns are constructed. Here is to be found an explanation of their importance for subsequent reactions to environment, and especially their influence upon the transitional period of adolescence, which forms a bridge between childhood and maturity. It is because of this transitional quality that we may hesitate to call adolescence the most important stage of life.

It stands without doubt as a most significant palimpsest of combined experiences, incorporating the past with the present and predicting the future. But can one, in assessing the comparative values of the various parts of a bridge, think only of the span and negate the importance of the abutments from which it springs? If these were inadequate or not sufficiently sunk, the whole structure would not stand the strain for which it was intended. Neither could be of use separately for the purposes of transit: the abutments must carry the weight of the arch, while this fulfills the purpose. The symbolism of the bridge is not completely satisfactory from all points of view, however, although many are unassailable, because, in spite of the fact that the adolescent phase is the means whereby the person crosses from childhood to adult years, the abutments are unequal in this respect, transit must always take place from one direction only. On the one side we have an abutment which is short but of the utmost power, quickly passed in comparison with the other, which lengthens out into the long road of maturity. Time is a one-way street. There is no return except through memory, phantasies, or illness, in all cases a *psychological substitute* for return.

There are other similarities that we can find between the building of bridges and the study of the adolescent. In order to insure the efficiency of the bridge, it is necessary to possess a thorough knowledge of the materials to be used for its construction. We must also take into consideration the soil into which we must excavate to place the abutments; compute the loads which the bridge must be expected to carry; their impact, caused by the speed, which sets up vibrations in the fabric of the bridge. We should know the force of the prevailing winds to realise what must be allowed for wind pressure; the climate, in order to gauge temperature effect, as well as the other forces and stresses which the bridge must be capable of withstanding. We may apply this need for knowledge to the conditions which would make for the safety or dangers of adolescence in the case of any particular boy or girl. The materials to be used are the component instincts, and all that we mean by the psychological make-up of the person. The ground in which the abutments are sunk resembles the home-life of the child on the one side, of the future environment on the other. The loads, technically known as the *dead* and the *live* loads of the bridge, remind us in the first instance of the burden of the physical and psychological changes which confront the adolescent; in the second, the traffic of contacts with persons, who make up the human element of daily life, which sets up equally exacting vibrations, which must be allowed for when we consider the power of resistance of the bridge. Wind pressure, temperature effect, and other stresses or forces find their counterpart in emotional conflicts which come from within and without the young person, and may do untold damage if the original structure is not strong enough to bear the strain. Again, those responsible for the care of the bridge must be ever on the watch for deformation in the materials used and the effect of sudden flood or tempest while the bridge is under construction and use, just as we must be if we are to bear our responsibility to the young folks in our care. We should know and watch all these factors if we are to be adequate maintainers of the bridge.

We have already suggested that one of the special functions of this difficult phase is to bring again into the focus of the present the old tendencies of the past, its joys and sorrows, its conflicts and its triumphs. The same old rôles of childhood will now be re-enacted, but with costumes and gestures of the new period; the other actors and the supers on the stage will be changed. No longer will they be the home folks, but others, whom we persuade to speak their lines and carry on with the same business as before, so that we can repeat ours, sometimes exactly the same, occasionally with alterations, so that we may improve our parts to our liking. This repetition may bind us to it endlessly without allowing any possibility for escape from its tyranny, or give us a second chance to reconstruct some of the weak places in the old design, to gain a new perspective through bringing the old situations into line through our increased power of discrimination, so giving a better balance for the future superstructure.

Sometimes, however, the events and stresses of adolescence add to the former instability, widen old cracks, and cause so much damage to the personality that the work of repair cannot go on at the same time as the reconstruction and the daily routine of carrying the loads. In this case we shall have to call in an expert, who, having made a careful survey of the injury, advises suspending the traffic for a time, while thorough repair is carried out in order that permanent damage may not occur, which would make further use of the bridge uncertain or unsafe.

It is for reasons such as these that we may indeed regard adolescence as one of the most important stages in the series of repetitions, because, although the repeat patterns may and invariably do continue throughout our lives, they usually compel our attention then by their exaggerated quality. By this means we may now observe what we may have overlooked many times before—both strong as well as weak places in the structure of the girl's character. Then we shall know better how we may assist to counteract some of these distortions which have taken place through warping, caused by early mistakes in training; to strengthen places where there is extra strain; correct false lines that have crept in, marring the original design, because of some early tragedy, as well as to augment beautiful curves which fear and anxiety have almost obliterated.

There are two other important factors which must be kept in mind when we contemplate the necessary work that should be accomplished during adolescence. One is to reinforce existing material by providing gratifications for the dynamic forces of fundamental component instincts upon which the future destiny relies; the other, to see that there is an adequate system of safety-valves and ventilation-shafts. In this way the dangerous trends of the same impulses may be discharged and carry off surplus emotion attached to them, which adolescence increases, often creating a tension too great for assimilation that breaks through in some unwelcome demonstration, and to keep the whole aired by new experiences which prevent stagnation.

In many ways we may also liken the time of adolescence to a re-birth phantasy, such as often appears in the dreams of girls of this age. If, as we have already suggested, the whole of childhood's mental and emotional experiences are once more revived swiftly and at high pressure during this short space of time, out of this kaleidoscope gradually emerges the woman, young, and with her nascent maturity eager to continue the work of shaping herself upon the reconstructed lines.

The function of re-birth in adolescence was realised long ago, and among some of the peoples whom we now regard as primitive races. We constantly notice rituals, which clearly represent re-birth phantasies, appearing among the puberty ceremonials and initiation rites, to which both girls and boys were submitted before admission to the adult community. The present-day version of these old customs is of course to be found in Confirmation, which includes the same idea, although only in part.

When we come to examine those old rituals closely we shall see that in many ways the ancient peoples showed a clearer appreciation of the psychological needs of the youthful human being than many in the present. The needs, however, survive, strangely unchanged in spite of their failure to obtain recognition, and the young folks are obliged to find their own fulfilment of them. The demand for these essential elements of impulse gratification or discharge during adolescence often forms a cause of bitter strife between the new and the old generations. The latter look on and disapprove, but will not supply substitute, approved methods of gratification. Moreover, the older generation shows no hesitation in denouncing them. It is interesting to observe that there is usually more outspoken hostility awakened by adolescent manifestations in the girl than the boy, although we notice similar exaggerations, vanities, and efforts at ruthless self-expression in both.

It would seem, upon unprejudiced study, that the adolescent girl is less popular at home and in society than her brother; that more allowances are made for his childish outbursts of bad-temper than for his sister's irritability or tears. His clumsiness, due to rapid growth, is more easily condoned when he knocks over a table than when she spills her teacup. His vanities are regarded as more lovable than hers; his crude methods of demanding attention from those around will be overlooked, while they are severely criticised in his sister.

The Flapper or Backfisch is constantly under ridicule or anathema for one thing or another, but there is seldom any similar publicity given to the misdeeds of her male contemporary. It is significant in itself that he has not even been given a distinguishing name. He disappears from the comic or popular Press as the object of jokes or censure. No one writes to the papers to complain of his excesses, although he frequently shares them with the girls who come in for the blame, such as the extravagancies of the flapper at petting or necking parties. In the joke he ceases to be when he can no longer figure as the "flapper's little brother," until he reappears as a young man. Why should this veil of protection be spread over him during adolescence as though the subject were sacrosanct and he inviolable?

Yet among the primitive races seclusion for a certain period was necessary for the pubescent transition of either sex. Both were treated with equal seriousness as future men and women of the tribe, who would later shoulder corresponding burdens and responsibilities for the general welfare. This change in attitude from the past to the present is interesting to speculate upon, and to compare with the response of the adolescent girl and boy towards their reception by the older generation and their consequent attitude towards one another.

We may find it profitable briefly to discuss here, as well as later, some of the instinctual tendencies and unconscious wishes which find expression in modern adolescents, through curious outbreaks of an emotional nature or in phantasy. They may impress us as examples of atavistic repetition, whereby the individual once more shows the experiences of the race without conscious realisation of so doing; or it may seem to us that the original puberty rites were merely a direct result of demand and supply where primitive impulses were concerned, and so both simply represent a certain stage of development in the human mind, whether ontogenetic or phylogenetic. But we will return to discuss this further in the next chapter. We should also like to suggest here that the present attitude of the adults may represent a corresponding repetition of ancient custom, although so deeply disguised as to be almost unrecognisable without specific research.

We have already postulated that an essential element of adolescence is to provide for reconstruction of weak spots that have been left owing to difficulties in early years. But adolescence may not always fulfil its opportunity. We may only too often see an averagely happy childhood, which promised well for the future, fail in its fulfilment under too great strain from conflicts with which the natural physical strength or psychological tenacity of the young person was not capable of resisting. The immature psyche could not respond to the increase of heavy demands which swept in from too many directions at once. When the unabsorbed shock of adolescent stress goes unnoticed and unaided too long, disastrous consequences may be feared, which it is hard to eradicate later.

One of the most curious phenomena of our present-day culture is certainly the fact that adolescent manifestations frequently seem to arouse intense hostility and an unwillingness on the part of adults to recognise their urgency. They neither realise nor cater for the needs of those undergoing its stress, although naturally all of us have passed through the same or similar conflicts, which one might suppose would produce a belief that others may suffer at this time. The vague observations that adolescence is a "difficult time," the persistent attempts to avoid giving any definite information to adolescents concerning themselves or their mental and physical changes, leave them blindly struggling with their conflicts and ignorance, as well as with this strange behaviour of their elders. A straightforward meeting of the problems, or even an honest attempt to do so, would in itself dispel many of the discomforts of that age, among which should be reckoned the failure to obtain information or explanation of the feelings aroused by the upheaval of old values and a stirring of new ones. Another wish that is generally found then is that they should be openly regarded as approaching maturity. The grudging acceptance of this fact by adults, especially in the case of girls, be it outspoken or merely sensed by its victims, tends to provoke hostility towards their elders, or to increase it, which is a marked characteristic of this phase.

The puberty rites among the primitives were often cruel and severe, it is true; but can we say that the conflicts endured by modern adolescents, sensitive enough to be affected by lack of understanding, are less agonising because they are principally psychological instead of physical? Ancient usage left the young people without any doubt that they were relinquishing childhood, and were soon to be received into the company of adults. The exact extent of their own duties and privileges, as well as those of their older neighbours, was strictly laid down, and no question could remain as to their subsequent functions in life. They were told precisely what would be expected of them in the future, both positively and negatively. It was explained fully what was obligatory for them from now on, and equally clearly what early habits must be surrendered with the assumption of adult estate. They learned also what was taboo. The uncertainty of life's requirements is one of the chief difficulties of many adolescents, and we find them striving to discover new rules for life, sometimes through experiment, sometimes by research into books of all kinds, but rarely by the direct method of questioning adults, since they have already proved this a failure for obtaining information.

We have referred to this modern trend of civilisation to be reluctant to face the questions of adolescence, apparently to simplify their responsibilities. The hints which are given are vague or so veiled that they convey little to those they are meant to enlighten. Alarming warnings, nevertheless, are uttered in language which still the boy or girl can scarcely understand about the dangers of adolescent cravings, which are sometimes not even an accurate representation of facts. But still they are terrifying enough to produce, or rather reanimate, old fears, which add to the current conflict instead of reducing it.

It is a perturbing thought that most of the little booklets, written ostensibly to help adolescents, seem to agree that nothing need be dealt with but the temptations and evils of the age, and avoid giving any constructive help or explanation of existing difficulties. They want bread and are offered stones in these warnings of hideous consequences of tendencies which are normal enough then, and in themselves harmless. Medical men and ministers of religion are often strangely the authors, or reputed authors, of these pernicious little books, or perhaps they merely allow their professional status to give weight to their already ponderous utterances. How does this come about? If their actual knowledge of the subject justified their selection to write these pamphlets, one would suppose they would be aware the warnings were false statements, or at best twisted misinterpretations of the truth. In this case it is surprising that men of professional standing should consent to give publicity to a misrepresentation of facts, although they usually hide their identity and make use of their profession to sponsor their views.

If, on the other hand, they believe what they write, their scientific knowledge must either be insufficient for their task or they are suffering from psychological blindness to facts through some personal repression. Yet parents, teachers, and others put this class of literature into the hands of young people, possibly without reading it first, either not realising the possibility of inaccuracy or not caring and knowing maybe enough about the subject to question whether they are passing on the truth or lies which will poison these impressionable young minds.

This state of affairs sounds culpable set down thus, and we are forced to wonder how it can happen. It may well be considered as one of the riddles connected with the adult attitude to which we have referred before. But what possible reasons can there be to account for such strange behaviour, which in fact produces an effect exactly contrary to that which the adult apparently wishes to achieve?

Upon careful examination of particular instances, it would seem that this failure to recognise the possible effect of false information, or even the fact that it is inaccurate, is often the result of ignorance of these matters on the part of adults, probably due to some sex repression, and also shows the existence of a residue of personal psychological difficulties on their part. It will likewise frequently illustrate the tendency to repeat, but in this case the repetition echoes the behaviour of the last generation towards themselves that they are now passing on to the next. In addition, it provides an outlet for their own sadistic impulses, which the ancient puberty rites enunciated plainly and consciously in the initiation ceremonies, which must have furnished gratification both to those who carried them out as well as to the masochistic desires of the candidates.

When we come to discuss the problems which are associated with the emotional conflicts of adolescence we shall see the sadistic impulse especially clamouring for an outlet, both directly and indirectly, either in its active or passive form, which includes the element of love gratification in which it usually plays a strong part, even if disguised, at this age. It is interesting to observe that these sadistic and aggressional impulses possess a tendency to arouse a similar desire for emotional gratification in those who are in immediate contact with the adolescent, and that two or more persons will frequently enjoy mutual satisfaction together.

We should reflect that in the struggles of adolescents for self-expression this component often becomes dramatically clear. Young people who are strong and healthy are anxious to prove their power in a battle of wills, just as much as they show a marked preference at this age for games in which trials of skill, physical endurance, or courage are conspicuous among the components of the game. The older opponents in contests of every kind are upon their mettle, and we generally find them offering dogged resistance to the young contestants, frequently submitting to defeat with a very bad grace, should it occur.

The physically weak adolescent, or one whose psychological balance has been impaired by unfavourable experiences in childhood, will often show great reluctance to compete with any rival. Games will provide no attraction or be a source of absolute torture, and we shall find both boys and girls shrinking equally from any action which would bring them into direct conflict with parents or authorities.

We may also notice an arresting correlation between this desire for emotional or mental contests and pleasure in muscular activity, as well as finding that the interest in games may correspond with, or in some cases be substituted by, love of handicrafts which necessitate muscular effort. The study of the comparative values of various activities will be extremely useful when we come to consider the problems of adolescence from the point of view of providing sublimations and safety-valves which will give gratification to the instincts as well as drain off surplus emotion connected with the sadistic and aggressional impulses in useful and constructive ways. Left to break through where they will or can without guidance, these tendencies will often find asocial discharge in mere revolt and destruction, which will ultimately prove as disappointing to themselves as needlessly wasteful of energy, which rightly directed would be of the utmost value to the community.

Through considerate understanding and guiding of these dynamic forces arising from the component impulses we may accomplish a more satisfactory future development of latent powers than by merely producing a series of stunted inhibitions as the result of trying to eradicate and curb the exuberances of youth by prohibiting forms of activity they have chosen because no others were at hand. We often quote the old saying, although sometimes with an apologetic smile at its triteness, "You cannot expect old heads on young shoulders." Yet at the same time we behave as though we require our young folks to resemble ourselves in mature tastes and preferences, and to possess a similar experienced attitude towards life, which can only result from extensive knowledge of the world, by which ultimately we have selected our philosophy. We deny them the essential qualities of youth, the inevitable results of abundant energy, natural keenness to explore the unknown, to accumulate experiences to prove whether they get the same impressions as others have described.

We must also realise, along with the factor that they, being essentially young, fresh, and eager to try all that life has to offer, that their minds as well as their bodies will, if healthy, be restless at this age, and therefore differ from us who, being older, are becoming tired in body if not equally so in mind. We have lived. They are at the threshold. We can kill their youth by inhibiting their activity, but we cannot revive that which we have killed, except with the utmost difficulty. If youth be ignored in the attempt to be old before the time, because we seem to scoff at the ways of the young, it cannot be regained. If we show maturity in such an unattractive guise through our own disappointment, so that those following fear to grow old in case they might resemble us and halt half-way, we have sinned against the new generation.

We may be jealous of their youth, because maybe we in the past also denied it by trying to be old prematurely, putting on the semblance of years and experience for fear others should laugh at our inexperience. We are envious now, perhaps, and therefore try to keep the young from their birthright even as we, thinking, with the strange talion logic that obtains in the depths of the unconscious mind, that by so doing we may yet make the balance even. But this cannot be. We are better able to recover our lost youth vicariously by helping the young to obtain every advantage of their growing-time, by giving them the sun and the air and all the blessings of freedom, as well as our good will.

They will be grateful, even if they show it brusquely, which those who do not understand call *rudeness*. We shall understand all that it meant to them when we find in the future that it bears abundant fruit.

CHAPTER II

THE ADOLESCENT GIRL AMONG PRIMITIVE RACES

In order the better to understand many of the problems of the adolescent girl of to-day we must retrace the history of her evolution from the earliest records which are available. Not only do the old views upon the girl in relation to her seniors and their attitude to her throw some light upon the situation which still obtains, but we find similar fears and phantasies existing in the unconscious minds of modern girls which were current then, even if they have had no chance to learn about the experiences of adolescents in the past.

The fact that this should be the case is not only arresting in itself but it also explains much of what is so hard to grasp in the attitude of the older generation to the younger, and the desires of girls for gratification of certain impulses which become so plain during this age. A comparative study of both demonstrates how the mind of primitive peoples tried to deal with the problems associated with this stage of growth frankly and in a symbolic manner, which we so frequently try to ignore or repress.

When we come to read books describing primitive customs in bygone ages, or those which still survive in remote parts among backward races of the present, we generally find that it is more difficult to obtain accurate or detailed information concerning the customs which have prevailed among the girls than among the boys. This is due to various reasons. In the first place, explorers or anthropologists engaged upon research have, in the past, been men in contact with men of the tribes. It is usual in all parts of the world for puberty rites to be kept strictly hidden from the sight and knowledge of the other sex. Therefore it is possible that the men of the tribe have no very great knowledge of what does happen in the case of the girl's entry into womanhood, or, should they know something about the rites, might pretend that they do not, because it would be beneath their dignity to do so, or against tribal custom to reveal them to a stranger. It would certainly be contrary to all primitive conventions for the male scientists to question the old women of the tribe, who are entrusted with carrying out the girls' puberty rites, because of the usual regulations regarding the seclusion of women, as well as owing to difficulties relating to speech. In many parts of the world each tribe has two languages, if not three: one for the men, another for the women, and the third in which they are allowed to communicate with one another. It is strictly forbidden generally, upon pain of death, for the women to know the men's language. Therefore this increases the difficulty of gaining information concerning female puberty rites. Complications might even arise if the services of an interpreter were requisitioned. He might pretend ignorance of the women's language, or it might be true, and in any case it would be hard to determine whether the information he produced would be correct.

The details of instruction given to the girl at puberty are not so available for this reason as those handed down to the boy, also because those concerning the latter are usually carried out in the presence of the whole male population, whilst the girl is initiated in seclusion and secrecy. We read thus, in W. D. Hambly's interesting book, *Origins of Education among Primitive Peoples*: "Modern anthropological literature is replete with information which may be used to illustrate the methods and ideals of primitive man, who undoubtedly concerns himself with the general and specialised education of boys. On the contrary, there is a paucity of evidence respecting the training of girls; but the lack of direct evidence by no means indicates that primitive people have excluded young females from the benefits of preparation for tribal life. Peoples of rudimentary culture are extremely reticent concerning all rites of a sacred nature, and there is little prospect of augmenting our knowledge of the training of primitive women unless the number of specially trained women investigators is greatly increased. Women are extremely unlikely to favour the male anthropologist with a description of their customs, and even the men of the tribe, provided they are fully acquainted with the proceedings of the other sex, are very taciturn when questioned about the women."

During recent years, however, several books have appeared which deal with these interesting problems of girls' puberty rites and initiation ceremonies, which have been either the work of women who have spent many years in the countries about which they write or written from information obtained from medical women, nurses, or missionaries who have extensive knowledge of the conditions prevailing among the women and girls in that locality. Nevertheless, for the bulk of information we possess upon the subject we must still consult earlier books of reference written by male scientists, who first put before us what they were able to collect by whatever means they could—observation or hearsay—although it is not so extensive as that which describes the ceremonies common among the boys.

Chief of these classics are the two long series of valuable books furnished by those veteran pioneers Sir George Fraser and Havelock Ellis. Especially in *The Golden Bough*, the first-named author relates customs, gathered from all parts of the world, concerning the puberty rites of girls and other matters connected with them which have since been corroborated by the women investigators, who, by adding a few details here and there, give us a clearer picture of the state of affairs existing in women's life in the home or as a unit in the community among the primitive folk.

In *The Origins of Education* W. D. Hambly also points
out the value of the pubertal seclusion for the purposes of
education, and gives a clear view of the subjects which were
considered as of the utmost importance in different countries, according to tribal habits and the ways in which
they obtained a livelihood, for the instruction of the adolescent girl, as well as the manner in which the knowledge was
imparted and by whom. But we will return to these particular questions in greater detail later on in this chapter,
as they are necessary in estimating the extent and directions
of educational development which has taken place during
the centuries.

Three women especially are associated with research upon
this subject: Alexandra David-Neel, who has written several
books and presented interesting papers to scientific societies
on the subject of the women in Tibet, including the poly-
androus tribes; Margaret Mead, who carried out a special
inquiry in Samoa; and Mrs. Seligman, who has obtained
some most valuable material respecting customs related to
the women and girls of the Arab and other native tribes of
modern Egypt.

Margaret Mead's book, *Coming of Age in Samoa*, gives
us an interesting account of the life of the girls there, from
childhood, throughout adolescence, to marriage. She seems
to have learned to know some of them well, and to have
liked them, too, during her residence upon the island for
several months, while conducting this research in connection
with the Columbia University of New York. Further knowledge was gained from those who had been many years upon
the island, who had a closer acquaintanceship with the girls
because of their professional duties.

The preface of this book contains one sentence which is
of peculiar interest to us. Professor Franz Boas writes thus:
"The results of her painstaking investigation confirm the
suspicion, long held by anthropologists, that much of what

we ascribe to human nature is no more than a reaction to the restraints put upon us by civilisation." If this is the truth, then we can in no way be surprised that we see the girl of to-day weaving her phantasies upon themes which were associated with rituals of a bygone age or race, and repeating in her day-dreams material similar to that which appears among the legends and folk-lore of ancient cultures.

Let us now return to a more detailed account of the most important beliefs connected with puberty in the past and see how the primitives set about preparing their young people not only to carry on the traditions of the tribe but also to equip them for the particular life and occupations of the locality in which they were going to live. We may see, if we study the puberty rites and customs of the various races about whom we have been able to gain fairly extensive information, that these tribal laws must at some remote time have been worked out with careful thought, since they so well serve the purpose for which they are intended. At first glance, perhaps, it may seem that they often resemble childish games, and show evidence of unnecessary cruelty or typical savagery. But when we examine them more closely we realise that primitive peoples, being firm believers in symbolism, chose these methods as the best way of impressing important matters upon the minds of the younger generation. Also, that they realised it to be essential to pass on certain information to maintain the health and strength of the tribe. It may be as well to point out here the well-known similarity between ancient customs or occupations, that were originally the serious affairs of life among these primitive peoples, and some of the familiar games of childhood. Karl Groos, in an excellent book, *The Play of Man*, explains that the fondness of the child for playing with bows and arrows and building wigwams is a survival of the serious interests of men and women in the early days of the world, although it is now an amusement.

In place of first importance we may mention *the period of seclusion* of varying duration, because of its prevalence among puberty customs in all parts of the world, during which tribal lore, ritual dances, and knowledge necessary for adult life were imparted to the adolescent. We may gather from the universal practice of this seclusion and instruction that the primitives have recognised that organised education was needful, and that it was not enough for the girl to be allowed to pick up what she could in her own home. It would also appear that this time was important in its symbolic significance as typifying death and re-birth, the end of childhood, and the beginning of the new adult life, in order to help the next generation to realise their fresh responsibilities as members of the adult community.

Next in significance among the initiation ceremonies we should mention those which comprise *the endurance tests*, some of which are connected with native ideas of beautifying the body by carrying out most elaborate designs in tattooing or scarifying, which one would imagine must be most painful. Yet the victim is obliged to submit to the operation without protest or uttering any expression of suffering, lest she become an object of ridicule in the tribe for the rest of her life. Other tests are connected usually with marriage-preparation customs, often the cutting of the clitoris, or a ritual defloration. Marriage will generally be arranged for her as soon as the puberty customs are completed, when she is allowed to return to the family.

Broadly speaking, we may divide these ceremonies and instructions into two classes: (*a*) those which concern the preparation of the girl herself for the future; and (*b*) the regulations to which she must conform to safeguard the community from dangers which will be apprehended from her presence among them.

The actual origins of these various rites and the ideas

behind them are in many cases impossible to ascertain. But by comparing them with other symbolic actions, beliefs, and fears which are to be found in individuals at other periods of the world's history, or even in our own day, we sometimes believe we are able to learn something of their intention.

To the primitive mind everything that is encountered in life, which is obviously highly important, and which they can neither understand nor control, seems to be of supernatural origin—that is, the work of gods or evil spirits—and connected with magic in some way. They attempt to deal with it, therefore, in a fashion which serves to explain it to themselves, and pass on the same theories, of course, to the girls whom they instruct. Having arrived at some method of explanation which satisfies themselves, they will, through symbolic representation, enact what they feel to have been the cause of the occurrence, and thus show the idea they can control it to some extent through this imitative magic. By certain charms or spells they hope to persuade the gods to give them the necessaries to support life, or to propitiate the demons to leave their homes unmolested and turn their attention to those of their enemies. For such reasons we find that a good deal of the girls' education is taken up with learning the most common charms and simple magic to safeguard the household in times of need, somewhat in the same way that our girls might attend a first-aid class to teach them what to do in an emergency before the doctor could be found.

It is the habit of very many persons to regard the lives of the savages as being ideally happy and simple, free from all restraint and responsibility, without work or hardship. They connect their idea of primitive folk with a musical comedy representation of some South Sea island, where it is always a sunny, languorous afternoon; where dances and love, which is always romantic with generally a happy ending, or one of sentimental tragedy, perhaps, but not too acute, are the order of the day and night. But they do not see behind the scenes of their island of bliss the actual hard work that has to be accomplished by some members of the tribe, usually the women and girls, so that the rest may be idle, and that the traders, who generally exploit the ignorance of the natives, may grow rich upon them.

They know nothing of the extreme complications of the marriage laws, or those governing inheritance; the long and arduous training which goes to the performance of the tribal dances, which express much that the foreigner never suspects; the fears that oppress the people arising from the teaching of their religion, about the calamities that may befall should an island deity be offended. They have not heard of troubles that can come upon a family from some feud with members of another totem group, nor the difficulties of avoiding death in savage warfare, by some beast of prey, or even as the result of a spell cast by a local witch-doctor in the pay of an enemy, if another mightier than he or she is not found immediately and induced by some means or another to take up their case. Neither do they reckon the dangers which arise from the elements: hurricane or cloud-burst, earthquake or a prolonged drought, that may reduce a prosperous people suddenly and completely to a state of famine from which there is no way of escape except by the migration of the entire tribe.

When we take this side of the picture into consideration we are forced to the conclusion that what we have imagined to be the most cruel and *unnecessary* factors of the initiation rites, the endurance tests, have a reasonable motive after all. Among these peoples it is absolutely necessary for the adults to possess a high degree of personal courage, and to be capable of endurance for the daily exigencies of life. Danger and privation are frequent, and they must be met with valour that will not fail before hardship.

It is well, therefore, to put before the young as an integral part of their preparation for the future, as well as a virtue that will win them high estimation in the tribe, the possession of courage, so that it may not escape their notice. Thus endurance tests justify their place at the entrance to adult life, to show that this resource will be needed to win through at a crisis; and not to falter under pain or privation is a sign of maturity.

This may be compared with a habit of many adolescent girls of to-day who, without knowing about these primitive ordeals, will set themselves the same standard tests of endurance and courage, and will seek to repeat the same actions of the past. Sometimes several will share them together, and react to them also in the same way, regarding with admiration and acceptance those who succeed in passing these tests without flinching, and feel any who cannot do so without signs of fear and pain to be worthy of pity and contempt. In this way it would seem to show that the primitive custom not only served to teach what was thought to be essential but at the same time provided an emotional outlet for the masochistic and sadistic impulses, which at this age are always particularly strong and need some kind of gratification. Should they gain no opportunity for discharge or be too strongly repressed, they usually become unduly inhibited.

The signal for the commencement of the segregation period is generally the onset of the first menstruation, which for the primitive marks the commencement of puberty, as well as for a great many of the lay public to-day. The girl is then hurried away to some special hut prepared for her in a secluded part of the forest or away from the rest of the tribe elsewhere. She will be attended by her mother, by some old women, or in some parts by girls who are not yet pubescent. The customs regarding the selection of the attendants at this time vary greatly, as also do the experiences of the girl during her seclusion and its duration.

It may, in fact, be modified to last but a few days or a

week, or stretch out over a period of months and even years. She may be kept in a cage or a dark hut alone in the forest, or slung up in a tightly laced hammock in a corner of the family hut. Sometimes she will be confined in absolute solitude, or with a party of contemporaries. She may be kept upon extremely low diet, or restricted to a very few articles of food, so that she emerge from this banishment weak and emaciated, or in other parts, especially in Africa, she will be fed upon a particularly fattening diet until she attains the rotundity which is there considered to be a mark of great feminine beauty.

The idea of slinging her up in the hammock is so that her feet shall not touch the ground; in other localities the same motive is carried out by putting her into a cage of wicker-work or some other material, frequently so small that she is obliged to remain in a crouching position, because it is impossible for her to lie down or stand upright. Darkness is generally another important element of this particular kind of initiatory ceremony, in which it is not difficult to recognise the death and re-birth phantasy. She must not put her foot to the ground, nor must the sun or direct daylight fall upon her, or she will be followed by bad luck.

During her seclusion the birth-idea is often increased by giving her a new name, by which she will be known when she returns as a woman of the tribe. This finds a present-day equivalent in the privilege of adding another name or changing an existing one at Confirmation, although it is seldom claimed.

We should remember the twofold purpose particularly in connection with the girl's seclusion, and its close alliance with menstrual prohibitions, because not only does it protect the girl from the dangers of sunlight and other evils, but acts as a protection to the community from the injuries that they anticipate from her. A menstruating woman is always thought to be a menace to safety, and she has to obey strict rules that limit her activities, which we will explain later; and the girl at her first menses is bound by still more stringent laws.

Many curious theories are current to account for the phenomenon of the menstrual bleeding. It will sometimes be held that a wild beast has bitten her, or that some demon has had sexual relations with her in the woods. She becomes taboo until the flow has ceased, and certainly until this happens she is not allowed to return to her home. Among some of the North American tribes, however, the adolescent girl is supposed to possess supernatural powers of various kinds, not always injurious, and especially that of divination.

It is interesting to observe how this idea of hiding the adolescent girl in the dark will reappear in the myths of the later stages of cultural development, and also among the phantasies of the modern girl. For instance, we are all familiar with the legend of Persephone and Demeter, the daughter who was condemned to leave her mother to spend each winter in the dim underworld and return again in the spring with the flowers. She is probably connected with these still earlier puberty seclusion rites, which later have become in an inverted way connected with sun worship and a fertility cult. We find also that frequently an adolescent girl will suffer from recurrent anxiety as the days get shorter, which will reach its climax about midwinter, becoming so intense that it will completely destroy for her any pleasure in the festivities of Christmas and the New Year. She knows nothing about the old beliefs and relative legends, and yet tells one how ill she feels, and weak, so that she fears she is going to die. One generally finds, however, that as the days lengthen she gradually revives and forgets the anxiety, until it returns again the following year. These death and re-birth phantasies will often be a source of intense suffering to the adolescent girl, although when she can she generally keeps them a profound secret from her most intimate friends and relations.

We have already mentioned that the period of seclusion is of importance from an educational point of view. Let us now inquire what some of the subjects are in which the initiate receives instruction. It is common to find that the choice of subjects varies with the part of the world in which she lives, and the kind of occupations by which her tribe gets its livelihood. Where agriculture is the main interest of the community it will be modified according to whether the work is mainly carried out by the men or the women. Should the men do the work in the fields, the girls will have to learn principally the preparation of the raw materials the men produce, the cooking and preservation of food-stuffs. They will be occupied also with the weaving of grass mats or those of palm fronds, the making of cooking-pots, baskets, and other household requisites as well as clothing, and the care of the children. Lastly, but none the less important, will be the learning of all the charms and spells that are necessary for the fertility of the fields and insuring a good harvest.

Among tribes whose chief support is provided by hunting, the girl will generally learn the skinning of the animals and how to prepare and cure the skins for use in the house or for clothes, as well as cooking and drying the meat for use in time of scarcity. This is the principal occupation among the women and girls of the Eskimo tribes.

The lives of the primitives are largely influenced by magic, domestic and professional, and there are a vast number of rituals for private use which must be known by the women as well as the men, so that each may use the appropriate spell at the right time to bring good luck or to avert disaster. The women have usually to attend to the making of certain ritual foods or drinks which will be needed to celebrate special festivals. The men and women of the tribe are generally separated for the rites of their religious observances, but we find that both sexes regard them usually as of vital importance, whether carried out by means of sacrifices, incantations, imitative magic, or by the ritual dances, which severally vary in importance from one place to another.

All these matters will generally be imparted to the girl at puberty, together with some of the most common rulings and customs concerning births, death, and marriages, as well as restrictions of intermarriage between various totem groups. She must also understand thoroughly the regulations regarding the menstrual prohibitions, and those which must be observed during pregnancy, child-birth, and lactation. The infringement of these fundamental laws is often punishable with death, and so we shall understand that it is essential that she shall be instructed in an impressive way, so that she will not forget them.

During menstruation, and in some parts during pregnancy, it is forbidden to her to touch the hunting-gear of the men or their weapons of war. She usually must not prepare nor cook any food to be shared with the rest of the household, but especially by the menfolk; she must not go near their bedding nor clothes lest serious calamity befall them or ill luck come upon the household. In some tribes the girl is given information about local methods of contraception and of procuring abortion, if and when children are not required. The number of children in a family will at times have to be severely restricted in case of famine, or when the tribe is nomadic and it is impossible to carry several tiny children as well as all the rest of the family possessions. The attitude of different tribes and races is extremely divergent concerning sexual intercourse between young persons previous to marriage. In some parts a girl is not considered marriageable until she has proved her fecundity by bearing at least one child to a prospective suitor. Among other tribes, however, pre-nuptial intercourse is punished by the death of either or both of the offenders, and the virginity of the bride is essential.

We are also told that in many parts of Australia the facts of procreation are not known among the primitives, and that fatherhood as such is unrecognised. Sexual intercourse is in no way connected with the birth of offspring, but it will be said that a woman becomes pregnant because she passes a stone or tree, where dwells an ancestral spirit, and he has entered her to be born again. Other tribes will ascribe the birth of a child to the woman having swallowed a fish while bathing, or because a flower fell upon her shoulder. Naturally the girls of the tribe receive this information too, although we are forced to wonder whether the women are quite so ignorant as they are supposed to be, or if this is only what is told to inquisitive strangers who visit the locality upon research.

Nevertheless, one comes across equal ignorance of the truth among the uneducated classes in modern present-day civilisations, sometimes also among those whom one would suppose to have had correct information given them at some time in their lives. The birth phantasies, or rather procreation theories, of adolescence are often just as picturesque and fanciful, similar to these beliefs of the backward peoples. These, of course, we meet again among the Greek myths, such as the impregnation of Danæ by the golden shower, and in countless fairy-tales, where the birth of the long-awaited infant follows upon the queen swallowing some curious object provided by a fairy or because three red poppies floated in her bath.

The ignorance concerning these matters may, on the other hand, be due to sexual repressions and to guilt connected with the subject, as Professor Sigmund Freud has pointed out so clearly in his book *Totem and Taboo*, which gives us so much enthralling information upon this subject.

CHAPTER III

THE ADOLESCENT GIRL IN THE FAIRY-TALE

Fairy-tales occupy a particularly interesting place in the history of fiction. It would seem that they are to be found in some form among all peoples, in all parts of the world, and in every age. For what purpose they came into being is a question which may well claim our attention for a short time. Who made them, and why should they bear such a remarkable resemblance, when they form part of the mental entertainment of children as well as their elders in parts of the world between which there have apparently been no direct communication?

To answer this last question many theories have been put forward, similar to those which attempt to account for the same affinity which has been observed in legend, custom, and myth. Chief among these has been the view that all peoples are descended from a common Aryan stock, fragments of which have migrated to all corners of the world, bearing with them their customs, myths, legends, and fairy-tales. Yet we find the likeness also among folks who cannot be traced as having an Aryan descent. Other investigators have been doubtful of this opinion upon many grounds, and prefer the rival one, that they were carried from one country to another by settlers or by captives of war. In connection with this view we should bear in mind that raids were often made upon neighbouring or even distant tribes in search of women, either as wives or slaves. In this case we can imagine that they might try to amuse their children, or those of whom they had charge, with the tales of their own homes. Yet another supposition, perhaps the most modern as well as the most plausible of all, is that they are the crystallised day-dreams of peoples dwelling in all ages and lands. Thus they are similar because their wishes are alike, which are the basis of the phantasies. They appear in all epochs, and give equal entertainment to divers folk because fundamentally the strata which build up the human mind are the same from the lower stages upwards, and that a particular development of mind with corresponding wishes will create for its enjoyment myths or fairy-tales which adequately enough express the ideas that are current in such a person.

This is doubtless true of a very large number of the fairy-tales which have been popular throughout the ages, but there is also another point to consider. Who made them, and for what purpose were they made, other than that of amusement? Internal evidence would seem to show that another motive of these stories was that of warning or instruction. We may believe that the obvious moral which is attached to this class of fairy-tale points to the fact that they were early ways of teaching children ethics. They would represent to the child that it was good to be kind to the poor, to the feeble-minded, the old, and to animals, adding the magic element in the form of rewards and punishments to add point to the stories. These would appear to be some of the earliest forms, and can be discovered among quite ancient and primitive races, contemporary with the puberty rites described in the last chapter.

It would seem that we can learn a great deal about the origin and purpose of the particular tale from its content and structure, and in this way distinguish the different groups of fairy-story which have been familiar to us from childhood. Those intended for the instruction of the child will show the obvious moral attached to the actions of the young persons described in them. For instance, the kind child who helps the old woman and speaks kindly to her will have gold or pearls fall out of her mouth, while the rude one produces frogs or snails. A typical warning story is that of Red Riding Hood. The little girl runs into danger because she did not obey her mother's instructions to refrain from speaking to strangers in the wood, a lesson that may still have the effect of terrifying nervous children, and will sometimes follow them throughout life, implanting a fear of strangers, the origin of which they forget, although the anxiety remains and makes social relationships almost impossible.

But what are we to believe concerning the structure and motive of the fairy-tale where an adult gets into trouble for ill-treating the adolescent girl? Surely grown-up people would not willingly put themselves in such an invidious position before their youthful hearers? How may we account for this variety?

We have already mentioned the day-dream origin of fairy-tales, representing wishes. These are probably specimens of this type, and show us the phantasies of the young people themselves, made either to entertain themselves or one another as mutual phantasies, to give themselves some sort of consolation for their troubles in a world which provided them with little in reality. There is also another possibility of their invention, which is that they might have been made up and told to children by one of the foreign captives in a household where she was unhappy, and so found her compensation in a phantasy of ill-treatment by some tyrant, who would be her own employer disguised for the purpose of the tale.

This suggestion might easily furnish us with a solution, especially when we consider that these girls were in many cases quite young themselves. Regarded from this angle, the tale of Cinderella, for example, in all its variants that can be found all over the globe, takes on a new significance. The slave in the household entertains her master's children with this day-dream of her own. She, by means of identification, is the Cinderella, eagerly awaiting the coming of the

Prince and longing for the downfall of her mistress, as well as the two ugly sisters, who would be the elder daughters of the house, who had all the fun while she had the hard work and the crusts to eat.

There is also an additional interest which may be extracted from our reading of fairy-tales, which does not fall into those already suggested. This is the wealth of detail to be gathered directly and indirectly concerning the ideas, wishes, and home-life of the adolescent girl during these dim ages which are represented in these stories. Nowhere else can we gain such a complete commentary of these subjects as in the representative phantasies of the individual and the race in which they were evolved. We may learn here of the daily doings of the young people: the occupations, work, and pleasures of all classes of society in the various countries where we collect them; their joys and their sorrows, their position in their homes, local customs concerning abandonment in times of famine, marriage customs, as well as the adventures they would have liked to have, the magic spells of witches to overcome, the rewards from the fairy-godmother to compensate hardship.

Except from details of customs introduced during the tale, it is exceedingly difficult to determine the age of any particular story, and then we can never be sure whether these may not have been introduced at a later period in an attempt to bring a still older version up to date. We may keep this in mind, however, that the atmosphere of the tale will probably approximate with the period at which it started on its travels, and also contain a good deal of local colour from the land of its birth, or represent those of the childhood of the narrator, even should she have moved into another country. We may often, when reading these old stories, with this idea in mind of trying to place the age of a tale, be able to do so by noticing the typical occupations described in it, or some custom introduced which was a daily occurrence at a certain time, or by the marriage regulations that are introduced.

It is for reasons such as these that the fairy-tale is of such peculiar interest in this investigation of the position of the adolescent at different times in the world's history. In this way we may gather information which will no doubt be accurate enough to give us details of the home-life and family relationships in the past, as well as their feelings about the things which happened to them, and their ways of trying to escape from their troubles, which are impossible to obtain in any other way. History is remarkably silent concerning the daily routine and occupations of its growing girls, even if it should give us scanty information concerning the boys, their sports, pastimes, duties, and education at times.

In order to study the life of the girl in the early days we are obliged to glean fragments from whatever source we may, and in legend and fairy-tale we have a rich field, since, strange as it may seem, when the heroine is a girl, we will usually notice she is an adolescent or in the few years which immediately precede puberty—that is, from twelve years old upwards. Why this should be so is not easy to say.

The country from which any particular variant of a story comes will give us the specific details of her life and the prevailing customs of the time in which it was written, the duties that were assigned to her in that state of life in which she found herself, her amusements, and the current beliefs in magic or witchcraft typical of the time and locality. We are shown clearly the differences in the lives of the various social classes, the young princess and the wood-cutter's daughter, the girl brought up in the home of a prosperous merchant or the beggar maid. For this reason a comparative study of the basic fairy-tales with their local variations would make an exceedingly interesting research, besides providing valuable material that cannot be derived from other sources, as well as indicating the prevalent ideas about adolescent girls at various past ages, and the girls' own wishes and fundamental tendencies also, so that we may compare the output of the unconscious mind then and now.

We may thus learn as much about the psychology of adolescent girls from these fairy-stories as from any other human document they have been instrumental in originating —that is, a diary, adventure story, or a day-dream. They show us how the environment in which a girl grows up will be woven into her life with elaborate variations, and how she will seek to alter the dull routine of her home-life with romantic adventures. It is also interesting to notice the differences in atmosphere that are provided by the psychology of the country or race from which they spring. That is, the tales which come to us from France have a quality quite different from those which were collected from all parts of Germany by the Brothers Grimm. The tales of Andersen show us quite a different type of mind again from those stories which we may collect in Sicily, Japan, or from the North American Indians. The tales from the Arabian Nights are something apart and could never be confused with the stories heard in the Hebrides or from Denmark. Not alone is the setting distinct, but the subjects dealt with and the handling show us the work of another kind of mentality.

Let us take a few of the most typical and widely spread stories, and see what may be gained from a summary of their content or the main theme around which they are written. We usually find that the growing girl chooses as her favourites those which she thinks most nearly resemble her own conditions or represent her wishes, although to the casual observer the likeness may not be great nor apparent. Still, when we come to examine the deeper layers of the mind, it is no uncommon discovery to learn that what a person believes or feels about herself or himself may differ completely from the view held by the family or friends. It frequently happens, therefore, that the most popular tale will have been adopted when quite young, and that the unconscious attempt will have been made later to model reality and the personality of the reader as closely as possible upon the adventures of this heroine of fairy-lore.

It may be suggested here, by way of protest to this last remark, that the modern girl does not like fairy-tales. She prefers detective or adventure stories. This is doubtless true to a certain extent, but then we may reflect that after all both of these varieties in which she takes such keen delight often have a good deal of the magic or fairy-tale quality about them. They are a modernised version of many of the old themes. They will doubtless be preferred by the girl who is passing through a boyish phase, or by one who at some time in her life has had a keen desire to have been a boy. The girl, however, who has a more feminine ideal will still be drawn to romance and fairy-lore, although she, too, may like to find it in an up-to-date setting, and needs to find a fanciful version of the apotheosis of the girl heroine. At this age we so frequently find this wish showing signs of life, which requires fostering because it may often be deliberately suppressed by the girl, for fear that her preference might make her an object of ridicule among her friends and contemporaries.

It might seem that the traditional fairy-tale was on the whole more popular a generation or so ago among adolescents, but there are several reasons which will account for this apparent change. In the first place there were not so many books written then available for the young girl's reading. She was supposed not to open her mother's exciting novels. So when her interest in romance came over the horizon about early adolescence, and she began to want to know more about love, courtship, and the choosing of a mate, she found that her main source of gratification was to be found in reading about the adventures of the girl who was wooed and won by a fairy prince. She, through identification with the girl in the story, went through the same tribulations and enchantment, was saved by some magic spell or the good offices of her fairy godmother, who finally made her more beautiful than her tiresome elder sisters, and carried off the matrimonial prize from under their noses. The cruel stepmother was suitably punished too, because, having chosen a fate, thinking it should befall a rival, she was condemned to suffer it herself. Her father generally proves an indulgent if weak parent, who is delivered ultimately from the tyranny of his second wife by the help of his daughter.

Not even the most astute parents or teachers ever imagined how much erotic pleasure and gratification the adolescent girl derived from her study of these simple tales: how they fed her hunger for romance and sexual information of a sort, which they refused to satisfy by other reading, or they would have denied this too. But besides giving her an opportunity for gaining all these escapades through identification, and to enjoy the thrill of the dangers from which the beautiful but unhappy maiden was rescued just in time by the prince, or the excitement of waiting with the haughty young princess who had sent her unwelcome lovers on wild adventures and wondering if they would be successful in their quest or not, she must have experienced additional glamorous delight from the picturesque setting of the story in some far-off country, about which she knew little or nothing—some land of mystery, so different from the drab everyday world, of which the adolescent is usually just a trifle bored. The lavish colour of the Oriental stories would enthral one girl as much as the northern icefields of the Andersen stories, or the dark forests of Teutonic fairy-lore.

Many an adolescent even to-day would rather like to be stolen away by the fairies, like Kilmeny, if only for the sake of finding out whether her parents would organise a great search-party for her, or leave her to come back some time! Would they really lament for her and go in mourning all their days? Or perhaps she might find it a pleasant alternative to going back to school, where she was not interested in the pursuits of her contemporaries, or because she was tired of looking after her younger brothers and sisters, and helping with the housework after her lessons were done.

Nowadays, of course, the cinema supplies the place of the reading of fairy-stories to a great extent, and in many instances furnishes the girl with exactly the same elements she required from the former interest. We shall still find the same themes represented, although they may be rather differently disguised. Still they will give her the identical chance for vicarious adventures, colour, and romance of the rather impossible order otherwise performed by enchantment of magic rings and cloaks of darkness. She can get away from her own life which she feels so dull, and share the exciting adventures of the love-stories of other more highly favoured damsels, or so she believes.

But let us return to the question of the root fairy-tales in antiquity, and see whether by grouping them together according to their main theme we cannot find their close resemblance to the legendary myths and hero tales on the one hand and modern fiction on the other, represented by romantic novels, or even detective tales and movies.

We may classify the more familiar stories into the following seven sections, beginning with the earlier types.

I. *Warning Tales and Moral Lessons* of the Red Riding Hood variety, and a good many in the collection of Hans Christian Andersen; usually not very popular with young folks.

II. *The Animal Group*, which probably belongs to remote antiquity and possibly will be descended from the beliefs in the animal totems, where certain families had sacred and helping beasts, which must never be molested except for ritual purposes. Calamity followed the slaying of the sacred beasts, and there was supposed to be a great affinity between the totem animal and the families descended from it. The turning of men into animals by enchantment also was a likely concomitant of the same idea, and related to the were-wolf beliefs and the fears of dangerous creatures which turned out to be princes in disguise. (See later *Beauty and the Beast.*)

III. *The Cinderella Group*, containing the well-known figures of the unfortunate maiden, persecuted by stepmother and ugly, jealous sisters. The kindness of the fairy-godmother and the final rescue by the prince, and happiness ever afterwards.

IV. *The Sleeping Beauty Group*, a very large one, showing many variations, but reflecting the pubertal seclusion, as the spell generally worked when the princess was fourteen or so, and remained under it until waked by the prince and claimed as his bride. The cause of the spell is interesting, as it is usually represented as occurring because of some negligence on the part of the parents, which brings about the calamity, either because they forgot to invite a fairy to the christening or failed to carry out some condition imposed upon them when the child was promised to them, having long been childless.

V. *The Bluebeard Group*, the girl bride who gets into trouble for curiosity and disobedience, akin to the legend of Pandora, and many others, which relate to the dangers of sexual curiosity. This begins to show the dangerous side of marriage, the cruel husband, and the final rescue by the brothers.

VI. *The Beauty and the Beast Group.*—This shows two interesting factors: the sacrifice of the daughter to save the father, and the fear of the girl for the unknown lover, whom she regards as a repellent beast, until her gentleness or love releases him from the spell and he resumes his human shape.

VII. *The Brother and Sister Group*, especially familiar among the Teutonic and northern tales of Grimm and Andersen. We find this as a favourite motif: the brother and sister wander away, sometimes being abandoned by the parents in time of famine, showing fairly ancient customs; or the theme slightly varied, a pair of young lovers, brought up as brother and sister, who after much tribulation finally marry each other. The theme is interesting as showing a frequent attitude of brothers and sisters in any age who have great affection for one another.

There is also another group, which although exceedingly interesting psychologically is not so frequent as those tabulated above. This is the father and daughter love. It is represented by a king, who, having lost his wife, usually at the birth of a daughter, vows that he will never marry again until he can find a woman who equals his dead wife in beauty and virtue; or the queen has extracted this promise from him when dying. Years pass by and he seeks the world over but without success. Finally, the daughter grows up and is found to exceed her mother in loveliness, so that her father falls in love with her. Sometimes he knows the story of her birth; at others he comes across her as a stranger, because she had been put out to nurse as an infant. The girl proves her virtue by resisting the advances of this elderly suitor, is eventually delivered by a young man, and accepts her bridegroom in the person of her rescuer. This theme is closely connected with that of the virgin sacrifice, when the vow of the father condemns her to death or to be devoured by a monster, to save himself or his land from devastation, from which fate she is rescued in some versions by the young lover, as in the legend of Perseus and Andromeda. The same subject is introduced into the fable of the Patient Griselda, but with this difference. In this case the mother is still living, and the father offers as excuse for making love to his adolescent daughter that he is trying to see if by that means he can cause her to complain.

When we come to examine the attitude of the daughter to the father at adolescence, as well as his affection for her in a later chapter, we shall see what alterations occur in this mutual love, and the changes that follow one another as the years of adolescence pass by. In a great many fairy-tales the father does not appear in a particularly favourable light. He is usually represented as weak and foolish, the tool of a selfish and cruel stepmother, meekly submitting to watch her tyranny towards his own daughter, and passively regretting the loss of his first wife. The father who sacrifices his daughter to save himself from a dangerous situation is another variant; but we sometimes meet the kindly, indulgent king or merchant who searches the world to find a suitable husband for his girl, who will succeed him in his position as well as be a protector to his daughter. It may perhaps be worthy of remark that if the girl is represented as having a happy existence, she usually is shown as the indulged and haughty maiden, unwilling to accept any suitor, feeling that they are all unworthy of her, possibly also because none of them will come up to her father in her estimation. She does not want to leave him, and therefore makes all kinds of excuses not to do so. She will usually, by design, surely, rather than accident, be described as the only child, only daughter, or the youngest, who comes in for this overwhelming share of her father's love; and there is often no mother. If other sisters come into the story they will frequently be half-sisters, or disagreeable or unpleasant in some way, which is a not uncommon feeling for the girl to entertain about rivals in her home. But we shall be examining these problems of family relationships in a subsequent chapter, when we shall be able to recognise still more clearly how accurately these old fairy-tales portray the psychological undercurrents of home-life, and the emotions entertained by each member of the family towards the rest.

Another point of interest to which we may give some brief attention is the clear distinction shown between the happy girlhood of the rich young daughter, although she may also be discontented at times, who shows plainly enough that she wishes to remain as long as possible the irresponsible child, absorbed only in amusement, who does not want to grow up, nor to marry, which would mean leaving her parents and home, or setting out for her husband's country. Sometimes this difficulty will be solved by the chosen suitor receiving half the father's kingdom and settling down with his bride. We may see her, too, playing the haughty tyrant, condemning her unwanted suitors to impossible quests, from which they will probably never return, or setting them riddles to guess of which she only knows the answer, to prove her superiority of knowledge. Often the father's response to her vagaries is to get some soldier of fortune to compete and to win the hand of his daughter to humble her pride. But in these instances we often find fate once again proves propitious, and the soldier or the beggar, as the case may be, is found at the right moment to be a prince in disguise, or that he has been brought up by foster-parents of humble birth, and that now his identity is declared.

If the happy, wealthy, and idle girl is unwilling to exchange the home of her childhood for an unknown future, we may see the poor girl only too anxious to rid herself of a life of endless hard work and no pleasure for any bridegroom who comes along, however uninviting he may seem at first sight. She is kind to him, and virtue will be rewarded by finding he is really once again the prince, who was bewitched or under some enchantment. We see her represented as having to herd sheep or geese, bake, and go out to gather firewood. It was only natural that she would be ready to follow any possible fairy prince at first call into whatsoever far country he might lead her. A great many of the fairy-stories which have been handed down for so many generations by word of mouth, long before they were ever printed, were her phantasies.

This remains true always: the happy child always strives to stay in the golden dream world with loving parents and the surroundings she knows so well. She comes to look upon the idea of growing-up, marriage, and a husband whom she must obey, as a horrible fate, where she may encounter a Bluebeard; but the unhappy child looks forward eagerly to the future and sees the golden time *ahead*, when she is no longer at the beck and call of all those older than herself, where she, too, may go to the ball in a frock as radiant as the stars, and does not have to stay at home wearing the discarded frocks of elder sisters.

One more topic of considerable interest before this chapter reaches its conclusion. That is the subject of the girl's mother in the fairy-tale, because this is a strange problem. If, as we should suppose that sometimes the mother herself were the narrator of the story, one would imagine that she might sometimes represent a mother who was good, kind, and desirable. But this does not occur. If she should have been of this variety, she will invariably die in the girl's childhood, and the girl continues to mourn her and to wish she were still on earth. This mother cannot live in the fairy-tale. When a mother is alive she will approximate closely to the stepmother type: she is cruel and jealous, doing her best to get rid of the girl, and often making her husband take her away and leave her in the forest, as in the beautiful Russian tale of *The Frost*.

It would seem that the reason may be as follows. In the first place, this type of tale shows clearly the girl's own phantasy, and naturally follows her own unconscious idea of the mother as her rival, and projects many of her own thoughts upon her. The mother can only be loved in retrospect, when she is no longer there to interfere. The living mother, who claims the father and orders her about, is no longer loved, but disliked or even hated—a psychological equivalent of the stepmother. The loving-mother figure will always reappear as the good fairy or the fairy-godmother, with her magic help and willing sympathy for the girl's misfortunes. She is the mother-substitute, whom the adolescent girl of to-day so often seeks as her friend, and of whom the real mother is often desperately jealous.

We may often trace the history of the descent of the fairy-tale down through the ages, following its path from the ancient myths of the gods or heroes to a later stage, where it will pass into two branches: one the fairy-tale proper; and the other turns off into religion and becomes incorporated with the legends of the saints. There are quite a number of fairly early legends, usually local ones, where young girls of the same age are befriended in their troubles by the saints, or the Madonna herself, in much the same way as the fairy-godmother of the other branch. Thus each age revives the same themes, with a different setting which will be acceptable to its hearers, or in such a way that will best represent the lessons the elders want to bring to the notice of the young people, as well as those which show us the phantasies based upon the conscious or unconscious wishes of the young people themselves.

CHAPTER IV

THE ADOLESCENT GIRL IN THE PAST

To procure accurate information concerning the adolescent girl in the past is not easy. One has to look for it among records of other affairs and other persons, since it would appear that her welfare was not considered as of particular importance until she became ready for marriage.

What girls did in the past is perhaps still easier, however, to discover than the more intimate problem of what they thought and felt, what impressions they received from the life that went on around them. This may be conjectured from very rare information that has come down to us through the ages or legends which have survived respecting the lives of a few outstanding characters. But usually it must be gleaned indirectly. It is interesting, nevertheless, to piece together what we may, and to see if we can thus sketch a fairly coherent picture of the past, with the girl as central figure.

In our second chapter, which dealt with the life of the girl among the primitives, we were concerned mostly with those who lived in Africa, Australia, and the Peloponnesian Islands, or among the old tribes of North American Indians, among peoples whom we should regard as savages, in fact. The last section was devoted to stray information picked up from fairy-tales, which reflect vague "olden times," according to the place where they originated. In many we cannot determine the period to which they belong with any degree of certainty. The environment described provides some clues to conditions, which still hold good for the present chapter, but they have the additional virtue, which we have already mentioned, that besides giving us some little insight into the girl's occupations and duties, or amusements, they also show a vivid picture of what she thought about. That is, if we are prepared to accept the hypothesis that they are based upon wishes, warnings, and the psychological undercurrents of family life. These appear to remain fundamentally the same with very slight modifications throughout all time, as we shall endeavour to show subsequently.

If we pursue the investigation of the fairy-tale further we may gain information about all countries, because it is impossible to find any civilised or uncivilised land without its fairy-lore. Here we will discover also that in *them* the adolescent girl plays a very important part, which would seem to directly contradict the idea that in early days she was not greatly esteemed. This may perhaps be accounted for thus. These stories, which we have been considering, are domestic; they were for the instruction or amusement of the *home*, and as an integral part of family home-life the girl had to be considered. Judging from evidence supplied by the fairy-tale, the girl always occupied a position of importance in the home, for one reason or another, if not in the interest of the public.

It was publicly that they were not of much account. State records, public documents regulating the education and upbringing of boys, may be found carefully preserved, but nothing of the sort for the girl, until questions of marriage laws arose, and problems of inheritance and dowry. But then she was regarded as a woman. Her girlhood had legally ceased, adolescence remained unrecognised, so we are no better off than before. We must return to the records of home-life, few as there are, to instruct us as to what happened to them.

In this chapter for many reasons it would seem better to limit the research to Europe and America, with the exception of a brief reference to ancient Egypt, which in early days of civilisation seems to have been almost part of the history of ancient cultures around the Mediterranean as to be inseparable from it, and to omit the vast regions of Asia and the Far East. One of these is that Oriental views upon the position of women and the unchanging customs of those distant lands have in all probability shown little alteration in the position of the adolescent girl, except comparatively recently. Here we have in mind the aim of tracing the girl's history in the past to find an explanation of her attitude to life in the present, and the problems of her environment. By tracing each succeeding stratum of development we hope to establish a better understanding of changes that came about with the passage of centuries, and to compare these with the almost changeless psychological elements. For this reason, and because the history of women and girls in the East remains practically a closed book to the stranger, it would seem necessary to leave it for another, who knows the subject from within, and therefore understands the special problems that can only be elucidated by intimate knowledge of the countries, languages, religions, customs, literature, and above all the history of their home-life throughout the many centuries of their ancient culture.

Perhaps the first gleam of light to be shed upon this dark subject in ancient times comes from Egypt. Amenhotep IV, usually known as Echnaton, one of the most progressive rulers the world has yet known, brought about innovations during his short reign which were not universally accepted until many hundreds of years later. He set aside the polytheistic worship of the gods of his ancestors and established the monotheistic cult of the sun's disc, instituting himself as the chief priest and representative of the deity. But he was not only in advance of his age in matters of religious faith, but also in his ideas concerning family life, for he refused to accept the custom of the country and take another queen even after his beloved wife, Nefertiti,

had presented him with seven daughters and no heir to
succeed him. We have also evidence to the fact that he
regarded her with tender affection, as well as the seven little
daughters, whose portraits have become familiar to us as
the result of German explorations. These girls, portrayed
with all the natural grace and charm of young adolescents,
may well be the first real representation which we have of
the young girl in art, except in the conventional figures,
which are no portraits. In a separate small gallery in the
Berlin Museum we find the contents of the "House of the
Sculptor," found during excavations in Amarna, who was an
artist holding a position similar to that of a Court Painter
to Echnaton. We see there a model of his house, the same
little pots of dried colour, and the brushes which he used for
tinting the plaster figures and plaques that he made of the
royal family. Round the walls are these very plaques, cast
from actual matrices, which were found in the ruins of his
studio, and from these we catch some glimpses of this long-
ago royal household, so that we feel we know something of
what they were and what they felt for one another.

In one we see the king in the garden with Nefertiti. He
is offering her a flower. In another he is sitting with his
daughters. They are little cameos of their home-life. A fresco
at Tel-el-Amarna, the king's city of palaces, shows two of
the adolescent girls reclining upon flat cushions caressing
one another, with the natural grace which disappeared from
portraiture with the death of Echnaton, returning to formal
methods of representation that gave us a lifeless figure and
set, masklike face. We must recollect, too, that this family
lived about 1370 B.C.

After this the curtain falls, and we see nothing of the
girl as a living, real human being for a long while. We may
find young slave-girls upon wall-paintings, as dancers or
musicians, or the portrait of some youthful princess painted
upon the lid of her sarcophagus, but they remain strictly

impersonal. We know that the adolescent princess passed her time waiting for her bridegroom, amusing herself as best she could; that the young daughters of the peasants worked in the fields or as slaves in the houses of the well-to-do, but we have no idea what any of them thought or felt about their lives.

We are obliged to accept what observation offers us for long stretches of time. Greece and Rome give us little else. The peasant girl helped her mother in the house or herded goats on the hills outside. When times were bad or in warfare they could be sold as slaves or carried into captivity by the conquerors. The adolescent girls in the slave-markets were of interest mainly because of their beauty or their strength, and how much hard work could be expected of them before they fell sick or broke down under the strain. That the young daughters of the wealthy had their games and their amusements we can gather from the evidence of the vase-paintings, the Tanagra figurines, and vague mention here and there by contemporary writers. But here the young girl is not conspicuous. We know very little about the young Iphigenia, for instance, except that she was doomed to be sacrificed to fulfil her father's vow. She probably accepted her fate in a dutiful manner, according to legend, requesting only a short respite to bewail her early death, which, after all, was not required as the goddess Artemis obligingly substituted a hind for the sacrifice, and dedicated the girl to her service as a priestess instead. What she thought about it actually we have no means of discovering.

Girls, rich or poor, were then completely the property of their parents, and lived or died in those days according to their convenience, and no questions were asked. When they grew older they were esteemed as useful for the making of marriage alliances, for the bride-money they might bring to the home, or as mothers and potential mothers of great men, although little seems to have been done to help them to become such, except the training they obtained at home, which was good or bad according to the sort of mother who was there, and supervised their training and bringing-up, as well as by her example.

Sparta seems to have recognised the need for something more reliable than this, however. Not only were the sons taken away from their homes and parents at a certain age, housed, and trained to be warriors, but the girls were similarly educated systematically to become the fit mothers of warriors, which is probably the first instance of organised education for girls that can be traced, if we except the instruction which was given to girls during the puberty seclusion of primitive races. Yet it is doubtful whether these customs may have gone back as early, or earlier, in the world's history. What effect it had upon the psychological development of the young Spartan women we once again do not know from any records made at the time.

Recent fiction, nevertheless, can fill some of the gaps for us in a convenient fashion, by giving us some vignettes of past history compiled from its contemporary sources. In the interesting novels by Naomi Micheson we find an attempt to reconstruct these early days for us, and in some of her stories we find glimpses of the life of a young girl in these far-off days. In *Cloud Cuckoo Land*, *The Conquered*, *When the Bough Breaks*, and *Black Sparta* we gain some impression of how the world must have appeared to the wondering eyes of an adolescent girl then, and how little it offered her that was pleasant, except in rare cases.

Time passes on, and we find that the obscurity lifts a little in the period which saw the persecution of the early Christians. Among the records of the first virgin saints and martyrs we have records of many young girls who were going through the typical, mystical, masochistic stage of adolescence. The glow of romance then centred around this focus, and records of their heroism remain, which must have been envied by many girls of a similar age in the succeeding centuries.

These sadistic or masochistic tendencies, which we pointed out as characteristic of adolescence, when describing the initiation rites of the primitives, found their fulfilment once more in the persecution of the early Christians. We see in them also some of the same elements which occur in fairy-tales: the sacrifice of the maiden, the idea of death associated with marriage, the finding of a mystic husband in Christ through martyrdom, which provides a similar satisfaction for the young girl's desire for romance as the rescue by the fairy prince. The gratification to be obtained through erotically tinged suffering made death welcome to them, and took the place of a well-developed masochistic phantasy by transferring it to reality.

Religion eventually interested itself in the cause of the young girl. We find that some of the women's religious orders undertook to accept adolescents into their convents for the purpose of education, without the necessity of taking the veil when the term of instruction should be ended. The following quotation is to be found in that most excellent mine of information upon these subjects, *The Pedagogue's Commonplace Book*, compiled by Edith Rowland, from a treatise by Thomas Fuller, a divine of the early seventeenth century, giving an account of female education in the remote past. He writes thus:

Nunneries also were good shee-schools, wherein the Girles, and Maids of the Neighbourhood, were taught to read and work; and sometimes a little Latine was taught them therein. Yes, give me leave to say, if such Feminine Foundations had still continued, provided no vow were obtruded upon them, haply the weaker sex might be heightened to a higher perfection than hitherto hath been attained. That sharpness of their wits, and suddenness of their conceits (which their enemies must allow them) might by education be improved into a judicious solidity, and that adorned with Arts, which now they want, not because they cannot learn, but are not taught them. I say, if such Feminine Foundations were extant now of days haply some Virgins of highest birth, would be glad of such places; and I am sure, their Fathers and elder Brothers would not be sorry for the same.

These girls were in the minority, however. Generally, throughout Europe at this time, the young girl was brought up at home, spinning and learning all the domestic arts which she would require later when she in turn became the housewife, whether her future home were the cottage of the peasant or some country manor-house or castle. In those early days women were required to have a considerable knowledge of a great many different things, although to be able to read and write were the accomplishments of the very few. To make every piece of clothing needed by every member of the family, men and women and children, as well as the domestic staff, from the raw materials, such as the fleece of the sheep or the growing flax, was no idle pastime. They would have to attend to each stage in turn, the drying, cleaning, dyeing, spinning, weaving, making, and decorating, which all needed considerable skill and artistic ability, as well as intelligence, that a great many persons might not willingly admit these women and young girls of the past possessed.

In addition to these last-mentioned occupations we must reflect that food also had to be dealt with from its growing stages upwards also. Not only was it necessary to provide the household with food, when it was fresh and plentiful, but ways of drying, curing, and preserving it had to be resorted to, so that to provision the family during the long winter, or maybe throughout the whole year when the harvest failed or was very scarce, was no easy task. Supplies of all kinds had always to be laid up against possible famine or probable hard times.

These two sections of women's work alone might well give the growing girl plenty to occupy her hands and her mind, but she was also expected to know something of the art of healing, the making of simple medicines and remedies from herbs, as well as the dressing of wounds. Besides this, it was considered her province to look after the poultry, bees, and small animals, as well as the growing of fruit for preserving, green salads, and vegetables, or herbs and flowers needed for the medicaments she concocted. She had social duties to learn, too, and various accomplishments necessary for her to be acquainted with, such as music and dancing, the singing of ballads and country folk-dances or part-songs which were formerly great favourites in the country districts. If she had a quick invention, and were clever at telling amusing stories, she became a popular member of her family or circle of neighbours in the long winter evenings, as well as in the household where she worked if she were in service.

What happened to the young girl if she did not stay at home? Many adolescents of the peasant class, when the parents were too poor to struggle with the problem of feeding and housing a large family, were sent out to work in other homes. What sort of life they found there depended upon the kind of household into which they went and the ways of their employers. Details of their life and environment, whether in towns or the country in early times, as well as during later years in remote country districts, are best filled in from domestic fairy-tales, which give us such a good picture of the day's doings, and in many instances what the young girl felt about the duties which were assigned to her.

Girls of the well-to-do classes, or even the nobility too, also left home upon occasions. It was the custom in most European countries for the young girls, as well as their brothers, to be sent into the royal household for a time for the purposes of education and culture, or, failing the palace, to the castle of some relative or into the manor-house of the neighbouring gentry. This plan was adopted very generally; sometimes an exchange of children would be effected, or they would be sent from one country to another. This was usual in the case of the young prince or princess, who was often sent to a foreign Court. In the case of the latter, frequently with a view to subsequent marriage alliance, as in the case of several young Scottish princesses, or on account of an infant betrothal, which was the reason of Mary Queen of Scots being brought up at the French Court.

We are able to gain some interesting details concerning a few of these girlhoods, because young princesses at that time seemed to have carried out a great part of their education by learning to write elaborate letters to their parents. Formal, to our way of thinking, they may be, but all the same they frequently include most interesting glimpses of a girl's life about the Court as she lived it and saw it.

It is a long jump from these much earlier days which we have been describing to the Tudor times in England, but it would seem that there is very little definite of a personal nature to be gained before this time, except from outside sources, until we reach this wealth of material from the adolescent letter-writers of the Tudor times. We may get a rare view here and there of the girls of the time attached to various royal households, as those who worked so busily at the Bayeux tapestry under the direction of the wife of William the Conqueror, in which we can also see them represented making this record of his victories and other contemporary events. Some experts have considered this to be untrue.

Here and there among the writers of these centuries we find a stray picture of a girl appearing in the poems of Chaucer in England, or of Boccaccio in Italy, while we must remember that Dante's Beatrice, when first she enchanted him, was but nine years old, and a few years later became his great inspiration, although she died soon afterwards. We have Italy again to thank for portraits of adolescent girls in the work of one of the most famous of the Florentine painters. Botticelli must have found this age especially attractive to him, since his chief models nearly always show the immature beauty and tender grace of the adolescent, rather than the more robust matrons, usually so popular with artists of that time. The same quality appears in many of the well-known works of Leonardo da Vinci; but of course it is familiar to most that he had a particular affection for adolescent boys rather than for girls.

Another famous figure of an adolescent girl stands out conspicuously from among the shadows of the early part of the fifteenth century. That is Joan of Arc, about whose girlhood in the little village of Domrémy, her visions and her "voices," most of her biographers have collected as many details as possible.

Although it is a novel, a book which is of undoubted value in our investigation is Sigrid Unset's notable work *Kristin Lavransdatter*. This was so well esteemed in her own country that it won for her the Nobel prize for literature of that year. It has been translated into English under the same title. It shows a remarkably vivid picture of a girl's life in Norway in the latter half of the fourteenth century, a period just before the Black Death devastated Europe. The first volume especially is of interest, since it describes her life during childhood and adolescence, although the other two provide us with information concerning her struggles during her early married life, when she was really still in her adolescence, throughout her womanhood, and finally shows us one generation later in the home-life of her daughters and their bringing-up to womanhood. We are first shown the young daughter living at home, helping her own mother with all the many occupations and activities of the household, and describes the festivities which took place at different times of the year, and the journeys she took with her father. Later her parents decide that she needs a wider education and knowledge of the world than their village can provide, and she is sent off to spend some time at a convent for the purpose of finishing her education, and later to Court to add a final polish. Her adventures while away from home are exciting enough, but we should remember that they probably fell to comparatively few adolescents, but were representative of the customs of the times, brought together for the sake of increasing the interest of this book.

Another fascinating volume, which shows us family life about a century later in Germany, is the *Chronicles of the Schönberg-Cotta Family*, compiled by Mrs. Rundle Charles in 1895 from Martin Luther's *Tischreden* and letters. It describes the home-life of the Luther family, when he and his sisters were young, giving a very good impression of the occupations and thoughts of young girls of this period, especially concerning the differences in opportunities which befell their brothers and their own limitations. The family must have been typical of many fairly well-to-do, thrifty people of those days, who loved their children and gave much time and thought to their upbringing. Their attitude and behaviour towards them seem nevertheless hard and stern to our present views, and the punishments meted out to the children and adolescents extraordinarily severe, yet the young people themselves seem to have taken them for granted.

About this time, or slightly earlier, a book appeared in England which must have created quite a stir at the time. Although called the *Babees Book, or a Little Report of How Young People Should Behave*, it concerned the *young people* far more than those we should now reckon *babes*. Here we have detailed regulation to determine behaviour suitable for every possible occasion, and even if far more space is devoted to the boy, his sister is not entirely overlooked. The book is of course difficult to procure, but when this can be done it well repays careful study and any trouble taken in getting a sight of it, because it reflects so vividly what instructions were deemed necessary to inculcate good manners in those days.

Let us now return for a few moments to the young letter-writers of the sixteenth century, to which we have already referred. In this Tudor period in England, as well as in France, there was a group of young girls, all practically about the same age, over whose education particular care was being expended, some of the best scholars of the day acting as their instructors, one of whom especially, Roger Ascham, tutor to our Princess, afterwards Queen Elizabeth, left records of his royal pupil, as well as his views upon education, including that suitable for girls. Elizabeth, Lady Jane Grey, and Mary Queen of Scots were all indefatigable letter-writers when they were adolescents, and their work is available for us without much trouble in memoirs of the time. A collection of the early letters of Mary of Scotland, bearing the title *Queen Mary's Book*, Poems and Essays by Mary Queen of Scots, but also containing many letters to Elizabeth, the eldest daughter of Henry II of France and Catharine de Medici, who was a dearly loved friend and companion of the childhood of this girl, has been edited by Mrs. Stewart-Mackenzie Arbuthnot. The collection begins with letters written when Mary was twelve, and although it is thought that many of them were school-time exercises, yet they still bear marks of her individuality.

When we reach the next century we find that wider interest is beginning to be taken in the education and upbringing of children than was ever accorded to it before. Different from the *Babees Book*, in that it is for parents' enlightenment, and not for the instruction of the young, the philosopher Commenius wrote an important treatise in Czech for some of his patrons upon the education and welfare of children of both sexes. It was called *The School of Infancy*, which included the *School of the Mother's Lap*, which was afterwards translated into German in 1633. We should again remember that among these early writers the period of infancy was regarded as practically an equivalent of its legal significance, and covered the time of adolescence as well as childhood.

In England especially, due probably to the fact that the education of the young Tudor princesses had given new stimulus to the idea of training of girls in general, we find material suddenly becoming rich and varied, which has been so scarce to obtain before. This was a century of letter-writers and diarists. With the girl's eager search for means of self-expression, she took to this task with enthusiasm and considerable ability. We have several excellent diaries of this time, or collections of letters which give us in abundance what we have sought in vain in the past.

Some of the most celebrated of these are to be found in *The Memoirs of the Verney Family*, the first two volumes of which record the period 1600–59, the time of the early Stuart Kings, the Civil War and Commonwealth, compiled by Frances Parthenope Verney from letters and family documents found in attics and lumber-rooms; and the third, put together by Margaret Verney, 1660–96, now to be had in two volumes, which comprises the family history to the end of the century. These not only give the news of the day, but also an account of the doings of this adventurous family, and their interesting comments and opinions upon current experiences and the exciting events which happened around them during the entire century. They give us an excellent summary of the part the mothers and daughters of the household took in the family affairs, and from it we are able to grasp what the woman's part and position was in that time.

Lady Newton has also edited two other valuable books from the records of her husband's family, the Leghs of Lyme. The first of these absorbing volumes, *The House of*

Lyme, relates the history of the family from its foundation in the time of Richard II until the end of the eighteenth century; the second, *Lyme Letters*, expands the information given in the first with the correspondence of different members of the family between 1660–1760, commencing with a review of the political life at the time of the Restoration, and description of the part taken in it by the Leghs, and continues to recount their experiences almost to the end of the next century. The first volume is perhaps the more interesting of the two, as it is more personal and less political. We find in both, however, rare flashes of insight into the ideas and adventures of the young girls of the family, especially when they have been high-spirited young ladies and the pets of their fathers, acting as household secretary.

Both these two sets of family histories show us that the usual scribe was often a young daughter of the house. Fresh from her education, and anxious to show off her newly won accomplishments, she is only too ready to write her father's letters, and to be the link between scattered members of the family, as well as the home confidante, who is let into everybody's secrets. She shows herself her father's favourite, too, because it is for him that she generally undertakes this task. It may be an additional interest to her, too, that in this way she can do what her mother cannot, or only in a very limited way. Because in these early days many daughters were, in learning to read, write, and do simple arithmetic, obtaining a key to knowledge which their mothers did not possess, and found in this a bond which united them to their fathers.

Later we hear of the young daughters of the poet Milton acting as his amenuenses, when he became old and blind, as well as exceedingly irritable. This sharing of some interest, work, or pleasure with the father is a theme that we find constantly appearing in reality or in the phantasies of the adolescent girl, and is a problem to which we will give more particular attention in the chapter upon the girl and her father.

The seventeenth century was one that was unsettled in many ways. The Civil War, in which so many of the families of England were deeply involved, sometimes with relatives on both sides, left lasting impressions upon the sons and daughters that have had effects like those so vividly described in the *Memoirs of the Verney Family*. It is remarkable, too, that in this century the settlers began to find their way across to the New World, taking with them their wives and daughters, to make the beginnings of the American colonies, afterwards to be the United States. These girls must have suddenly found that lives which may have been uneventful before began full of thrilling adventures and new experiences beyond the dreams of their phantasies, or indeed very similar to many of them, and as dangerous as the heart of the most adventurous young adolescent could wish. It is interesting, too, to reflect that it is from these pioneers that the young American girls of to-day are to a great extent descended; and if not all of them in actuality from those who settled there first of all when the first settlers came, from others who left their homes and tried their luck in a new country—an enterprise which always shows both courage and determination. These girls seem to have inherited the spirit of their ancestors in many of their ideas concerning methods of dealing with modern problems in ways which have made their elders in the two hemispheres hold up their hands in horror, and wonder what the young folks may do next.

These people who are so terrified that the whole human race is becoming degenerate because of the enterprise of its adolescent girls would probably never have crossed the seas, nor allowed their relations to have done so, to act as pioneers, nor for the sake of their own liberty of thought.

They would have stayed at home and rejoiced at becoming martyrs in secret, no doubt feeling injured and thinking it was not nice of the rest to have thus demonstrated the faith that was in them by not only having the courage of their opinions but the honesty and love of adventure to carry out these phantasies of setting forth into the unknown.

It is, of course, from the records of family life that we find the most valuable information of the childhood and adolescence of girls who afterwards left some mark upon the world's history. We often notice that distinguished women have been the especial favourites of the father or have been an only child, whom the father had brought up and educated with as much personal attention as though she had been a son. Freud, in one of his well-known books, points out that some of the most illustrious men in history were those who had an unswerving belief in the love of their mothers; and we may perhaps not be far wrong in assuming that the same is true of the daughter who is sure of the love and support of her father. She becomes more self-confident and able for this reason to accomplish the work she feels incumbent upon her instead of waiting anxiously and hoping someone else would do it, in case she might not carry it out properly.

We find interesting corroboration of this theory in the lives of other famous women of more recent times, as well as in those who lived considerably before the period which we have just been reviewing, who became leaders and or-ganisers in a sphere which was then one of the very few open to them, namely, religion. They were the founders of reli-gious orders for women, and it is interesting to note that later in life, when they became the heads of their institutions, they indeed took over the mother-rôle, repeating the old situation, but in a reversed form. They were then the strong mother to the weaker adolescent daughters, instead of that of the father to herself, which in a way reflected the cult of the ancient mother-goddess Demeter with her daughter Persephone, and was reminiscent of the god Zeus, who was given mother-attributes through the legend of his giving birth to his daughter Artemis or Diana from his head. It would make an exceedingly interesting study to investigate the differences to be found in the girl's development when the father or the mother has been the dominant personality in the house, and of whom the distinguished daughter was the favourite.

St. Catharine of Alexandria, for example, according to legend, shows the influence of her father in many ways. It is recorded in Mrs. Jameson's *Sacred and Legendary Art* that the king, her father, loved her, and ordained seven of the wisest masters

that could be gotten together; but Catharine, divinely endowed, so far excelled them all, that they who came to teach her, became her disciples. When Catharine was about fourteen, her father King Costis, died, and left her heiress of his kingdom.

Later, when her councillors pointed out that she should marry for the sake of her kingdom, her reply was as follows:

He that shall be my husband and the lord of my heart shall also possess four notable gifts, and be so endowed that all creatures shall have need of him, and he shall have need of none. He shall be of so noble blood that all men shall worship him, and so great that I shall never think that I have made him king; so rich that he shall pass all others in riches; so full of beauty that the angels of God shall desire to behold him; and so benign that he can gladly forgive all offences done to him. And if ye find me such an one, I will take him for my husband and lord of my heart.

Which was as good as saying: "If you can find me the replica of my father, who was just such an one as this, I will have him, but no other can come up to my ideal."

Her quest was never substantiated, and she put a heavenly bridegroom in the place of an earthly one in a vision, finally gaining her gratification in martyrdom at the order of the tyrant Maximin, whose advances she had refused with scorn, keeping her father-fixation throughout her young life. The life of Queen Elizabeth of England offers us a similar father-image predominating, and providing an ideal for a daughter, so that she spent her life trying to identify herself with him in every way possible, and breaking down when the elements which represented her feminine side refused to be denied. Her girlhood and the experiences of her adolescence, spent like that of her cousin Mary Queen of Scots, practically in captivity, must have contributed much to the moulding of her mature character, and accounted to a great extent for the tragedy in the lives of both these women.

St. Teresa d'Avila, born in Castile in 1515, gives us an instance of the influence of family affairs showing themselves in the development of a remarkable personality. Here we find an important part being played by a brother, of whom she was especially fond. In her writings she tells us that

they read together the lives of the saints and holy martyrs, until they were filled with the most passionate desire of obtaining for themselves the crown of martyrdom; and when they were children of eight or nine years old, they set off on a begging expedition in the country of the Moors, in hopes of being taken by the Infidels and sacrificed for their faith. . . . As they had been disappointed in their hope of obtaining martyrdom amongst the Moors, they resolved to turn hermits; but in this also they were prevented. (*Sacred and Legendary Art*, by Mrs. Jameson.)

Teresa lost her mother at the age of twelve, a loss to her irreparable; what her destinies might have been, had this parent lived, it is vain to speculate. The few years which follow, exhibit her as passing from one extreme to another. The love of pleasure, the pride of position, the desire to be loved, to be admired—all natural to a young girl of her age, endowed with very extraordinary faculties of all kinds, made her impatient of restraint. . . . In fact, at the age of sixteen, there seems to have remained no settled principle in her mind but that thoroughly feminine principle of womanly dignity. Her father, however, seems to have been aware of the dangers to which she was exposed and placed her in a convent, with orders that she should be kept in strict seclusion.

It was in the year 1561 that she conceived the idea of reforming the Order of the Carmelites, into which several disorders had crept. . . . Such, however, was her success that at the period of her death she had already founded seventeen convents for women and fifteen for men.

This seems to have been a most remarkable record of achievement for a woman of these days, and to have carried on the zeal of her early youth.

Yet from the account of her attempt to find martyrdom at the hands of the Moors in the company of her brother, she reminds us of the romantic child or girl in early adolescence of any period, trying to put adventurous phantasy into reality. We find a similar instance quoted in a book written about children several hundreds of years later, but so closely connected that it may find its place here. The book is entitled *Chapters from Childhood*; the author, Mrs. Soskice; and the children described, the young Madox-Hueffers, grandchildren of the Pre-Raphaelite artist Ford Madox-Brown. We find here the story of their attempt to lead a mission, founded upon the crusade of the moment—Socialism.

We three little ones had a special mission of our own, although it was all part of the same work. It was the reformation of policemen. . . . We felt nervous when we undertook the work, but Olive told us that that kind of agitation was quite within the law until the policemen had actually begun to rebel against their chiefs. I think she looked it up in some sort of Blue Book before we started. She was always getting worried and looking things up because she was so anxious that no mistakes should be made.

Here is the character of the anxious adolescent among the more care-free children whom she is looking after.

What we had to explain to the police was that it was most unfair to put a man in prison merely for taking what he needed from another man who had more than the first man had.

Helen [another young adolescent who comes into the picture] really thought that there might be some chance of our being arrested and dragged off to prison, but she said we were not to mind because other people had been through far worse. . . . She was very brave, although she had a cough, and was so thin and delicate. . . . Helen thought she was going to die quite soon because of her weak chest, and other people thought so too. But she wasn't at all frightened. She said it was absolutely the only way of finding out for certain several things she wanted to know. She was not religious. Once she put Mary's doll out on the bedroom window-sill in the soaking rain, and made us pray to God to keep it dry as a sign that He really did exist and was able to do anything He wanted. When we took it in in the morning, you wouldn't have known it for the same creature. Helen said it was a sure sign that there wasn't any God, because if there had been He would have been only too happy to have saved our souls by anything so simple.

From these quotations it would appear that essentially the nature of the adolescent girl changes little through the ages, although her environment may undergo such entire transformation. Whatever their surroundings, we find representatives of similar types: the high-spirited darlings of their fathers, ready to work or play with him, or after him; the romantic ones so eagerly demanding martyrdom, however they may best procure it; the anxious or domestically minded young maidens, only too happy to follow their mothers and to learn all they have to teach them about the management of the house and the children, to be ready for the time when they shall attain to this dignity. We have the gay and giddy ones, too, on pleasure bent, fond of dress and entertainment, like young Teresa d'Avila, over whom their elders shook their heads, and prophesied danger ahead, and tried to shut up in convents or their later equivalents, the first boarding-schools for young ladies, to teach them to mend their ways and to turn their attention to the more serious affairs of life.

Looking back through the ages we see this same censoriousness active continually in the attitude of the old generation towards the new. There is always apparently the same attempt to try to make the young people keep back their eager steps in line with their elders who cannot go so fast, even if they wanted to do so. To refuse them too much help, even if they do not actively hinder them in their progress, is a course of action which we find repeated over and over again as the centuries pass by. The tradition of the past can be used as a tyrannical prison in which youth may be held fast and waste a great deal of energy in trying to escape.

Now let us see what the early part of the eighteenth century achieved in the way of assisting the young girls of the world to throw off their shackles, helping them to a wider freedom than the environment had offered before, and what advantage they took of it, as well as the attitude which was adopted by their parents occasionally, who looked on so disapprovingly.

Whether it was due once more to the fact that a woman occupied the English throne or some strange aftermath of war and revolution, but the reign of Queen Anne was a memorable one in the history of domestic affairs. We find that girls' secular schools were being started then up and down the country, distinct from the convent education, which by this time had of course fallen out of repute, because of the Reformation. There was a famous young ladies' seminary in Queen's Square, where the fashionable daughters of the day attended for their instruction. It was probably limited enough to our mind, and comprised little more than reading, writing, arithmetic, and the use of the globes, some singing, a few tunes to play upon a harpsichord or spinet, and no doubt a great deal of time given to the inculcation of good manners and deportment.

We read in old memoirs of this time that the then newly built church in the Square, dedicated to St. George the Martyr, was the scene of some of this instruction. The school possessed a coach, and passers-by were often interested witnesses of the young ladies being driven there to practise the necessary accomplishment of getting in and out of this elegant vehicle with the requisite ease and grace. Later the visits to the church were discontinued, and the same lesson was held indoors, an arm-chair and a footstool doing duty for the more exciting vehicle. This school afterwards moved to Harley Street, and is interesting as the place of education of Elizabeth Barrett and her sisters, as well as many other well-known young girls of a later day.

Once more the diaries of young girls of the eighteenth century provide us with details which fill gaps in the chain of information about home-life and the amusements of this time. Chief among these must be reckoned that of Fanny Burney, who, as the daughter of a fashionable dancing-master in Poland Street, became acquainted with a large circle of interesting people of the period. Among them was Dr. Johnson, and she left us her impressions of him, as well as of the other folks she met and the things she did from her fifteenth year for the next seventy years. She also wrote several novels, the best known of these being perhaps *Evelina, A Young Lady's Entrance into the World*, which was doubtless founded upon her own varied experiences of London life and manners. It gives a good idea of what was then considered the correct thing for a young girl to do and those which were severely frowned upon. Fanny had a marvellous zest for life and a great eagerness for friendship, which won her the affection of a great many friends and admirers, some of whom she kept for many years.

It was the custom in those days for many country families to come to London for the season, and if they did not possess a Town residence to rent one in the new quarter that was springing up after the Great Plague and the Fire, to the west of the City. This was Bloomsbury, with its squares, the first definite attempt at town-planning that London had known.

The regulations, still to be found tucked away in some arbour in the corner of a square garden, give us the far-off echo of the doings of the younger members of the families who lived in the houses which faced them upon their four sides, their privacy jealously protected by gates thrown across all the streets which led into them, and which remained until some forty-odd years ago. Tiny lodges were built beside them where pensioners from the Crimean War afterwards kept guard, and opened them only for the carriages of those who lived in the squares and their bona fide visitors. The rules hanging up in the summer-houses give us a strict list of the games which might or might not be played in there, with the strictest prohibition against any games being played on Sunday, and the instruction that the men- or maid-servants of those living in the houses were not to be allowed to use the Gardens.

Until recently it was by no means uncommon still to be able to see about in this neighbourhood, upon the iron railings in front of these houses, on each side of the steps leading up to the front-door, the extinguishers for the torches of the link-boys, who would walk home beside the sedan-chairs of the owners of these houses when they came back from their evening parties. For the young girls of those days would go off to their balls in sedan-chairs when the family did not hire or own their private coach.

Dickens and Thackeray have left us many pictures of the life of the young girls of this time, and we find a vivid picture of what the young adolescent girl thought of her world of school in the account of Becky Sharp's exit from education at the commencement of *Vanity Fair*, when she threw her presentation Bible out of the window of the coach. Adolescence was a much shorter period then, regarded from the point of view of public opinion, than it is at present, although psychologically it may have been much the same. We find in those times that girls were considered women when they left school, which may have been thirteen or fourteen, fifteen or sixteen, according to the views and position of their parents. The schools were the luxuries of the wealthy then, or at least the well-to-do; or the young people may have all been educated together by a resident tutor. The days of the resident governess were hardly to be found before the nineteenth century. For the girls of the middle class there was a very poor substitute of the dame school, and for the poorer classes and in country districts no public education at all in the eighteenth century. But at the beginning of the nineteenth century agitation was raised upon this question, principally by the Society of Friends, and the result was that they founded schools for boys and girls in different parts of England and Wales. Scotland had village schools which were attended by boys and girls alike, of a higher standard than those of a similar grade in England; and the value of a sound education seems to have been more seriously appreciated in that country than in ours at that time certainly.

We can discover various little glimpses of the young girl at school or being educated at home by her industry recorded by the needlework sampler, which, it would appear, most girls produced to show that their education had not been neglected. It usually comprised the practical instruction furnished by working in cross-stitch the letters of the alphabet, both large and small. Religious verses or those of filial piety would fill the space beneath, and then there would often be a most elaborate border or design surrounding the whole, worked again in cross-stitch with gay-coloured silks, often of really great beauty. One often wonders whether the girl was left to choose her own design and verses, or if different schools had their set patterns which all copied more or less faithfully. Sometimes we find particulars of the school, and words like these appear: "Taught by E. Cuthbert," or upon another, "Wrought by Patty Lucas at Mrs. Garrett's school at Chelmsford in ESX. being 9 years old in November the 17. 1753."

The usual age for the working of samplers seems to have been from eight years old to thirteen. Those done by the younger children are very simple as a rule, and consist of one or two plain alphabets and perhaps a red-brick house with a blue slate roof and yellow windows; but the older girls worked the most elaborate and often artistic pictures. It may have been that the girls would work two, one simple one when they were little, and improved upon it just before they were about to leave school.

The verses which are to be found upon them are often of a singularly wistful nature, and must have given their young needlewomen a very sad view of life. But then it was generally thought safer to bring up the young to take a serious view of their responsibilities, and to think of life as short and exceedingly wicked, to be upon the safe side. These are a few examples of sampler verses, which show what the parents or teachers thought suitable maxims for their young folk, if the choice was not left to the girls themselves. If so, they proved that the mind of the young adolescent girl was turned to a very sentimental variety of piety.

> Let dress take up but little time,
> And not in gaudy clothes to shine;
> Reflect how short must be thy stay,
> How vain to deck a piece of clay.

However, if many parents were of the same kind as those we meet in the *History of the Fairchild Family*, that masterpiece of 1818 by Mrs. Sherwood, we may imagine that it may have been chosen to occupy the fingers of some unfortunate girl who was considered to be too vain, and that working these precepts might cause her to reform her ways.

Yet lines of this kind are the rule rather than the exception. Here is another:

> Sweet is the flower of youthful prime,
> But withered by the hand of time.
> Then let me deck the charms of youth
> With virtue and unfading truth.

SoPhia Steele Wrought This Sampler in the year 1829 age 11.

One can hear the note of pride in the following lines on another sampler, decorated with a map of England, Wales, and Scotland disappearing shyly off the side and top.

> Susan Temple is my name,
> And Britain is my Nation
> London is my dwelling-place,
> And Christ is my Salvation.

Here is another variant of the gay young lady's work

> Harriet Nelson is my Name,
> And with my needle I work the same,
> So all the world may plainly see,
> What care my parents took of me.

If one takes the trouble to look carefully into the verses which are to be found upon most of these samplers and compare them with the dates when they were finished, one is often rewarded by finding that some event of public interest may have influenced the choice of the verse traced thereon. For instance, one that is a treasure of the writer's own collection has lines of unequalled sadness. It calls down vengeance of heaven upon the foes of the country, and reflects solemnly upon the transitory quality of all human happiness. The date which reminds us that the British Army was at that time suffering defeat repeatedly in America, and that the news of the Black Hole of Calcutta had probably reached England not long before to appal all those who heard of it, helps to explain them. Another cause which may have influenced the seriousness of this girl was that just at that time John Wesley was going up and down the country crying to all who heard him to repent and so avoid the danger of hell-fire. One cannot help feeling that such occurrences may have assisted in the choice of her lines, and added enthusiasm to her fingers that diligently worked one set of verses after another down the long canvas, as well as being a reflection of her anxiety for her own safety in this world or the next.

The preaching of Wesley and the great religious revival that spread over the country affected the parents of the adolescent girls, it is true; but we may imagine that the girls themselves, who were just at the most impressionable time of their lives, were still more profoundly shaken by it. We have some information at least about the effect produced by the intense emotion aroused by his preaching from within the household of the preacher himself. A good many details are available of the doings of young Hetty Wesley. The excitement produced by the religious fervour in the house was evidently too much for this high-spirited girl, and produced symptoms which we should now ascribe to neurosis, but which were then afterwards, when discovered, believed to be the result of possession by the Devil.

At first the noises which disturbed the family, usually when engaged in their prayers, were not connected with Hetty, but at last were traced to her; but how she managed to produce them was never made clear. They were of the same type which provoke considerable attention from time to time, and are often at first supposed to be the work of some poltergeist agency, although upon closer examination they are generally found to be the work of some unbalanced adolescent. But this was not all. Small fires would also suddenly break out in cupboards and in attics which were not often used. A faint smell of smoke or burning would penetrate the room where the parents were, and a search would be made, while the alarm increased. The prevailing theory was that it was a manifestation of the uneasiness of the Devil, and his wish to be revenged upon the preacher for robbing him of so many subjects. At last, however, suspicion fell upon Hetty, and she was made the object of family prayers that God would change her heart and cause her to confess her wickedness. They were practically services of exorcism, and after a time the trouble ceased. It would appear that Hetty committed her acts of incendiarism and other practices in a condition bordering upon somnambulism, because she seemed to know little or nothing about them, or tried to give this impression.

Time passed, and gradually the world became more nearly approaching what to many of us are familiar conditions of our own childhood and adolescence. On the way there, it developed into the days of our grandmothers, who sat up all night with their hair elaborately dressed to go to the coronation of Queen Victoria, and bade a tender farewell to any of their relations who were bold enough to commit themselves to the hazardous journey behind a locomotive propelled by steam, rather than to the old and trusted stage coach. Our mothers told us of the days when they were never allowed to see their fiancés without a chaperone, and the only moment alone with them might be stolen when letting them out of the front-door in the evening. A chaperone was necessary, too, at every ball, and the waltz was as much in disfavour as the various dances of negro origin which have caused so much dispute in the present day.

In a little book, published in 1825, called *Hints from an Invalid Mother to Her Daughter on Subjects connected with Moral and Religious Improvement in the Conduct of Life*, by Anna Williams, we find the following wonderful passage, which sums up this attitude of the early nineteenth century.

Under proper restrictions, I am inclined to believe that of all the various recreations invented, either for the purpose of relaxation or dissipation, that of dancing is the most harmless; but it must be confined to proper society, reasonable hours, and kept within due bounds. Within the latter appellation you well know that I do not include that immodest though fashionable dance the *Waltz*. I have ever strictly forbidden your attempting it; and I charge you on the blessing of a parent, never to engage in it. The introduction of so licentious a dance amongst English women is a national opprobrium; they have hitherto stood so proudly pre-eminent for the purity and decorum of their manners, and their chaste style of dancing. But to Christian morals it is derogatory and repugnant in the extreme, and cannot be witnessed by a pure mind without disgust.

This little book is inscribed upon the inside of the cover, "Mary Kent, Radley Hall, The Gift of her dear Papa." What Mary thought about all these pious maxims we do not know, and one is left wondering whether she ever experimented upon the waltz or followed the advice contained in this volume and refrained.

Even we can remember in our adolescent days that we were not supposed to go about in London without an escort of some sort. That we were warned about stopping to look in the shop-windows. We were told that no young lady ever rode in a hansom cab by herself, or went on the top of an omnibus. It was supposed, too, that if we played tennis we did not run about too much, because it was not nice to get hot, and that croquet was thought to be a much more ladylike game.

Then bicycles were introduced. This meant the emancipation of the adolescent to a remarkable degree. She learned to ride and went out with her brother or a party of other girls and boys for a picnic. The former inevitable chaperone had now to be left behind, because she had not been able to learn to ride a bicycle or had had scruples that such a thing was quite out of the question on grounds of modesty, because "one had to sit astride it, and that was too dreadful." Automatically the girl became free of her in this and other ways.

In 1885 was founded a school in Brighton, which afterwards became famous as Roedean. The Education Commission Inquiry of 1864–67 had thrown considerable light upon the question, and various foundations for the institution of public day schools for girls where education could be obtained at moderate fees throughout England were the result of its activity.

The educational advantages open to girls in America were, without doubt, in advance of those to be obtained in this country before this time. This may have been due partly to the fact that because of the conditions of the colonisation co-education had existed in a great many parts, as it had been common in Scotland; and we have also to recollect that many of the early settlers had been Quakers, who have always held a firm belief in the value of a sound education. We must remember that they opened a school for girls in Bristol in 1811, one year after they had founded one for boys in that same city; but in Philadelphia the Society of Friends had established their public school, the forerunner of the famous William Penn Charter School, which was open to all classes and both sexes in the year 1689. In 1750 the Moravians organised a school for girls at Nazareth, while at the end of the eighteenth century the school at Dorchester, Mass., permitted girls to attend from June 6th to October 1st, presumably when the boys were on vacation. In 1789 the "double-headed school" was established at Boston, and a private school for girls, known as the Academy, was opened at Medford, Mass., which was copied shortly afterwards by numberless others in various parts of the country.

The family life of the adolescent girls in the States can best be obtained from the numerous books that were published over there, and which have since enjoyed such immense popularity in this country. Chief among these is probably *Little Women and Good Wives*, by Louisa Alcott. A rather later period is described in that equally famous series, *What Katie Did*. All these books give an extraordinarily good picture of the young girl's life on the other side of the Atlantic.

Yet the adventurous side of the girl's life and doings was not the only one which was represented in the fiction of the day. Other books, which we should now consider extremely morbid, were written by adults, who considered them suitable to mould the minds of growing girls, were bought and presented by their loving parents, and appealed to the masochistic side of the adolescent, who appreciates the idea of suffering and revels in the idea of innocent martyrdom for a great cause. There were a great number of books produced in the middle and end of the nineteenth century of the Cinderella type, such as *Sarah Crewe*, that gave a pathetic account of the ill-treatment and persecution of a little girl who was left in the charge of an old and very sour schoolmistress, who bullied her in the best manner of the fairy-tale stepmother, but who was rescued in the end and lived happily ever after. Another favourite theme at that time was the adolescent girl persecuted, once more for righteousness' sake, by a beautiful but worldly-minded mother, whom she finally converted, however. There were numerous examples of this subject, but most of the readers of this book will probably remember the fragile young heroine of the *Wide, Wide World* and her heartless mother, who tied her to the bedpost and whipped her with the dog-whip for saying her prayers and reading her Bible, as well as many other stories of a similar type, providing any amount of emotional romance for the hungry impulses of the adolescent.

A careful and detailed study of the literature provided for the adolescent girl during the centuries would make a fascinating study in itself, since it would show us what her elders thought she would appreciate, or wished her to appreciate, what sentiments and examples they deliberately held up as her models; but unfortunately space does not permit us to pursue the subject here at greater length, as there is still a little more ground to cover concerning the girl of the past before we may go on to the girl of the present in the next chapter.

The next event of particular moment for the development of the freedom of the adolescent was the agitation that arose over the Suffrage Movement. In this the young girl became as much interested as her mother or elder sister, although in most instances she could only look on from afar, and did not often have a chance to take part in the struggle. The first petition for the enfranchisement of women had been presented to Parliament as early as 1867, but it was not until 1906 that the movement became a widely spread and public affair, when the Liberal Party came into power; and at a meeting at the Free Trade Hall, Manchester, Christabel Pankhurst and Annie Kenny asked what the attitude of the party would be towards the question of Votes for Women. Instead of an answer

the two girls were seized by the stewards and thrown roughly into the street, and when they held an indignation meeting they were arrested for obstruction and sentenced to fine and imprisonment. Both chose to go to prison, and the sensation caused by these events was an enormous advertisement to the cause.

The young women of England, many still in the stage of adolescence—mentally if not physically—naturally found in this movement and agitation a wonderful outlet for their typical fondness for *a mission*, for the opportunity of persecution and martyrdom to procure for them some romantic excitement to brighten the routine of the day's doings. It was similar to the zeal of the young Christian martyrs, which sent so many young folks then to a cheerful death. It reappeared during the Children's Crusade, and provoked the enthusiasm of the young schoolgirls at Taunton. They worked the banner for the Duke of Monmouth at the time of his rebellion, which brought them into the hands of Judge Jeffreys at his "Bloody Assize," after the defeat at Sedgemoor. Many years later it stimulated the eagerness with which girls espoused the cause of Bonny Prince Charlie, and they must have regarded Flora Macdonald with the utmost envy for the part she played.

But of all previous landmarks the world's history has given us, none has been so momentous for the adolescent as the experiences of the years 1914–18, the years of the Great War. But as this seems to be the opening of a new epoch for the freedom of the adolescent, it would seem to be better to leave the present chapter at this point and to recommence another section with the events which led up to the position of the girl at the present day.

CHAPTER V

THE ADOLESCENT GIRL IN THE PRESENT

It would seem to be the general opinion that the adolescent girl of to-day has reached the Golden Age, but it is doubtful whether she would agree with this view. We are apt to take into our consideration the aspect of the question which enjoys the greatest prominence in one particular age and to base our arguments upon that, without bearing in mind that the factor which is obtaining the greatest attention at the moment is not the *only* one of importance.

When we were occupied with the survey of the ages and the differences to be found during each for the fate and opportunities for the adolescent, we seemed to discover that the girl could find the chances she needed in each, if she had sufficient courage and initiative to make the most of them for the gratification of her impulses. The psychological basis of supply and demand for outlets for the various impulses seems to change but little within the external circumscription of the environmental influences of limitation.

To determine this we must study the important question of the comparative desires and possible gratifications. The duration of recognised adolescence has perhaps never been greater than at the present day, if we reckon this between the end of childhood marked by physical puberty with its changes and maturity, which is often confused with the recognised marriageable age on the one hand, or when the person seems to show physical maturity upon the other. But by what signs may be recognised mental or psychological maturity? To describe the condition of adult physical growth is a simple matter in comparison with the complicated problem of assessing a corresponding adult stature for the human mind, or to fix a definite line where the

adolescent girl changes her viewpoint and emotional reactions for those of the mature woman.

We cannot fix this by marriage. In the past, when the girl
was usually married in her teens, and to reach the age of
twenty-one without finding a husband was considered a
disgrace to the family or a slur upon the girl, they naturally
did not automatically achieve maturity with the wedding
ceremony, although it may have been assumed that they
did. These young wives and mothers were still psychologically adolescent, and must consequently have had corre-
spondingly difficult conflicts to conform to the requirements
of the mature standards which were thrust upon them.
Their typical fluctuating emotions and changing moods
brought down heavy censure from their elders, who certainly
used to expect that it was possible mechanically to produce
the finished article by suddenly altering external conditions.

It is one of the greatest problems of psychology that one
often finds extraordinarily mature minds and emotions in
quite young children, and that for some reason, which we will
try to investigate later in detail, some human beings fail
to make the transitions that are usual with the passage of
years and that ordinarily keep pace with physical development, remain mentally always children or perpetually
adolescent.

In fact, if we are to believe what some psychologists or
medical men would tell us, the female mentality is always,
even at its highest stage of development, *childish* or at most
adolescent. They believe that it is only the male mind
which matures. In many cases this may appear true, but
it is doubtful if we should find a very high percentage
of male minds which have reached this perfect maturity, if
adequate tests could be applied.

To-day many persons believe it to be possible, through
simple statistics made from an hour or so's investigation of
the performance of certain actions or the working out of

more special problems, to ascertain the ratio of the individual's intelligence quotient and the chronological age. This means in simple English what is his or her mental or intelligence age in comparison with the years of life. It is humiliating, perhaps, to hear from the results of these tests made upon large numbers of people that the average intelligence of the adult man or woman is somewhere between the twelfth and fourteenth year. And this is certainly well within the prescribed limit of adolescence.

The development of the mind, which may roughly be assessed as that of the intellect plus the emotions, varies considerably in different ages and countries from the effect of cumulative education and culture. Thus the mind of a peasant in some remote part, who has never learned to read or write, or has had so little schooling that it is soon forgotten, will be upon much the same level or possibly far below that of our ancestors living in towns of a grade of culture very much higher, but when reading and writing were not yet regarded as necessary knowledge for the average person. The adolescent girl of to-day, for instance, is possessed of more general information than her grandmother and great-grandfather, of a certain type, although her intrinsic knowledge gained from experience of life will be smaller in comparison in some directions, wider in others. The amount of knowledge and technical skill required for living even a simple life increases every ten years in ways that are difficult to estimate, and this demand causes a heavy strain upon personalities who have not a fairly considerable reserve of energy and intelligence to enable them to adjust quickly and easily to requirements made by each fresh decade.

Adolescents who grow up in these rapidly changing conditions of life, still fresh and elastic in mind, more readily learn to adjust to the new conditions than their older relations, who are fundamentally longing to arrest the world's progress, or even to force it back into the old familiar tracks with which they were familiar when they were young, so that they might avoid the pain of conforming to the new conditions. This being the case, we are not straining the point to say that the adolescent knows more about the world as it is to-day in many ways than we who belong to the last generation.

If we make a thorough investigation we find that the average person shows a marked tendency to stop short in early maturity and never advance beyond this point, which becomes their high-water mark of achievement. Thus we find that many professional men and women gain a certain distinction at the end of their academic training. They enter the adult world with some honour won, some book, perhaps, written as a thesis for a degree, or they have gained some coveted post through competitive examination. That attained, and their name becoming connected with this certain subject or discovery, many of them remain at this point. They never advance beyond it, and find it impossible to accept new theories or investigate even their own much farther than the freshness of their youthful energy took them. This seems a great pity, because it would seem that men and women begin to age mentally as soon as their minds and emotions cannot adjust to new conditions or assimilate new ideas.

It is the people who manage to keep a great deal of the eager inquiry of the adolescent mind in spite of their maturity who accomplish so much. They retain their vision of what might be, have enthusiasm enough to attempt something the realisation of which is not certain. They have faith in themselves, to take risks without assured security. It appears that the mature mind has in a large measure adopted *Safety First* as its characteristic slogan. Those who are still mentally young have their eyes directed towards the future rather than upon the past. This is essential for adolescence in order to meet with success. We always need a future to look towards; immediately we cease to turn our eyes thither, and remain satisfied with the present or seek consolidation in the past, we cease to grow or to develop. We are on the way to the slow experiences of decay and death.

This may seem trite and boring enough, but it is generally true. We may look round at the people with whom we are acquainted, and prove it upon them, if we do not want to apply the test to ourselves. This attitude of looking backwards rather than to the future is the great gulf dividing us from the coming generation, making them feel we are out of sympathy with them. This again is true. We are out of sympathy with them and what they represent, for this great reason—that their lives are before them and the best of ours lies in the past.

Should we listen to the remarks of the typical adult, such a person whom, without hesitation, we should call mature, we realise immediately that he believes the Golden Age to be past. It ended simultaneously with his own youth. He will tell you the young people of to-day will never be his equals. No time will ever be so great and so interesting as the dear old times. Listen to the snatches of songs which he hums or whistles. They will seldom be the latest popular ditties, but one he enjoyed in the heyday of his youth, when the song, too, was just out. He dares not reach out for the new things, and yet he often complains that the young people of to-day are so childish they cannot leave what lies behind them to advance towards the unknown.

Still the experiences of the Great War answered this question for one generation at least. The adolescent girl came into her own when and how she was needed. She left the schoolroom and became responsible and useful beyond her years in countless directions in which women had never before been called upon to prove their capability. The young people did it well. But their elders often cavilled at their easy achievement of what to themselves, had they only had the courage enough to own it, was terribly difficult—the hardness of having suddenly to readjust to radically new conditions.

The war and its requirements gave many the opportunity they might never have had otherwise of proving how capable they were of taking responsibility, of learning to do new things well and rapidly, of being free and living without the necessity of wondering what their mothers would have done under similar circumstances—simply because there never had been any similar circumstances. Some people expected they would all be willing to go back contentedly to the old conditions after the war was over. But that was impossible. The world had changed beyond all possibility of return. We had to go on from where we were. Those who went on did so because they were *living*. Those who could not had to be left behind—spiritually and mentally left to die out. If they could not advance nor accept things as they had become, that is to say.

This very real difficulty of adjustment on the part of her elders increases the problems and conflicts of the adolescent of the present generation. We must reflect that persons who are educating her are often those who represent just this type of pre-war woman, her mother or her school-teachers, who are not very young—middle-aged, let us say. Women who, although they may not acknowledge it to others, secretly regret the changes that have come about, and long for the old conditions with which they were familiar in their youth. This time that is unfolding with their daughters growing up around them is as strange and unknown to them as to the girls: more so, because they are in it as strangers and aliens. It is the country of the young. The old secretly deplore the freedom which is given to girls, partly, perhaps, because they are envious as well as jealous. This new freedom also makes it so much the more difficult to continue to keep the same firm control over them as when they were little children. They feel they are being left behind. The girls, in point of fact, know more about this world of to-day than many of these pre-war women.

One finds, only too often, that these women who are so deeply rooted in the past, their own childhood and adolescence, will prefer little children, and are shy of the older girls. They never know what to say to them, and feel that they are critical. This in itself is a confession that they realise differences between them. If we have interests in common and are in sympathy with those around us, it cannot be difficult to know what to talk about.

For this reason one cannot help regretting that teachers who are chosen to take the senior classes or to be the Heads of Girls' Schools should so frequently be women of this age and type, who are only willing to let the world advance at their chosen pace and according to their own ideals of progress.

This influence may have an irritating effect upon the type of adolescent girl who is of the robust, go-ahead kind. It will probably increase in her the tendency to rebel against all rules and authority, which comes to the fore conspicuously at this age. It is usually seen in the girls of strong character, although it will sometimes be found that weaker ones will carry on a covert rebellion, and love to lead a faction in the school secretly against authority. But it has frequently an extremely bad effect also upon the more clinging sort of girl, who has been seeking to hide herself in her home and her childhood all her life, and who is now as timidly clinging to the past as are her teachers. She will readily enough identify herself with the weak ones who are holding back, and feel that because they are doing the same she cannot do better than to imitate them. Of course she will be immensely popular with this element in the teaching staff, or with her mother, should she be of the same type. She will win the most golden opinions, and it will be said of her: "She is such a nice girl; not one of those modern young people, always wanting to be doing something she shouldn't and getting into all sorts of mischief. She is more like us when we were girls—so charming and ladylike!"

Unfortunately this feminine ideal of the past is one of the main difficulties we have to contend against. All that is childish, sentimental, timid, and a trifle silly has become hopelessly identified with the idea of being a woman in many minds. So also, equally unfortunately, has the idea that anything domestic, which often means that the wealth of knowledge concerning housecraft, is considered only fit for the backward, stupid, or very inefficient girls, not *clever* enough to do anything else.

This prevalent attitude which pronounces upon feminine attributes and suitable feminine occupations leads to many difficult conflicts. It has arisen to a great extent from identifications with succeeding generations of schoolmistresses who have held these views and acted upon them. It is increased further by the rigid line of demarcation which popular opinion has drawn between the terms masculine and feminine. The pioneer women who first worked for the education of girls were themselves possessed of the qualities which were then called masculine. They were not conventional when compared with former traditions of womanliness. They did not care for the very limited field of interests which were then considered the pursuits of women. Being energetic, they tried to push out and gain their own freedom by manifestly fighting for women in general. Those who were freed, helped, and educated by these pioneers naturally identified themselves with them, and the attitude gradually became crystallised into the axiom that any girl who was active, who had a love of adventure, and a fairly good equipment of brains, must of necessity scorn anything in the way of work in the house, which could be called domestic. It happened so, and the result was inevitable that domestic work and the making of homes were usually left to those who would have been inefficient in whatever sphere of work they had undertaken. This further alienated from these occupations women of brains who might otherwise have found scope for success and leadership in household management in their own homes, and the bringing up of their own children. Instead she wanted only to concentrate upon mass production in the way of educating those of the less intelligent mothers.

In this way the vicious circle has become a trap from which it is hard to escape. It is inconsistent of teachers when they come to point out to girls who are about to leave school that domestic work is as meritorious an occupation as one of the intellectual professions. The girls have already had an opportunity to notice over a period of many years that these same teachers who are now advocating, or pretending to do so, the value and advantages of home-making, pushed the clever or brilliant girls into scholarships or special training. It was also a cogent fact that they themselves had preferred something different.

The wish to have been a boy, or to become a man, connected with this so-called masculine ideal, is usually present somewhere in the psychological make-up of every girl or woman, more or less near the surface, as the case may be. The wish and conflict connected with its disappointment may not appear to have as much justification to-day as in the past. But nevertheless it appears to be equally strong in these days, when the education of the girl more nearly approximates to that of her brother than formerly, even if not stronger. At adolescence this wish becomes prominent with increasing poignancy in the girl of many types, and possibly for this reason. During her childhood the differences which she observed made between her brother and herself increase. The gulf widens imperceptibly, and to bridge it seems beyond her power and knowledge. She notices that her brothers and old playmates begin to seek each other's society or that of their friends' sisters, in preference to her own, and she feels painfully neglected. The adolescent boy usually does not want the boyish-girl. Should he want a mixture, then he chooses the girlish-boy, but the more normal ones prefer what they consider a "real girl."

They are also unwilling to accept her as one of themselves also, when a group of boys plan some expedition or outing. She feels her position has become definite but unpleasant, and she cannot get her bearings. Often she is unwilling to do so for the present, because to accept definitely her womanhood would seem irrevocably to throw away all chances of being able to become a real boy, if she surrendered to her fate and established herself as a real girl.

Of course it appears to be complete nonsense even to suggest that an adolescent girl can actually entertain any hope, however slight, that she can become a boy. But nevertheless unconsciously we find her juggling with the idea in countless forms, and refusing altogether to relinquish her childish phantasy of "Put me into boy's clothes, Mummy, and then I shall be a boy like Tommy." This is possibly one of the reasons why fairy-tales and magic will appeal so strongly to her at this age. The desire for the wishing-ring is never so active as now and in connection with this subject. In the fairy age anything might happen, and any transformation take place, and the old belief that anything we want sufficiently we can achieve in some way dies hard. The limitations of reality are of little importance in comparison with the strength of these unconscious wishes, and it is this conflict among others which makes the period of adolescence so difficult for the girl of to-day. She has so much, she wants more. She so ardently wants the best of both worlds, the advantages of both sexes, and the disadvantages of neither. She stands and hesitates, trying to make up her mind upon this as well as upon many other questions, and when she does finally make up her mind she is already more than half-way across the great divide between childhood and maturity.

PART II
HOME-LIFE

CHAPTER I

PHYSICAL CHANGES OF ADOLESCENCE

It is usual, when we come to consider this subject from the more scientific side, to distinguish between puberty and adolescence. Strictly speaking, the word *puberty* should be used to apply to the time when the sexual activity awakens, through the action of the ductless glands and the commencement of the inner secretions of the sexual organs, which also cause the appearance of the secondary sexual characteristics. *Adolescence*, however, is a process which is spread out over a number of years, and is technically regarded as commencing with puberty and continuing until we may believe sexual maturity to be complete. With respect to the full meaning of adolescence, it is customary to include all the manifestations and changes which may be discerned in young people at this time, psychological as well as physical—that is, changes in the mind and character as well as those that occur in the body.

It may be well to enumerate briefly and exactly what are regarded as the physiological changes of puberty, distinguishing clearly those that are generally considered the primary sexual characters and which the secondary. It is not uncommon to find that there exist among many people a rather hazy notion concerning these. Upon the other hand, we find that the adolescent girl will often react with a certain amount of fear and repulsion to these anatomical and physical changes when they become so definite that they force themselves upon her notice. Of course it will be seen from the list of anatomical and physiological changes given later that some of these are not visible from the exterior of the body; but the fact that the change has taken place is known by other signs which owe their existence to

H

the fundamental alterations within the body, as well as the inter-related mental changes which accompany them.

The action of the ductless glands and the part they play in these transformations of puberty have not been recognised until comparatively recently, and therefore the influence which their secretions have had upon mind and body was unsuspected. It has been now discovered, however, that any failure in development in these glands—or should they have been removed in childhood, owing to disease or from some other cause—arrests the process of growing up, which may signify so much to our minds. Still more strange, the secondary sexual characteristics of the other sex may appear. Too much or a deficiency in the secretion of these endocrine glands may also produce faulty development, or precocious development, either of which abnormalities have been found to improve with suitable treatment. It is usual at present to administer various glandular extracts and other preparations, but with the greatest care, because it has been demonstrated to be possible to bring about unwelcome psychological symptoms by unsuitable or unrestricted administration of these extracts. Neither is their use safe in unprofessional hands by persons who are not sufficiently experienced or aware of their function, because of the injurious effects which may arise from incorrect dosage, as well as the length of time over which they should be used. It is also necessary to watch carefully for signs of intolerance.

These ductless glands which most concern us in considering their effect upon the girl at puberty are, in place of primary importance, *the ovaries*; and the *mammary glands*, which account for the swelling of the breasts when they start to develop, and the accompanying deposits of fat which give the girl's body its characteristic charm and grace. In addition to these, however, we must also remember that it is frequent to find in cases of difficulty in reaching this transitional period, or in other physical and psychological abnormalities that may occur at the time, a super-activity and enlargement of the *thyroid gland*. This produces the condition known as adolescent goitre, with the familiar enlargement of the front of the neck, increased excitability, and often some attendant heart trouble.

Sometimes disturbance of the action of the *pituitary gland* will cause peculiar manifestations at this time. If the secretion is excessive, we find gigantism appear in children or adolescents; or should the secretion be deficient, a condition of obesity will be found. The limbs and face of the young person will resemble those of an infant, and the sexual organs retain a similar state of childishness from which they do not develop until treated. The mind of the person suffering in these ways remains at an arrested stage of development corresponding with that of their bodies. It has been ascertained that many adolescents who show precocious sexual activity, criminal tendencies, and grave mental derangement, are suffering from abnormal ductless glands.

The *thymus gland*, however, situated at the base of the neck, is larger and more active in childhood, and by the time puberty is reached it has usually diminished considerably in size, if it has not entirely disappeared.

Let us now return to the subject of the primary and secondary sexual characters, which develop in the girl at puberty. For the sake of clarity, it is as well to group them under the three headings of *Anatomical Changes*, or those which take place in the structure of the body and its organs; *Physiological Changes*, which are those concerning the new functions of the body; and *Psychological Changes*—but those will be found in the next chapter.

ANATOMICAL CHANGES

I. Primary Sexual Characteristics

(a) Increased size of the ovaries and commencement of their activity.

(b) Considerable enlargement of the womb or uterus, which during adolescence generally increases its size fourfold.

(c) Great increase in the elasticity of the parts through which the offspring has to pass during its birth. It is in respect of this need that it is now thought that too great or violent exercise during adolescence and the years which immediately follow it may be injurious to the health of the young women who afterwards become mothers. The hardening of the muscles which support the lower abdomen and the pelvic region naturally destroys this elasticity and thus magnifies the difficulties of labour for both mother and child.

(d) Notable increase in blood supply to the genital regions.

II. The Secondary Sexual Characteristics

(a) Change from the childish skeleton which approximated more nearly to that of the male, chiefly a widening of the hips and thus the pelvic cavity. Whether this is due to the increased exercise which the young girl now enjoys, this characteristic is not so marked as formerly. In point of fact, these secondary characteristics have all in the last few years undergone a remarkable change, due to what predisposing causes it is hard to determine—that is, whether they are mainly accounted for by the increased activity of the girl, alterations in the modern diet, clothing, or whether her attitude of mind can have influenced the shape of her body. Still, we cannot fail to note that the typical outline of the adolescent figure is different from what it used to be, if we consider the average, that is to say. In spite of this remarkable tendency of the age, we may still find a great many young girls who conform more or less closely to the former ideal of feminine beauty during adolescence, which set down these secondary characteristics as the typical anatomical changes to be expected at puberty.

(b) Development of the beautiful figure which characterises womanhood. The feminine figure is rounded, as opposed to the masculine, which is angular. The curves are especially marked in the hip, lower limb, and breast, and are produced by a deposition of soft, fatty tissue under the skin. The subcutaneous fat of a woman is more liquid than that of a man, and thereby tends to impart a rounded shape to the parts it covers. (*The Reproduction of Life*, by A. J. Cokkinis, F.R.C.S.)

(c) Enlargement of the breasts.

(d) Lengthening and thickening of the hair upon the head, also appearance of hair in the armpits and on the genital region.

Physiological Changes

(a) The most significant of these is the function of the ovaries, the production and commencement of the discharge of the ova, which means that pregnancy might occur as the result of sexual intercourse.

(b) Menstruation, which occurs suddenly in the young girl, and marks to her mind the dramatic onset of puberty, and which continues more or less regularly each month for a period of some thirty years or so until it ceases when the menopause is reached.

The psychological changes which accompany these bodily alterations of structure and the acquisition of new functions belong chiefly to the next chapter, but cannot altogether be avoided in this when we begin to examine the effect which the physical changes have upon the girl and her daily life. But there are also some well-marked symptoms connected with the general physical health of the girl which are familiar to all of us who come in contact with young people of this age that we must mention, as they are so intimately related to the premonitions of puberty, and will generally be found to precede those manifestations we have already summarised by a few years.

Puberty does not happen as suddenly as we might imagine, but is a summation of a long period of internal development, and the signs which become visible are but the ripening of the preliminary stages that then become recognised. It will be generally stated that the visible signs of puberty first make their appearance in girls about the twelfth or thirteenth year, although in some cases it has been known that little girls may commence menstruating when they are ten, or this manifestation may be delayed as late as the sixteenth year. Usually, however, menstruation is not the first of the pubertal changes, but is reckoned to appear about midway between the onset of physical adolescence and the end. The other physical alterations in the girl's figure will show even an unobservant onlooker that transformations are taking place more vigorously than before, and we see great changes occurring in her features as well as in her expression. The face undergoes swift change, and the childish contours disappear to make way for more adult lines. We may see a rapid increase in the size of the nose, although this is not usually so apparent as in the case of the boy. The length of the face itself seems often to extend perceptibly, and the cheeks, which before resembled those of a child, being round and chubby, will become more shapely. The line from the point of the chin to the ear changes too, while the hair, as well as growing longer and thicker, may become darker or take on some different character, such as becoming more wavy, or, should it have been curly in childhood, it may tend to become straighter.

The girl's growth is generally affected by puberty, and once again we may notice that it suddenly increases or stops altogether for a few years until the internal changes have become established. It would seem that individual energy is not always equal to the many different demands which are put upon it. Great increase of stature will often mean impaired physical robustness, or the strain caused by the development of the internal sexual organs will diminish bodily growth and great increase of muscular strength. One may also observe that too hard mental strain during puberty and adolescence may have an equally injurious effect upon physical growth, and especially deficient food, as well as various emotional factors which we will discuss in the next chapter.

It is extremely unfortunate that a girl should so frequently change schools or enter for some examination just at puberty or during the great stress of adolescence. It has been pointed out many times by those in a position to gain information on this fact that the girl, being more conscientious, is more frequently addicted to the vice of overworking than the boy. We should take into our consideration an additional reason for the girl, who is already being physically drained by various physical and mental readjustments requisite at this time, having to undergo a still greater strain. This is that in many cases, should she come from a home that is by no means well off, she will be expected to help with the housework and the children in the early morning before she sets off to school or when she returns, so that she must then sit up late at night in order to prepare her homework for the next day. This, of course, is a difficulty which the girl at boarding-school, or in homes where the financial situation is easier, does not have to face.

Indeed, we may often hear that mothers of adolescent girls offer quite vigorous opposition to their daughters joining clubs or the Girl Guides. They complain that it takes them away from home, and prevents them being able to give domestic help there which otherwise they would be able to do. As a rule the boys in the household are never expected to assist in this way, unless the family should live in the country and the boys are required to help in the garden or in a small-holding the parents possess. Yet in any case we do not find the boy suffering from this variety of overwork to the same extent, nor so frequently, as the girl.

For several years before the visible signs of puberty are established we may often find the girl suffering from headaches, bilious attacks, or strange, indefinite malaise—the cause of which is seldom determined—intense fatigue bordering upon exhaustion and inertia. These will sometimes be accompanied by more or less definite neurotic symptoms, which trouble the girl before the onset of recognised puberty and clear up gradually during adolescence. In point of fact it is often possible to find these strange manifestations have started quite early in childhood, and if an accurate history had been kept it would have been seen that they had made their appearance with a remarkable and clearly marked periodicity, that afterwards would be found to coincide with her menstrual cycle.

Those persons who have the care of girls of this age, whether at home or at school, are often puzzled as to the best course to pursue in dealing with their problems. Occasionally they may try to ignore all these premonitory signs, and continue to think of the girl as still a child far from approaching her maturity, and to treat her as such. We may, however, find the contrary attitude adopted towards her, with a surprising leap in the opposite direction, which assumes that the girl has suddenly become a woman immediately the first signs of puberty commence. With this idea she receives no more attention, and should any tentative questions be put by the girl they will be met with a response such as "I should have thought that you knew all about that," and nothing further. Both methods are probably devices of the adult to save giving any explanations or facing the situation, and the possible embarrassment she, too, may feel about the subject, which makes her unwilling to talk about it.

It often happens also that the treatment of the girl's physical symptoms may receive one of two opposite kinds of treatment. One is the sentimentally sympathetic, which gives her in many cases the idea that she is seriously ill, probably going into a decline like the heroines of the old-fashioned novels. One must admit, however, that this is not so common as formerly, and that the contrary attitude is the more frequent. This is the super-robust method of rousing the girl in order to "take her out of herself." She will be urged to behave as though she were feeling quite all right, the result of which is only too often that she forces herself on beyond the limits of her power of resistance, and consequently breaks down from overstrain. Why this course of treatment should be recommended will be explained later.

With her first menstruation the girl takes the definite step into womanhood, and it is usually a shock to her, however carefully and well she may have been prepared for its occurrence. Should she have had no preparation, or one that has been inadequate or even injurious in itself, it will naturally be far worse for her, because it has aroused vague fears of something about to happen, she does not know what. We may see a very great difference in this respect between the girls of to-day and those of yesterday. In the past it seems to have been the rule that mothers or older people never thought of warning nor preparing girls in any way, so that they, coming to the knowledge alone and ignorant of its significance, felt the full brunt of the shock. The results of this severe trauma we have learned only too clearly from hearing the life-stories of women who have undertaken psycho-analytical treatment because of some neurotic symptoms or menstrual abnormality. The usual idea which instantly presented itself to the girl who did not jump to the conclusion that she must have injured herself in some way was to believe that she must have contracted some terrible disease for which there was no cure. She would feel herself an outcast and unclean, for which reason she was afraid to tell anyone about her trouble, and to seek information or assistance.

This seems to have happened in countless instances. Nor was the information which eventually she did receive, when unable to disguise her condition any longer, much consolation. It was generally vague, unreassuring, and presented to her the worst possible aspect of the monthly rhythm. Often the adult who was trying to explain things to her would merely say that this was "what being a woman meant; this is the beastly side of life! It will always be like that for you now." She must be very careful never to let anyone know about it, especially men and boys. She must never take a bath nor wash herself *there* when she was unwell, and be careful not to get her feet wet then, because it was very dangerous—that was what her aunt had died of. Nor must she ride her bicycle, play games, nor take any violent exercise when she was like that.

The girl would go away feeling miserable, believing that life henceforward was to be a horror and a disease; that she and all women were outcasts on this account, and therefore she could never be happy again. No wonder that with these warnings dinned into her ears the girl of the past was often an ailing creature throughout her adolescence, probably largely through the agency of suggestion, and that nowadays we hear on the best medical authority that what was formerly known as *green-sickness*, a species of anæmia, has practically ceased to exist.

We now hear occasionally that girls at boarding-schools, certainly those of a more enlightened type, and, one may perhaps guess, without the knowledge of their teachers, discuss the subject without any hesitation or anxiety, comparing notes concerning this most vital and thrilling subject. The experience of those who have already arrived at this stage is sought, and it will be regarded by others who have not yet reached this dignity with pleasurable anticipation instead of fear. Why should it not be looked forward to? Why should not the seal of the entrance to womanhood, even if made in our own blood, not be considered a glory rather than a sign of humiliation and shame? In point of fact it is not a disease. The recurrence of the rhythm is perfectly normal. It need not be regarded as a degradation nor a guilty secret overshadowing our lives and making us miserable from one month's end to the next.

Although the initiation rites of the savages seem to us in some ways unnecessarily cruel, they at least gave the girl a welcome to her womanhood as part of their rituals. At the ceremony, when she was brought back from her seclusion, decked and adorned, she was definitely accepted as a woman of the tribe, and was not ultimately made to feel herself an outcast. She had won her tribal marks, obtained her physical adornments, and knew that the courage with which she had endured her tests and ordeals would be known to the rest of the tribe. This would make her honoured amongst them, not only by the women but the men also, so that in many parts the most gallant of the young males would come to bring her presents in recognition of her quality.

Ultimately, after her ordeals, she was received as a woman and potential mother, a position to be proud of instead of the uncomfortable idea that she had lost her girlhood's freedom, for which there was no adequate reparation nor compensation.

The first shock of menstruation and the consequent distress are, of course, partly psychological, but in this case the two are scarcely to be separated, because we find so often that the physical pain and the anxiety become so closely interwoven that the one stands for the other in course of time. It is no unusual discovery that the girls who suffered most, both physically and mentally, at their first menstruation continue to do so at each recurring period. Whereas those who were adequately prepared, and to whom it came naturally as something that may at times be inconvenient, it is true, but scarcely a calamity after all, suffer very little at these times, even at the commencement and usually not at all afterwards, except under special circumstances of exposure or fatigue.

It is wise, should we find that an adolescent girl suffers a great deal of pain when menstruation first starts, to take her to an experienced gynæcologist, who also knows something of the possible psychological factors which may contribute to her distress. In this case, should the cause be physical, it can probably be easily remedied, which can also be done should the origin be some mental trauma, although the form of treatment prescribed in each case would be different. Whatever the cause, it is not necessary to allow the girl to suffer, under the apprehension that it is part of woman's expiation of the sin of Eve. Formerly this was taken for granted, and an attempt to alleviate menstrual pain, as also that of childbirth, would be considered the weakness of a generation which was seeking to avoid its fate or direct interference with divine arrangements.

We still find, nevertheless, that a large number of people will make vague allusions to the girl's *age* when referring to troubles which frequently arise at puberty or during adolescence, and then dismiss the subject, as though there were nothing that could be done to relieve them. This attitude may be a direct descendant of the spirit which carried out the severe endurance tests of the initiation rites, representing an idea that one must suffer to become a woman, and the belief that it is good for her. Or again, it is possible that the women who shirk the issue of finding out what is best to be done for the girl who has a great deal of pain at her period never themselves experienced any particular discomfort at such times, and therefore imagine that the present-day girl makes an unnecessary fuss over nothing, not realising the devastating effect of long-continued menstrual pain.

There is also another reason for discounting physical or mental suffering which can be experienced during menstruation. By rights, possibly, it should belong to the next chapter, but it is difficult to ignore it entirely here, since it forms one of the main reasons of the modern prevalent attitude taken up respecting the girl's difficulties at the commencement of puberty. This is the wish to be man's equal, and to maintain the theory that the woman does not show any fluctuation in her activity, mental or physical, during the month. It has so often been said that this inequality in accomplishment is one of the greatest barriers that prevent her being considered of equal competence with the male worker, or to having a great career. Consequently many women, who are bent upon this or proving themselves man's equal in every respect, find no other way out of the difficulty than to deny any feelings of indisposition at such times rather than allowing for them, and taking full advantage of the interesting increase of intuitive knowledge which she may frequently be aware she possesses for these few days each month.

This subject has been dealt with in a most ingenious fashion in a novel which was recently published (1930), that shows the authors' extensive knowledge of women and their fluctuating emotions. In *Salome, the Wandering Jewess*, George Viereck and Paul Eldridge give us an account of a woman who set herself the task of conquering the moon, because she, like many of her sex, believed that its influence on the periodicity of life connected in ancient lore with that of the moon, was the greatest hindrance to her conquest of the world.

Taken in all its many aspects, it is a subject which can provide the most intense interest, especially from the two sides, that of the women themselves and their views upon it, and the attitude of the men of all ages and in most countries. From the earliest times, as we have already pointed out in a former chapter, we discover that men have had the greatest fear and horror of the menstruating woman, and took the most elaborate precautions to avoid her or to banish her from their presence during this time. They ascribed to her during these few days magical and limitless power for working evil upon them, and believed that to come in contact with her then would by some means either destroy their virility or interfere with pursuits which they held to be particularly their own.

As it is usual to find that women at this time do often

become especially envious of men, and may entertain hostile feelings toward mankind in general and those males in their immediate environment in particular, one is faced with this problem. Was the origin of the menstrual taboos and the men's fear the outcome of her hostile attitude towards them and her unreliable behaviour at this time, or did the men's laws and banishment of her arising from some primitive fear of blood provoke her desire to be revenged upon them?

The study of cause and effect is always a fascinating one, but in cases where the origin of causes can only be obtained by research into extremely remote times, and when, as in the present case, the subject of the investigation is one that becomes quickly shrouded in almost superstitious mystery even at the present day, to sort them out becomes almost impossible. Still, it is useful to keep both possibilities in mind, nevertheless, when considering this question, and to piece together what evidence we may find that can contribute in the least to the sum-total of data which can be ranged upon one side or the other to corroborate or oppose the hypothesis.

Some information, however, is contributed to this riddle from the Samoan Islands by Margaret Mead, whose book, *Coming of Age in Samoa*, was quoted in the chapter dealing with primitive rites. She tells us that there are practically no menstrual taboos or restrictions among the women of these islands at the present day, except that the girls are told by their mothers it is wiser not to bathe then, but that they have collected this idea from their contact with the white folk settled there. In the past a girl was not allowed to make *kava*, the local ceremonial drink, when she had her period, nor before puberty, but recently even this limitation has given way to expediency. In connection with this absence of taboos we read as follows—and taken relative to the suggestion we have already made that physical pain is the outcome of mental distress it would seem to provide illuminating evidence from the existence of a reversed state of affairs:

The menstruating girl experienced very little pain which might have served to stress for her her new maturity. All of the girls reported back or abdominal pains which, however, were so slight that they seldom interfered in any way with her usual activities. In the table I have counted unusual pain whenever a girl was incapacitated for work, but these cases were in no sense comparable to severe cases of menstrual cramps in our civilisation. They were unaccompanied by dizziness, fainting spells, or pain sufficient to call forth groaning or writhing. The idea of such pain struck all Samoan women as bizarre and humorous when it was described to them. And no special solicitude for her health, mental or physical, was shown to the menstruating girl. *From foreign medical advice they had learned that bathing during menstruation was bad, and a mother occasionally cautioned her daughter not to bathe. There was no sense of shame connected with puberty, nor any need of concealment.* (*Coming of Age in Samoa*, p. 145, by Margaret Mead.)

PSYCHOLOGICAL VIEW OF PHYSICAL CHANGES BY THE GIRL

In the last chapter it has been suggested that in many cases the larger proportion of the girl's troubles at or during adolescence arises from psychological causes. We find also, if we come to examine these, they are derived in a great measure from the past. The present events and experiences will through a certain amount of similarity revive old echoes of childhood's fears, old feelings of guilt and doubts which, although they may have been quietly sleeping for a number of years, suddenly flash up in memory and will not be content to listen to reasoning from the experience of the present.

Let us for our starting-point take this important focus of puberty and try to see what significance it may hold for the girl. We have suggested that during the few years preceding puberty it is not unusual to find that several physiological symptoms may appear, often, it is true, of a quite trivial nature, but which nevertheless may cause considerable inconvenience to the girl or her relatives.

There are several points of interest that we may find if we look rather more closely at these recurring indispositions. In the first place they are apt to repeat some tendency to illness to which the girl was prone as a child. They may always, or nearly always, follow some emotional crisis, and lastly, but by no means of least importance, we will discover, should we have taken the trouble to keep a diary of their occurrence, that they reappear with the greatest regularity between the same dates each month. Each of these factors offers us an interesting problem. Let us take them separately.

They repeat some tendency to illness which was wont to occur when this young person was a child. When we come to study the life-history of any particular child, from the point of view of her physical and psychological health, we often notice that there is usually one organ or part of the body which always seems to bear the brunt of any disturbance of health. We may attribute this to an inherent weakness. We may be quite correct in our assumption, but we may also, if we examine the events of the child's life a little more closely, find that not only did this part of the body seem always a little more weak than the rest, but that, at the same time, some trauma of infancy occurred which was also connected with it. Again, upon investigation, we may learn that at birth or during early infancy there was no particular defect or delicacy, but that it seemed to arise at a certain stage afterwards, and was then repeated from time to time.

For the sake of illustration, let us suppose a baby who at birth was strong and healthy and in whom there was no sign of gastric trouble until it was necessary suddenly to wean her, because of an illness of the mother, which necessitated her removal to hospital. Foods of all kinds were experimented upon for the infant, but all of them proved equally unsuccessful until a nurse tried some special preparation in very small amounts, which she fed to the babe with the greatest of care, and gave the now frail little creature endless attention. The result was that the baby thrived from this time onward, and became, naturally enough, devotedly attached to the nurse.

During the later life of that child, however, from time to time gastric disturbances would happen, and the few years that preceded puberty were punctuated by this recurring digestive trouble, which settled down into bilious attacks with severe headaches of the migraine type. After menstruation had set in they would come the day before the period;

still later upon the first day, and gradually disappeared altogether except on rare occasions, which came to be noted and yielded interesting material. From the same hypothetical case we may go on farther and see what can be gained from other sequences that were to be found.

The second point we put forward in connection with the recurring indisposition was that of the illness or malaise following some emotional crisis of much the same type as the first experience, and that it would then produce the same kind of results. In this case we are imagining we find that the gastric disturbance often reappeared also when anyone else in the house was ill, and there was very little attention to spare for the child until it was observed to be ill too, when it became once more the centre of solicitude.

The doctor would pay a visit to the nursery as well as to the sick-room of the other patient, and a special diet would be prescribed. After that the child would recover quickly and be happy again for a time until the next recurrence of the indigestion. Later on another element always seemed to enter into the sequence of events, which were becoming known in the family as "Peggy's Specials." A family picnic would often produce it, or some particular outing or treat, from which the child would then be of necessity excluded, although outwardly she had been looking forward to it eagerly for a very long time and at which someone was to be present to whom the child was much attached. But let us see what were the results actually gained by the attack.

The child stayed at home in bed, it was true, but reaped an enormous harvest of attention because most of the picnic party came to condole before starting. Someone, usually the same old nurse, stayed behind to look after Peggy. The other guests at the party all heard about the sad event, inquired after her especially, and sent messages to be delivered when the rest returned home. Then came the visits

and news-telling in the evening; often some little present
by way of compensation, and quite often a special visit
from the guest of honour, who spent a little while with the
sick child, being very tender and sympathetic. This is what
happened at a great many of the recurrences. We may see
how it repeated the traumatic event of childhood and provided outwardly at least a number of compensations. But
besides these which were obvious, it supplied still other
wish-fulfilments for the child, as well as being a way of
escape from a situation in which she was perfectly aware
she did not shine.

Parties were to her a terror. She realised that she was
miserable when she was one of a bunch. She was fat, snub-
nosed, and unattractive, quite unable to hold her own in
conversation with a number; unused to playing with other
children of her own age. She preferred grown-ups when she
could get them to herself, and when they were ready to
give her their whole attention, taking enough interest in
her to try to find out what she wanted and what she
had to say; when they were, in fact, doing exactly what
the old nurse had done, giving her all their attention.
She had always declared that this was what had saved
Peggy's life. No one else had been able to feed her,
although the whole household had stood round and offered
suggestions and advice.

So it happened that every crisis that upset the stability
of Peggy's world, the going away of people to whom she
was used, or whom she loved, would revive the same response
which had automatically followed when she was a few
months old. Every threat to her peace or her pride stimulated
her to repeat unconsciously the old attempt to gain in this
way what otherwise she could never win, but always had
the pain of seeing her elder brother and sister go off with.
Both were rather brilliant and popular in their own way.
They were difficult rivals, because they were so many years

older than Peggy; quick and active in body and mind. Peggy was a slow-goer always, but got there eventually, although usually when everyone else had gone away and the race was over, all having forgotten that little Peggy was competing too.

The years before puberty were extremely trying ones for the girl, and it may be as well to continue our illustration of repetitions in the life of a child from her experiences, because it is easier, perhaps, to see them in one girl than in a series of different ones. Again, she was slow in her development, slow in her school work, slow in play, slow at everything but thinking and reading. One book a day would have been the allowance she would have liked, but her reading was restricted, because it was thought to be bad for her to read too much. The elder sister had practically disappeared out of the schoolroom when Peggy was growing up, but was carrying on a more or less ardent affair with Peggy's governess at the time. Peggy thought this scarcely just, because it took a great deal of her time and attention away from herself. The old nurse had deserted her too, and had concentrated her attention and affections for many years now upon a younger sister, thus leaving Peggy quite alone. The brother was at school then, and alternatively they played and fought during the holidays. From somewhere, she did not know where, the girl felt dark clouds gathering around her; for some reason, she did not know why, she felt afraid of going on, and thought that she would like to die before she got to the next stage. What this might actually be she would not have been able to say, had she been asked. But then no one would have asked her about it, because no one had the least idea that there was anything troubling her. She would never have thought of confiding in anyone nor of asking what it was that people were talking about when they seemed to whisper mysteriously about girls growing up as though something peculiar happened to them then.

It appeared that something happened, but she could neither guess nor find out what it could be. Sometimes she thought it might be having teeth out to make room for others to grow; or cutting one's wisdom teeth, about which jokes were often made in her family. Then again she was afraid that when she was fourteen she might be revaccinated, as she knew her sister had been. She wondered whether she would be able to go through this ordeal without being a coward. Perhaps, too, it might just be Confirmation, but she thought she would like that. Yet she always came back to the idea of the vaccination. She was afraid her arm might bleed, and she would not like it. But still consciously Peggy did not know anything about menstruation. As far as she knew, she had seen nothing of it, heard nothing about it, and yet she was so much afraid of something that happened to girls when they were growing up, or rather before they were reckoned grown-up. She felt she would rather die than face it, or, better still, if only it were possible to do as Sleeping Beauty had done—go off to sleep and not wake up until she was a beautiful young woman ready for a lover to come and kiss her awake!

Here we have a curious picture of the girl's unconscious acceptance of the symbolic truth underlying the fairy-tale. Because it is probable that the finger-pricking motif around which the story of the Sleeping Beauty is woven is a picturesque reference to menstruation, and the sleep but the echo of the girl's puberty seclusion, from which she was released by her betrothal or pre-nuptial rites. Many of the old puberty rites, about which the girl had not then heard, although she had always been an eager reader of fairy-tales, myths, and legends, whenever she could get them, are reflected in many of her fears. Thus the ordeal of the tooth-drawing, although this was more frequently practised in the case of the boy than the girl; the idea of the scarifying in the vaccination, when some blood might be drawn, only.

too closely typified the fear of bloodshed, which is always revived to a certain extent in the menstruation anxiety.

It was a time of great trouble for her, and the girl wished to die rather than risk not being able to face her ordeal without proving herself a coward when the time might come. We pointed out in the chapter upon ancient puberty rites that death and rebirth phantasies are repeated constantly by them in a symbolic form; and we will remember the beautiful legend of Persephone and Demeter, the story of the adolescent girl and her mother—the girl who dies and is reborn with each recurring spring. But of this subject we will have more to tell in the chapter on the girl and her mother.

Let us return to the story of Peggy and her troubles. It has already been mentioned that she was late in developing, and it was a severe worry to her that her parents, especially her mother, treated and clothed her almost in the same way as the little sister, seven years younger than herself. Especially in the way of clothes and going to bed, which Peggy could not see was just. Her appearance and her clothes bothered her considerably. She was still fat; and her smocks, falling from yokes cut across her chest, which was beginning to develop although she did her best to hide it, seemed to accentuate her squareness. But her mother just laughed when she made any complaints and told her not to be vain.

Then suddenly one morning she found to her great alarm that her nightgown was stained with blood. She could not imagine what could have happened, and spent a miserable day trying to wipe away the few drops that would keep coming, whatever she did. By evening her clothes were considerably stained and were noticed by the maid, who was helping both girls to go to bed. The old nurse was out for the evening. Peggy said in an off-hand way that she must have scratched herself somehow, and went to bed believing that she was afflicted with the same disease as the woman in the Bible with the issue of blood, and that it was a token of some awful and mysterious sin. These uncomfortable thoughts kept her awake until late that night. She wondered how life would ever come right again, and what would happen when the rest of the family knew about it, which she supposed would have to happen some time.

In the morning her old nurse came to her, and having been told the night before by the maid what had happened, gave her a sanitary towel and a piece of tape, and said that her mother would speak to her after breakfast. It was the custom for this mother and daughter to read a few verses of the Bible together after breakfast, and the girl waited in agony until this was done for the mother to say what she was going to. What she actually said the girl could never remember. But she gathered that what had happened yesterday was something to do with being a woman, and it would always be like that now. That was what she had been afraid of. She would always have to be very careful never to let anyone know when she was like that; never to wash then, nor get her feet wet, because that was what her aunt had died of. She must not bicycle either, because that would be dangerous. With those uncheering views impressed upon her, she was dismissed, and she went to her lessons with mixed feelings.

All day long the thought rang in her mind, "Now I am a woman, not a child any longer—a *woman!*" Just as when her little sister had been born she reiterated the words "I am not the baby now!" until nightfall. And a second thought joined the first, "I wonder whether Mother has told my Father that he has a second daughter now who is a woman." But she did not suppose so, because it seemed to be something to be ashamed of. She wished it were possible there were a ceremony like christening, which proclaimed her a woman to the family and the whole world. Then she would be able to feel she had been honourably received into the company of women, admitted into their fellowship, initiated through the knowledge of this secret thing that had happened. But all went on as it had before, except that she used to feel sick and dizzy and she had the most violent pain at times, which made her wonder how to sit up straight in her chair and pay attention to her lessons. It was not much fun, after all, this being a woman, Peggy thought.

That was the whole history for the time being. The bilious attacks lessened, and she was told that probably this other thing had taken their place. She wished she knew all about it, but she never asked and no one thought to explain.

Several details of this typical story of the girl undergoing her first menstruation are interesting because one finds them with very little variation repeated in large numbers of adolescents. The longing for the ceremony to admit her into some secret society of women is certainly reminiscent of primitive custom, and the point of hoping her father would be told, because it suggests the natural tendency for the girl to seek her father under these circumstances. Once again it reminds us of early usage. In many parts of the world the first rights to the adolescent daughter went to the father, or to anyone else whom he should appoint to represent him, which was afterwards found in the custom of the father choosing the bridegroom or selling his daughter in marriage to the suitor who made the best offer for her.

These are some of the psychological reverberations that may arise in the girl at puberty, but there are others, which are also to be found in the illustration we have given. The hint that the girl connected what had occurred with the idea of disease, sin, guilt, and penalty. These are, of course, always closely bound up together with the idea of blood. It is the same association as that which occurs in the Bible story which leapt into the girl's own mind immediately. The conception of guilt and wrong-doing related with that part of the body is generally linked to some early warnings, or even threats and punishments, that have been made to practically all children at some time or another for playing with or touching their genitals. It may also be associated in a great many cases with vague and frightening warnings, all the more alarming because of their indefinite character, about sitting upon the seats of public lavatories in case they might catch an awful disease that way. What the disease was, and how it could be caught thus had never been explained either, but all these warnings having been once uttered to the child, she naturally links them together, when it appears to her that something which is most unnatural has happened to her body.

There is no more terrifying moment in our lives than when we feel that an old threat or warning has come true. If the threatened punishment has fallen upon us, it proves that we must therefore in some way have been guilty of the related sin. Now if *that* warning is found to be true, and apparently divine retribution does fall upon us for one particular sort of wrong-doing, God may at any moment take vengeance upon us for all the other sins we have committed and about which we have been likewise threatened. In the course of their short lives children used formerly to be told horrible things about the wrath of an Avenging Deity. They are spared a good deal of that to-day, but still plenty of threats and punishments are used towards children in the mistaken belief that fear is the most effective educational principle that exists.

When we come to read books or special chapters upon adolescence and the typical characteristics of changing personality one may expect to find in a young girl of this age, what do we find? Picking one at random, we see these lines:

In women, the psychological changes are much more rapid than in men. They are, in fact, almost sudden—and they are far more profound and subtle. Menstruation is the shock that makes the sudden change. A girl becomes immediately conscious of her womanhood, and every month she is reminded of it. She is no longer an open book, no longer an unreserved and outspoken child, but becomes reserved and delightfully shy. Her mental outlook becomes intensely romantic, everything is changed, and all her thoughts are tinged with the dream of womanhood and the ideal of love. She may not be conscious of the physical side of sex, she is usually unconscious of sexual desire, nevertheless, the wonderful change in her body, in its shape, structure, and functions, impressed her conscious and subconscious mind so profoundly that the whole of her mental and physical life undergoes a complete transformation. All her thoughts are tinged with the ideal, the spiritual side of sex.

This is what one medical man believes to go on in the average girl's mind, evolved apparently out of what *he* thinks about what *he* sees. What a pity he cannot change places with a really shy adolescent for a few days and suffer with her the tortures of the damned, and then we might find he would alter his opinion about her becoming "delightfully shy!" And we might in the next edition of his book be rewarded with a picture that is nearer the real state of affairs, and the thoughts that are in the mind of the actual and average adolescent girl about these changes that happen so suddenly to her body.

If the picture which is here laid before us is the truth, what a happy time adolescence must be for the girl! If this were the case, how can we account for the frequent nervous breakdown, which sends the young adolescent girl to the consulting-rooms of the specialist, the numberless instances of severe conflicts which appear in the minds of these young girls and about which we only hear when we have won her confidence? Are there, then, *no* adolescent conflicts, *no* troubles which may arise over these sudden changes in her body, in her emotions and even her thoughts, that seem to come from a region to which she has never before had access and which many of them feel is a proof of extreme depravity?

But let us continue with our study of the girl as she shows herself to be, and to suffer, and then we shall be better able to judge the truth of the picture we are given by the medical scientist.

In the shyness and reserve of the adolescent girl which some readers may challenge immediately as being inappropriate to apply to the young girl of to-day, we realise that it is here she shows her most intense fear of the future and the new world that seems to be opening out at her feet. In a great many cases, when we come to investigate the true history of what the girl thinks about herself, we may find that one cannot always take for granted the adolescent's *apparent* attitude of fearlessness and nonchalance to mean what it seems to indicate. It may only be too often a disguise to cover her most anxious moments, although one must admit that the modern young girl, who has been brought up without quite so many repressions and inhibitions which beset former generations, is frequently not so severely troubled with shyness and self-consciousness as were the girls of previous times.

Still, in spite of the changed environment of the girl, there are only too many still to be found whose mothers and teachers are doing their best to bring them up upon a plan, copied as faithfully as may be from the education they received when young, with not only similar results, but consequences which are, in fact, worse. The girl who is being brought up upon the methods of a former generation has this great disadvantage. She knows it. Her power of observation is keen enough to notice the difference between her life and the freedom which is enjoyed by other young contemporaries. Also, there is still another drawback, none the less serious. Her friends know it too, that she is made to conform to old-fashioned standards, and even if they do not laugh at her or tease her about it, they do so behind her back, which is a fact she also recognises most probably. No one likes to be an object of ridicule, especially on account of something over which one has no control.

Another difficulty creeps in here as well. The loyalty of the adolescent girl is often conspicuously strong, and she does not like to admit even to herself that the people who are in charge of her are very much behind the times. Thus she is faced with the problem, bitter as it must be, of having to oppose her school-friends and take the part of her parents, whom she must really know are doing something that is silly. She will have to do her best to defend them, and at the same time stifle her own feelings of agreement with the attacking force. That is, of course, if she does not become an out-and-out rebel and go her own way in spite of the home rules and regulations. But that will be a matter to discuss among the conflicts that arise in the home.

One constantly comes across girls, however, who are loyally taking the part of their parents, even in their own conscious thoughts, while inventing phantasies which give us a clue to the truth, as well as providing considerable relief to themselves from this intolerable situation. Most popular among these will be the *foster-child phantasy*, as it is usually called. Its theme is that the girl is not the real daughter of the people who pass as her parents, but has been either stolen by gipsies, put out to nurse, adopted, or numberless other possibilities. She will wander away from her reputed home to find them, and in her wanderings experience all kinds of adventures, exciting, tragic, or humorous according to the disposition of the particular girl, and at last finds her own parents, with whom she lives happily ever after. We all know this story. It appears in countless disguises in juvenile literature all the world over, only the details vary, the outline but seldom. Sometimes it will show a rise or a fall in the social position of the girl, in the difference between herself and her reputed parents. Still, it always gives us the hint that the girl who makes up this phantasy very often tells it to others as a story, writes it, or even reads it as her favourite, is not particularly happy at

home, whether she admits it or not, and that in her unconscious mind at least her parents leave much to be desired.

We shall find phantasies that resemble all the old fairy-
tales, each girl choosing the type which best seems to
illustrate her own particular difficulties or give her vicariously her dearest wish-fulfilments. It will be possible to
learn a great deal about the mental life of the girl from
these phantasies or day-dreams of hers. But it is not often
that we are in a position to know anything about them. It
is usually characteristic of adolescent phantasies particularly that they are kept jealously guarded, and treasured
as private property, simply because they deal with that
part of the life of the girl about which she is most sensitive.
To tell them to others would be to disclose her secrets and
to run the risk of being laughed at. The main groups of
phantasies we had best leave for the other chapters of this
section and divide them appropriately as they belong,
because they are both important and extensive, so that it
takes time and space to do them justice.

This tendency on the part of the girl to hide or disguise
her feelings during adolescence, and to adopt one type of
behaviour in order that no one may suspect that she is
wanting to do exactly the reverse, leads to a great deal of
misunderstanding and suspicion between the girl and the
older generation. Although these people who criticise the
adolescent so unadvantageously and harshly were once in
the same plight themselves, and may sometimes tell one
of the agonies of shyness and self-consciousness from which
they suffered when they were young, they do not ever seem
to imagine that these girls feel exactly as shy and awkward.
They do not seem to see through the disguise of the too
brave front, that is but an attempt to cover the shyness, or
their attitude of grim determination to see the thing through
may give the impression they are off-hand. The onlookers
believe them to be morose and sulky. They take the manner

of the girl at its face value, without having the wit to realise that it is but plate armour adopted to try to control the self-consciousness. It will take so many forms, and is nearly always only too successful thus far that the poor girl will not be thought shy but *rude*. This she will probably infinitely prefer, because she is extremely ashamed of showing her real feelings. Sometimes misguided but quite well-intentioned people believe that they can laugh an adolescent out of shyness, and doubtless find it very amusing to themselves to try, making fun of her plumpness or her long legs, her big feet, or red hands. Usually, however, it makes the girl's condition far worse.

She is worried about so many things then—her behaviour, her appearance, her clothes, and whether she is doing or saying the right thing. Suddenly she feels that quite different standards are expected of her now that she begins to go to grown-up or semi-grown-up parties, except the few fortunate ones who have been making the transition slowly all the time from their babyhood, so there is no perceptible break now or an actual starting of new habits. These few fortunate ones, whose self-confidence has been respected during the whole of their lives, go on happily, not bothered about these things. They do not even think about them. They behave when strangers have to be encountered exactly as when they are with their own family or old friends, and they will be popular because of this absence of party manners or difficulty about settling down in a fresh environment.

It is largely a matter of following the traditions of the family, after all. As we shall see later on, the girl imitates very closely the habits of the family in these respects, unless she has a mother who swamps her daughters altogether. For instance, the mother who is or has been a beauty or famous as a good hostess may be irritated by the want of equal good looks in this transition stage of her adolescent daughter, and her gaucherie arising from inexperience. She may be unwise enough in her annoyance to make some sarcastic remark about the girl in her presence before visitors, or conspicuously leave her nothing to do to help with entertaining. She would probably consider it her duty as a hostess to see to everything herself, and forget that the daughter needs a little help to put her on the right track in social etiquette, and certainly a great deal of help to make the best of her appearance to tide her over this awkward time in such matters as adolescent difficulties over her complexion and rapid growth, concerning advice about clothes and the like. All these little things, small and unimportant as they may seem to the outsider, whose own adolescence is far away, make a great deal of difference to the girl, whose self-consciousness often arises largely on account of the physical changes that take place in her body at this time, and she has not yet gained enough experience to know what to do about them. The medical expert we quoted earlier in this chapter seemed to think that the adolescent girl always appreciated these changes and that they filled her with keen pleasure, taking for granted that the changes that occurred to the adolescent made her, like the fairy-tale princess, radiantly beautiful; but in point of fact the adolescent girl may go through a transition stage which is anything but beautiful, which will cause her the utmost discomfort and be partly responsible for her shyness, which she finds anything but delightful, and self-consciousness, which is a misery.

Girls are not often brought up nowadays upon the theory that they should be seen and not heard, but the mother who is herself a brilliant conversationalist, which often means that she has a keen wit and a somewhat caustic tongue, usually has rather silent daughters. Why, is not difficult to guess. These girls will prefer to go out by themselves and to have their own friends apart from the family, so that they may escape from the burdensome atmosphere of being overwhelmed by the mother's cleverness, as others are by her efficiency. Yet the shy woman who does not find it easy to make friends will have shy daughters too. The capacity for making friendships is a most complex one, and provides some of the weightiest problems the young girl has to face, so intimately are they connected with her home conflicts and those of her parents.

The friendships of adolescents are of extreme importance. It is not infrequent that puberty and the beginnings of adolescence produce a temporary feeling of isolation in the girl. She suddenly feels separated from the children who used to be her most intimate friends by what has occurred to her. Something has come between them now which they cannot discuss. They can no longer share all their experiences; and she is often not immediately accepted by the girls older than herself. She is obliged to wait, therefore, and win gradually a new recognition into a set of her own, as well as to find a new place in the world of her environment.

Sometimes, to act as a compensation to this feeling, we shall find her seeking the society of quite young children for a time. It is not at all uncommon to notice that the young adolescent girl is very good to little children or even tinies for a few years, playing with them and enjoying telling them stories. It gives her self-confidence, and lets her feel thoroughly grown-up in comparison. Or she will attach herself to grown-up persons, who will take the place of the mother to whom she often becomes estranged at adolescence. This naturally is an attempt to put the foster-child phantasy into real life, and to find a new and helpful mother, whom she needs so much just now. Still, in whatever environment she may seek her escape from her problems and herself, she resembles the adolescent Melisande, alone and fighting her conflicts, which seem to have rushed upon her all at once.

CHAPTER III

EMOTIONAL CONFLICTS OF ADOLESCENCE

Under the happiest conditions, however, adolescence must of necessity be a time of conflict for the girl. In her uncertainty about being able to satisfy the demands which are being presented to her and that require a new type of reaction, she is obliged to find new standards for herself which she frequently thinks is a difficult task.

Once more in the attempt to answer this problem we must retrace the steps by which she has come, through babyhood and childhood, and discover there the pattern that has been already laid down for her behaviour. Old-fashioned books upon the subject would have us believe that at this age a new person suddenly appears, with a different character, viewpoint, and mode of action. But when we come to examine the adolescent, not only when she is beginning to enter this transitional stage, but take some interest in her antecedents, we find that upon all sides there are the traces of series of repetitions following one another out of the past.

It has been briefly sketched in the last chapter how the years representing the introduction to puberty and adolescence often revive tendencies to illness which were first noticed in her childhood, closely connected with psychological sequences. Also, not uncommonly, we remark that old psychological trends reappear for a time, if not for long, which had been thought to be outgrown. This causes us to think that in this phase of starting upon a fresh stage of life all old resources at her command, those already familiar, and therefore assessed for values they may possess, will be used once more in time of need when newer responses fail.

K

The uncertainty of the adolescent is largely composed of not considering herself able to appear thoroughly at ease in some new situation. The adolescent girl feels herself very much at a disadvantage through being called upon to manage unfamiliar situations without the requisite knowledge how to do so. The only background which will help her here is when she arrives at the stage of having done these same things several times, and therefore learns by experience what to expect and how to act. It is for this reason that we may often notice the adolescent girl repeating little girls' tactics of not liking to go out to parties by herself and suchlike. She will surrender part of her former independence for the time being in order to have someone there whom she knows, so that she can follow this lead and go back to this shelter and companionship, should strangers not appear to want to talk to her. Often this feeling shows the reverse of reality. The girl, being shy, does not want to try conversation with the strangers, and would rather stay with her escort than try to chat with people she has never seen before.

This reversing the situation is a very favourite one during adolescence. We may remark that it moulds the girl's thoughts and controls her actions in many ways. Once more it is to spare her pride, even in the secrecy of her own thoughts. Part of the girl's reactions, and a large part at that, is to keep up this pretence that she isn't shy, and that she knows perfectly well what to do in any predicament that offers. For this reason we often notice that she is a mass of disguises. To cover her shyness, she will appear too familiar or friendly. For fear of finding herself with nothing left to say, she will never stop talking; and so that people should not think she was not enjoying herself, she will laugh and giggle incessantly. Alternately she will try to behave in an ultra grown-up way, and sometimes go back and see what can be done by playing baby.

Probably no one is so anxious to be thought quite so

grown-up and sophisticated as the girl who is in the first stages of adolescence. For this reason we will find her copying the expressions and mannerisms of a woman of the world, because she believes that simple behaviour might lead others to think her still a child. She follows the same principle with her clothes. Left to herself, she would choose a wardrobe suitable for a woman approaching middle-age, who was anxious to appear as youthful as she could, and never notice that it was inappropriate for herself. Guidance in this matter is difficult in the extreme, because the girl is now only too ready as a rule to think that her elders are doing their best to keep her from growing up to serve some end of their own, against her interest. Another difficulty in the matter of an older woman trying to give her advice upon clothes is that, whether she be the girl's mother, a relative, or friend, if the girl is really fond of her, she will probably wish to imitate her clothes because she admires them as well as herself.

Afraid of not emphasising her new grown-upness enough, she generally overdoes it all round. This will apply equally to her love of decoration. Often she will be exceedingly fond of jewellery or beads, trimmings and flowers, but wants them all at once. Not being content with one beautiful thing which shows off both itself and her own young beauty, she crowds on too much, which cancels the lot. She loves bright colours, and does not hesitate to mix those which an older person would discreetly avoid putting together. It would seem that at adolescence there is this great urge for self-adornment of all kinds, and that the tendency to redundancy shows itself everywhere, reminding us that the experiences of the individual repeat the tendency shown by the development of the race.

Among the primitives who are so important to us in this study, the adolescent girl was adorned and believed it would show the wealth and importance of her family to have as much on in the way of personal decoration as possible. Through the succeeding centuries artistic taste has shown the tendency to demonstrate the appreciation of beauty in adornment through decreasing ostentation, which is usually the inclination also of the older restrained and discriminating person, as opposed to the redundancy of the individual girl or the preference of the savage for bright colours and multitudes of gaudy beads.

Dr. Cyril Burt, in his books upon delinquency in young people, points out that it is the general experience that when an adolescent girl pilfers or steals it is most frequent that she takes small articles of adornment or the money to buy them. Younger children want money for the movies or for sweets, and boys steal for cigarettes or other articles which they feel necessary for the rôle of the grown-up man which they want to adopt, which all show the same tendency.

During adolescence we find that many things take on a symbolic value for the girl over and above their intrinsic value. In the same way that jewellery and smart clothes appear to some as the hall-mark of being grown up or beautiful, we often see that the adolescent girl will go through a stage of candy-eating or develop an inordinate appetite for pastries or ice-cream. The adult, who watches her choosing ices or "cream fancies" with a cup of strong tea for her lunch instead of a more solid and substantial form of nourishment, feels that she is extravagant and frivolous, and would often like to compel her to lay out her money upon something more sustaining, like that which she herself has ordered, and probably consumes every day of the week when her work makes it necessary for her to have her midday meal in a restaurant.

But the girl who lays out her pence upon pastries and a cup of tea buys glamour and romance at the same time. She feeds upon the brightly coloured stuff with her eyes, and nourishes her artistic sense and her developing adolescent soul in a way that the poached egg of the older woman does not, and possibly in a way that the older woman never had the originality or independence to be able to do. "We do not live by bread alone," we are told. Our souls require feeding as well as our bodies. Who can tell what endless compensation can be got from such a meal as a relief from a drab existence, a colourless home-life, and a dull job that absorbs the rest of the girl's time? The very liberty of choice in looking down the menu and selecting anything that takes one's fancy, rather than being given a helping of the uninteresting food which is served at home, is a symbol of adult independence, and makes her realise herself as an individual rather than just one member of a family, a factory-hand, or one of the students at some secretarial college or other training-school.

The girl needs many different ways of showing herself as well as others that she is an entity and not merely one of a group. There is a great deal of attention given nowadays to the supposed need to inculcate in the adolescent the value of the team-spirit. But we sometimes feel that this may be a dangerous tendency all the same, should it mean a too wholesale return to the herd-instinct. It is recommended especially for the soul's welfare of the adolescent, and yet it may actually be the cause of crushing personal individuality, which we must also admit is needed for life, and stifling the new growths by thrusting them back into childish dependence.

The young person needs help to become *a self* in order to realise her personal responsibility, which may not be reached at all in the ordinary conception of the idea of the team or herd, where all will act together and think together, until one can hardly distinguish one from the other.

The adolescent who wants to hide away from the world, to be still the little girl tied to her mother's apron-string, or clinging to the hand of an elder sister, will welcome it of course, because her own uncertainty will enjoy the protection of the crowd. There is, then, no responsibility to face for oneself. If everyone does things together and shares what risks there are to be taken, they appear smaller. It is a revival or even a continuance of childhood, and also takes for granted the existence of a responsible leader, who fills the parent-position and tells everyone what they are to do and how to do it.

Being grown up should comprise the ideal of being an independent human being who has some individual contribution to make to the team, if you will, but not to be just *one* exactly like the rest, or one revives a conception of life which resembles that of the coral insect. The girl who is to grow into a mature woman must learn during adolescence, if not before, to stand on her own feet, or she will never be able to show herself a leader in her turn, the mother of a family, or joint head of a household. She needs to find her own essential mode of self-expression, one place that no one else can fill in quite the same way she can, because of her own peculiar personality or assets. The development of what each person has to offer for such reasons is what we may miss entirely if we are too insistent upon the mass production of team work. Everyone will then do the same thing in the same way, whether they are fitted for that sort of self-expression or not. It is often too wasteful of the capacities of our adolescents, but naturally it forms a wonderful labour-saving device for those who are trying to occupy or find recreations for the young people, and it sounds quite morally excellent, at the same time so unselfish and altruistic.

We may group our adolescents for the moment to illustrate this particular phase of the problem into those who are anxious to grow up, *to advance*, to find a means of self-expression for themselves, and those who are just as ready *to escape* the inevitable development of their age, and to do their best to hide away in the past childhood, which means the reverse of what we have been describing. These girls will try to stay children as long as ever they can. They like to wear the most juvenile clothes possible; they continue to live their lives at home or in as close imitation as possible of their home and childhood. They are only too willing to join in the group game, and to be one of a multitude where their doings will never be noticed and they have the minimum of personal responsibility. They are open to every suggestion about what they might do to amuse themselves and to occupy their time, and will be looked upon as the very angels of the team spirit.

But they remain children all the same, and one is forced to wonder what will happen to them if ever they are faced with the necessity of becoming units, to stand on their own feet and decide for themselves about the responsibilities of life. What sort of homes will they make? Could they take the position of mother of a family and manage the household, or would they allow it to manage them, and still shrink from all decisions that would be necessary and allow life to slide by somehow?

The usual fate of these girls, however, who have clung so tenaciously to their childhood is that they remain unmarried or become childlike, almost doll-like wives, who require their husbands to be a mother or nurse-maid to them. Or they may take up some work which enables them to live in some institution or community of women, where they all still do everything in the same way as they are told, living by rule and regulation, because they have never learned to do otherwise, and would be much too afraid of life to do anything else. They may grow up to be old women, but mentally they remain children or timid adolescents who cannot advance farther because the uncertainty of life frightens them, and the sense of the protection of the multitude is so reassuring.

It has been *the cultivation* of this particular type of woman, conservative, clinging, and docile, which has, although certainly preferred by a large number of different sections of the community and for various reasons, led to the belief that the woman is a more primitive and rudimentary being, possessed of a more simple and childish intelligence, than the man.

One of the reasons for the unpopularity of the type of adolescent who is regarded as characteristic of the present day is that she is trying to struggle away from the old tradition of womanhood and insisting upon finding herself. She is usually a strong type of girl mentally and physically, with plenty of enterprise to realise what she would like, and tries to get it with courage equal to the risk of rebuff.

We may often wonder whether the physical component has not got a great deal to do with the formation of character. This is true to a certain extent, but not entirely. It is by no means common that what we call reaction-formation and compensation enters into the scheme of things, and we find a strong character in a most frail body. A girl with apparently every physical handicap that a malign fate can supply makes her mental activity accomplish an individual intellectual development, far in advance of that achieved by those who have perfect physical health. The activity of the mind will compensate for enforced bodily inaction, because it is necessary to find methods of securing some outlet for energy that provides gratification for the essential instincts before life can be lived with any degree of happiness.

The girl strong in body may also have a strong character, of course, and be capable of getting a great deal of satisfaction and enjoyment out of life, as well as being a most useful member of society. But she will generally be a doer rather than a thinker. The girl, strong physically, seeks her outlets usually in sport, organisation, outdoor games, and occupations connected with country life, and needs these ways of finding her fulfilment to prevent her splendid energy running to waste. She will procure the keenest pleasure from muscular exercise, and a sense of well-being equal to that which a more intellectual girl derives from the use of her brains.

It is for reasons such as these that it becomes unpractical to try to bring up girls upon a mass-production system. We should give them an opportunity to develop their own tendencies, and try to restrain ourselves from attempting to guide them along lines of interest which may be our own, or applicable to quite another type, because this seems preferable to us, or there are more openings in life for a girl with these proclivities. Such attempts at guiding the adolescent girl provide a large number of her conflicts from without, and which often struggle fiercely with those from within, which are at the same time competing for her attention.

There is another important group of conflicts from within the personality which made a considerable amount of stress both for the girl and those around her. Besides the two types of adolescent which we have described so far, each having her own particular reactions to difficulties, the weak or regressive and the strong and progressive character, there is another that often closely approximates to this latter class. This is the girl who has always wanted to be the boy.

She may or may not be a girl with brothers of her own, with whom she has been brought up. We find her in the family of daughters only, or among the ranks of only children. These details merely contribute colour to her wishes, as it were, but do not add much to the shape of her fundamental desires. To her especially the time of puberty and adolescence is a time of intense conflict and a continual fight against the realisation that do what she may she cannot become what she wants so much—to grow up into a man.

There are very few girls indeed who have not at some time or other wished to be a boy, either consciously or unconsciously, when some family occurrence or some prohibition arising from the argument "You must not do or have that, because you are a girl, and that is for boys only," has refused something upon which her heart was set. The fact that a girl is or is not satisfied with her own sex may be largely a matter of the experiences of early home-life in watching the behaviour of her father and mother. This is of the greatest significance, because the little girl will adopt the majority of her parents' opinions as a rule, especially the unspoken ones, and will be influenced immensely by her mother's acceptance or refusal to be happy as an adult woman, and her father's attitude towards her mother. It will not be so much what they tell her as what she observed from noticing them together, and realising what each means to the other, as well as that which she feels goes on between them when she is not there that will build up in her mind the full conception of what being a woman means.

Menstruation comes as a particularly heavy blow to the girl who has always made the boy her ideal. This stamps her irrevocably different, and each succeeding period reminds her only too poignantly of her disappointment. She will resent also the other physical signs of approaching womanhood, and try to disguise her developing breasts in every way she can. As a means of escaping the inevitable, as well as attempting to provide a compensation, she will often do her best to be as masculine as possible. She does everything in her power to avoid those things which she regards as essentially feminine. She is noisy, rough, cultivates more than the usual clumsiness of the adolescent, which comes from rapidly growing limbs, large hands and feet; drops things and knocks them over, feeling it the greatest compliment when her exasperated parents tell her she is as bad as an overgrown boy about the house. Still, her frustrated ideal will make her unhappy about it, nevertheless, and she feels that everyone is against her.

She wants to take up all the hobbies and sports which are usually considered typical of the boy. She reads boys' adventure and school stories, and does her best to get herself adopted companion by her brothers and their friends in their escapades. If possible, she finds ways of fighting them, to prove to herself as well as to them that she is as strong as or stronger than they. She will attempt all kinds of hazardous adventures, and makes her family thoroughly nervous about what she will try to do next.

These are her reactions when she is frankly doing her best to act the boy as closely as she can, and when her wish to change her sex is fully conscious. We notice other interesting manifestations which represent the *unconscious wish* of the girl to be a boy. It may come to the surface as ultra-feminism to disguise her wish, with the tendency of adolescence which cherishes the desire so dearly that it will be guarded from detection as much as possible to spare the pain of being known to want something that one cannot have. Or it may be so deeply buried in the unconscious mind that the girl herself is not aware of it, and she only shows her tendency by a general dissatisfaction with life, and a hopeless despondency at ever being able to do anything right or of finding anything that is worth doing. Having failed so fundamentally as to be only a girl when she wanted to be a boy, it causes her to believe herself doomed to failure altogether. It will be hard to get a girl of this type to take up any new interest or work because of the certainty of failure which she imagines will block her way. The only hope of her being able to get enough courage to start will be through a fortunate identification which she might happen to make with someone progressive.

Another manifestation of the same disappointment is an intense jealousy of boys, which shows itself in an aversion to them and everything that belongs to them. She does not want to have anything to do with them, and quarrels with them at every opportunity, going out of her way to run them down and tell people what inferior creatures she thinks them. She becomes a young man-hater, but does not seem to suspect the truth herself—that it is a sign of her envy. In this connection we find envy, hatred, and malice three close neighbours, and the girl may frequently take the opportunity, should it arise, to cause some injury to various kinds of males or to their belongings, although ostensibly it will happen as the result of an accident.

Her disappointment at not being a boy gives her a universal grudge. To whom she attributes the mistake over her sex, as she thinks it, may only be discovered indirectly, in spite of the fact that it is of the greatest importance, because her general discontent will exclude all recognition by herself of the true focus of her sorrow. It would appear that she sometimes blames her mother for the unhappiness, believing it to have been her fault that nothing goes right. In other cases she will consider her father prefers his sons and makes favourites of them, giving them everything they wish for, while she is always the one to go without.

She may believe it to have been Fate. She was born unlucky, and if only she could find some talisman to change her luck everything would come right again. It is easy to recognise what the symbol of the talisman means to her. She wants the token of masculinity of which she feels she has been deprived, and is vainly seeking something which she may take as its substitute. Some girls discover it in work, sport, or some other outlet for their disappointment. But it is difficult to gain a satisfactory compensation, because it will break down over and over again with the recognition that after all this is not the real thing, and what she really wants can never be attained.

Some girls may show their disappointment in a negative attitude to life in general by rebellion against home and parents; then afterwards beyond the home in school-life or authorities wherever they go. All man-made laws will appear to them designed hostility to themselves. They will do their best to break them whenever possible, and should they incur punishment for their actions believe this one more injustice of the world against the female sex, themselves in particular. They emphasise ways in which there is a double code for men and for women, always drawing attention to cases where the advantage seems to favour the man and ignore those where women have some privilege or preference. They will ardently support Women's Rights, and formerly attained intense gratification by joining the Suffrage Movement.

They utterly refuse to see that men will never take them for one of themselves, and that by trying to become imitation men they lose their power, which as women they could have in abundance, because thus they can supply what he needs, the woman element, which is a very great need, certainly, in the lives of most men. The more womanly, therefore, the woman, the greater power she has over the man, because she more completely fulfils this need, although his demand will often make a hypocrite of her, without his being aware of it.

It is interesting to examine more closely the focus of the girl's rebel proclivities, which tendencies often lead to actions that gain notoriety of a kind as forms of delinquency, and to notice whether they will be directed mainly towards members of her own sex or those of the opposite one, or if they arise from her instinctual emotions, her love, and her hate; her impulses to cause suffering or to draw suffering upon herself; her curiosity or her longings to attract attention connected with her desire for admiration and love.

We must leave these last for the chapter allotted to them, because they will often be connected with the girl's early love for mother and father. We must approach them gradually step by step as we retrace the old family situation which repeats itself during the unfolding of the girl's life-story. These few points upon which we have touched in the present chapter are not yet dealt with from all angles, but they will also have to be filled in as we go until the whole picture stands more or less complete, showing some details in high relief while others are left in sombre shadow.

INSTINCTUAL CONFLICTS

There is also another group of conflicts which troubles adolescent girls, arising from their emotions and impulses. From puberty onwards, as well as the few years before it, concurrently with the premonitory physical warnings which we have already described, fresh emotions or new manifestations of old ones find their way into the girl's mind, and at first provide her with considerable anxiety.

Some she may recognise as revivals of feelings she first experienced during childhood. In those days they brought down punishment upon her or scoldings, until she had learned to control their outward appearance, or at any rate to disguise them from the people around her. They will generally be noticed to be intimately connected with the tendencies to which psycho-analysts have given the name of the *Component Instincts*, and which play an important part in the early development of children. They appear conspicuously also during adolescence among the reanimation of former psychological mechanisms and forces, as well as assuming still greater significance later on in the formation of various kinds of neurotic troubles, perversions, criminal tendencies, or when sublimated act as the driving-force behind many creative or artistic forms of work.

They are generally grouped as follows, and in pairs:

Love and Hate, with which jealousy is related.
Masochism, pleasure derived from suffering, caused by the self or another.
Sadism, causing pain to others, or pleasure taken from the idea or thoughts upon this topic.
Curiosity, the desire to look or find out.
Exhibitionism, the desire to be looked at and admired; or to show off.

For the moment we may dismiss the first pair of instincts, since they commonly concern, in place of first importance, the girl's parents, brothers and sisters or friends, and consequently will receive attention in the special chapters devoted to these subjects, which makes it unnecessary to describe their details twice over. The others also near the surface, or, we might say, break through the repressing forces and seek means of expression during adolescence whenever they have a chance to do so.

We have already referred to ways in which the adolescent girl seems to seek occasions in which she may be caused pain. From time to time we meet those who before going to sleep each night indulge in elaborate phantasies of torture or of being beaten. Sometimes they accompany these with actual self-inflicted tortures or beat themselves, which may or may not be directly connected with some form of more direct masturbation that gives rise to sexual feelings of a pronounced type, causing great satisfaction, and ending frequently in a climax which approximates to the adult orgasm, after which sleep occurs. Dreams of a similar nature may equally produce gratification of this same wish, or we shall find the girl showing a marked preference for books giving vivid descriptions of these subjects. Naturally should she be able to find descriptions of the primitive initiation ceremonies of the savages, these will furnish her with peculiar interest, and she may proceed to experiment upon them forthwith.

The masochistic instinct of the young girl may also lead her to try to find friends with the opposite tendency, that of *sadism*, direct or indirect, and induce them, under cover of playing a game, acting or the like, to carry out some forms of physical torture upon her or each other. In other cases the pain which the girl desires may be mental, which she gains from the teasing, or bullying, of some older women, by which she will incidentally derive sadistic pleasure for herself.

In point of fact, we come across groups of adolescent girl friends fairly often, who will mutually enjoy exciting orgies of this kind of gratification from the inter-related instincts, under the guise of playing at endurance tests, torturing, Spanish Inquisitions, etc. They are quite unaware that the feelings they procure from them are of undoubtedly sexual origin, that act as a discharge for the gathering emotions connected with the sexual impulse, which takes on new colour at this time, but which the girl seldom recognises as such. It is interesting to note that these sadistic or masochistic games occurring among groups of two or more girls seem to take the same place that more definite mutual masturbation does among boys, although games of a highly developed sado-masochistic nature have been recorded in many parts among groups of schoolboys in the pubertal or pre-pubertal period.

We have all known girls who show definite manifestations of pure, undisguised sadism. They will want to tease or hurt their relations or companions, physically or verbally, and generally find only too many ingenious ways of doing so without having to resort to the phantasy method. This, however, does not prevent the fabrication of day-dreams of the same sort, which again take place in the interval between going to bed and falling asleep, similar to her masochistic phantasies, except that these sadistic ones usually concern other people. These sadistic day-dreams, as well as another related pleasure, that of hero-worship directed to some sadistic figure of ancient history or romance, which she has read about or seen upon the stage or screen, will give her intense delight, although she may do her best to keep this excitement to herself.

One of the chief reasons why she should keep these day-dreams to herself, including the thrill she derives from them, or impart them only to a very select group of like-minded companions, is that these component instincts, having been checked and repressed in childhood, all are imbued with a certain amount of guilt. To allow unsympathetic, that is to say *forbidding*, adults into the secret would be to run the risk of calling down censure upon oneself as in time past. The greater the guilt which is experienced now, the more significant was the part it played in the past, in all probability; the greater the pleasure derived from it then, and the greater the prohibition. All these steps may be reconstructed out of material shown by the behaviour of the adolescent, and often corroborated by her own early memories.

Everyone will admit that the third pair of component instincts, the desire to find out about things or to look, and its opposite, the wish to be looked at and to be admired, which may appear in its painful contrary tendency, the fear of being looked at or watched, are familiar enough among young people in their teens. They are so frequent and so obvious that there would seem to be little more to say about them, except to warn those who feel that they are some of the frailties of the girl, which ought to be promptly and thoroughly weeded out, to be cautious over the weeding operations. It is quite possible to pull up growths so roughly that too much of the root is dragged away, which will leave the plant sterile and the garden bare in the future, or turn some of these natural impulses into neurotic disorders or perversions through the unwise

L

handling. This transformation of instincts, which are suitable in their own place and in moderation, is brought about in order to avoid unbearable guilt or punishment on the part of the girl, or she is made so self-conscious about them that their gratification in any form whatever becomes impossible or a cause of constant anxiety.

Adolescent *curiosity* finds little sympathy with the adult in its form of inquisitiveness over the affairs of grown-ups. But it often, nevertheless, covers a justifiable desire to learn something about the life which is before the girl as an adult woman, and details that may be grouped under the title of sex information, which, after all, she ought to know now, even if it has been refused her before. One hears of terrible chaos occurring at a girls' school, which, after all, is representative of many, when a little group of companions were found discussing that all-important theme, *Where do babies come from, and why?* No one had or would have told them because of conscientious scruples. So the girls had each sought information from varying sources at her command, and they were holding a symposium on the subject. But because it was the natural history of sex in themselves and the human race, and not a nature study class upon the reproductive habits of flowers or birds, it was anathema, and the girls were all practically expelled. Adolescence suddenly brings the girl face to face with the desire to know so many things, and she cannot satisfactorily sublimate all the desires provided by this instinct through her scientific studies provided by the school curriculum.

But if the component instinct of curiosity may find a rough or chilly reception when it appears at adolescence, the other side of it, *Exhibitionism*, is usually frowned upon still more severely, in many or most of its manifestations. We have already touched upon the girl's love of adornment and dressing-up, so that she may win her own admiration as well as that of others who see her. She wants to resemble the girl who was turned into a beautiful princess in the fairy-tale by the agency of the fairy-godmother's wand, which represents the transformation from the coltish stage of Cinderella-adolescence into blossoming young womanhood without the difficulty of passing through it slowly and painfully.

We have pointed out that she needs careful help over this rather exuberant or elderly preference for clothes. But after all, we see as many girls nowadays showing their exhibitionistic tendency to *outré* dressing by adopting pseudo-masculine garments or being conspicuous in wearing clothes inappropriate to the occasion, even crudely ugly, in order to avoid what they believe to be *showing off* by wearing feminine attire that is in itself charming. They have been made to feel that it is a crime to make themselves beautiful because this is *showing-off*. It is the only way they recognise, and so they fly to the opposite extreme, but only accomplish the same effect by calling even more attention to themselves and their clothes, through untidiness or sheer ugliness of their apparel, than they could have done by other means.

The seeking of self-expression through clothes is of course an interesting study in itself, in its positive as well as its negative form. The fear of being conspicuous from which so many young girls suffer acutely, and the relative anxiety that people will look at them when they are walking down the street or through the lounge of an hotel or restaurant, where many persons are sitting, who may notice them, is intense. The antecedents of this fear are usually as follows: In childhood the little girl was showing too plainly the natural impulse of appreciating the admiring glances that were cast in her direction, and was rather harshly reprimanded for it. She was told that this was naughty, that no one would love a vain little girl, and it was something to be ashamed of. Perhaps the mother or nurse went on to emphasise the fact that this small child was not even a pretty little girl (although this may not have been quite true). Therefore, why should anyone want to look at her, unless to see if she had cleaned her teeth that morning or if she had a smut on her nose?

Results: the girl grows up morbidly self-conscious, obsessed with the idea that she is so ugly as to be repulsive, that she may always have a smut on her nose should anyone be noticed glancing in her direction. She feels that it is useless for her even to try to make the best of her appearance as she is so hopelessly plain, and continues to fret about it.

This treatment of the child may have been well meant in the beginning, but one may see that very unwelcome consequences arise from the thoughtless remarks. Why should not children be allowed to enjoy the fact that they themselves are pretty as well as being taught to gain pleasure from any other beautiful object? We encourage them, or try to do so, in æsthetic appreciation of other things; why should we exclude this important manifestation of beauty? They are quite observant enough as a rule to realise that their parents take more notice of other pretty children than plain ones. And in any case, what good is accomplished by causing them misery for years even if finally they do make the discovery that once again their parents were lying to them for some obscure reasons of their own?

If children were given a more sound appreciation of beauty in its fullest conception they would probably in the end be less conceited than those who are allowed to pick up opinions haphazard, and get a one-sided view of the value of good looks and what can and cannot be done with them.

Education of the young through awakening their sense of guilt is a limiting method after all. It impoverishes human nature so much if the only reason for refraining from a certain course of action is because someone will scold or punish if they find out about it. This furtive attitude to life is destructive rather than constructive, and yet people actually so often train young girls to be furtive either directly or indirectly.

The adolescent girl needs considerable assurance of her own power and assets. This search for reassurance often lies behind her attempts at showing-off, either in respect of her appearance, her self, or relative to something which she can do. If she has some real talent which she may exercise and so gain her applause that way, so much the better, because if she cares enough for her art her development of it will give her an ideal of achievement and teach her artistic discrimination in course of time. If she has no outlet of this kind, it is more difficult, but it is generally possible to find some direction in which the girl can gain the appreciation her soul longs for in a legitimate fashion by the cultivation of some talent or proficiency. This will help to keep the balance from tilting too much to one side or the other. The girl will thus be prevented from contracting distorted ideas about what she can do and what she cannot, learning to assess her own capabilities justly, without becoming morbidly sensitive about the criticism of other people, which is frequently pronounced at this time.

We have mentioned already that the girl begins to be conscious of more definite sexual feelings during adolescence than before, and may suspect in some instances what their significance may be. She will become alarmed as the truth filters into her brain, terrified lest this is something unusual and a proof that she is abnormal—the over-sexed woman she has read about. She may have gained some hints about this in one of the nasty little books which unfortunately get passed round to adolescent girls by people who ought to know better, but who, strangely enough, often give them away without reading them or pausing to wonder what impression they will get from them.

These feelings which often rush upon the girl now, accompanying the experiences of the first few months of menstruation, may cause her to seek relief by masturbation in a more adult form than those to which the little girl usually has recourse. The fact that she has done this, together with the realisation that it has both relieved the tension and provided pleasure, may in a great many cases make her feel still more depraved and guilty. Should she only be fortunate enough to meet with someone who can give her a wise assurance that after all this is a natural phase, and that it frequently happens at this time and usually passes off again into the background when her adolescence becomes more firmly established, it will be an enormous gain. She needs to know that in any case the practice is neither the sign of moral degeneracy nor a symptom of sexual disease, the forerunner of incipient insanity or any other of the alarming alternatives suggested in the little books upon purity and the like. Her mind might then be set at rest and a great deal of harm avoided for the future. But often she continues in these fears. The anxiety constantly preying upon her mind seems to increase her tendency to masturbate, to see whether the impulse increases or diminishes, whether it is becoming better or worse; if she is really falling under its insidious spell as the books or the warning adults have predicted. They forget the injurious possibilities of these dangerous suggestions, which may affect the adolescent at this impressionable age.

This trouble, as well as others, will frequently turn a girl's thoughts to religion at this age. It may precede the wish to be confirmed (our most definite survival of the puberty ceremonies of the ancients) which may have arisen from witnessing the excitements and preparations which accompanied the Confirmation of an elder sister or even that of a rather older school-friend. The girl generally develops a mild or even passionate devotion for the priest who holds the class for preparation, and the whole affair provides her with a wonderful outlet for her emotions, as well as her impulse for showing-off, since at this time and during the service itself she usually comes in for her fair share of special attention and small privileges. Religious fervour becomes for her a satisfactory vehicle for the time being of a new phase of phantasy-building as well as a means of discharging her pent-up emotions, and the recrudescence of childish guilt concerning sins of the past and the present.

Accompanying the tendency to find interest and an outlet for emotional tension in her own religion, we often notice that some adolescent girls will become absorbed for a few years in reading about ancient cults and forms of mysticism, especially those in which young girls were consecrated to the service of some female deity. Divination, fortune-telling, magic in various guises appeal to her immensely, and probably derive much of their strength from the dynamic of her curiosity in respect to her own future and the revival of memories of the past upon which she often weaves phantasies surprisingly like ancient belief and custom, although the girls in question generally have never had any opportunity to gain any outside information about them.

The other ways in which adolescent girls try to deal with their new emotions, their urge to find fresh outlets for their instincts and tendencies that have exhausted old and childish methods of self-expression, will find a place in the chapter where we will discuss their school-life, because we so frequently find them prominent then and there.

CHAPTER IV

CONFLICTS CONCERNING THE HOME

The problem of the adolescent girl as a unit in the home cannot fail to be an important one. It is also necessary to consider it from many different points of view, as well as to take into our reckoning the social class to which the home belongs. The position of the adolescent girl will vary in many ways according to this grading.

Among the more wealthy and educated classes the adolescent girl is at an important stage in her schooling, whether she is destined at the end of it, still several years away from the commencement of adolescence, to look forward to going home to spend the interval between leaving school and marriage in taking part in home interests, games, and helping her parents with entertaining and various social duties, or training for some career. As a daughter of the professional middle class she will probably be still more seriously and earlier considering her future, trying to make up her mind, or having it made up for her by her parents, what she is going to do to earn her own living in the future, or to be able to do so directly her schooldays are done; while the daughter of a working-class home often leaves school at fourteen and starts off to work then in the first job which offers, or at any rate seriously begins training or starts as an apprentice, almost at the beginning of her adolescence.

In this ambition of the present-day girl to find some work to do we probably see one of the greatest changes that has occurred in her bringing-up during the last few generations. Not so very long ago, in the time of our mothers or grandmothers, the idea of a girl being brought up to earn her living was unthinkable, unless she had lost her father or some similar catastrophe had befallen the family, which made it necessary. It would have been thought strange behaviour on the part of the girl or odd of her parents to have allowed it. It was believed correct for the young girl then to leave school at whatever age her parents thought fit, usually earlier then than at the present day, and afterwards to occupy herself as best she could until a husband could be found for her. There may have been very little for her to do at home, especially if her mother were a busy, energetic woman, who was unwilling to give any of her household duties into the hands of her daughter, however good this preparation may have been for the time when she should have a home of her own. The girl may have *gone on* with the little music or painting which she had learned at school, *taken up* embroidery or parish work. But even then it was not considered *very nice* for her to work too hard at any of these *accomplishments*, for fear people might think she wanted to use them professionally. This would have been regarded as a scandal.

Mediocrity was considered the hallmark of respectability in those days, and many energetic girls who had a real love of their art and enjoyed doing things thoroughly chafed at merely being allowed to play upon the fringes of the work in which they were keenly interested.

Naturally the girls of that time would try to get married as soon as possible in order to have homes of their own, and escape from the enforced and boring idleness of that of their childhood. Others, who could not settle down to this dull routine of doing nothing which really mattered should it be left undone, often incurred the wrath of their fathers and the grief of their mothers by whole-hearted rebellion and did something. They were, however, commonly held up as examples of filial impiety to their social circle, and were regarded as "rather queer" into the bargain.

One possible outlet for their energy was permitted: voluntary work connected with parish activities and other charitable organisations. But this often did not recommend itself to the girl's mind, because, like other amateur artistic outlets allowed her, it was generally carried out in a slip-shod manner. However, many fell in love with the curate, and did it to gain his interest or out of devotion to the vicar. There seemed no other way of escape for her in the home, and unless she were content to sustain her spirit upon these minimal interests, she had to find her focus of energy elsewhere, or through social activities.

The advance of civilisations and the increase of snobbish-ness, perhaps both combined, arranged that the old interests and occupations which formerly must have kept the women of the household busy were taken away from them. In the past these must have given plenty of scope for the use of all their faculties as well as providing ways of utilising whatever artistic gifts they had, in the making and decoration of household linen and other necessaries for a well-ordered home. But these gradually slipped out of the hands of the mothers and daughters, and were left to domestic servants as work not fitted for members of the upper social stratum, or it became the fashion to buy things ready-made rather than to make them at home.

Snobbishness played havoc here, and together with this tendency came the view that to take part in domestic work, to understand anything about the preparation of food or housework of all kinds, was menial; therefore women who did this were inferior because of it, since it could only interest or appeal to those of very inferior intelligence. Some curious theories seem to have developed in consequence.

At first, apparently the greatest sin was for the girl to take money for any work she might do, although she was allowed to give her services voluntarily. Therefore to be a wage-earner was the thing that could not be tolerated. Later, when it became more general for girls of good family to take up a form of employment, even domestic work, provided it were upon a sufficiently large scale, and not carried out in the home, *and* was sufficiently well paid, became acceptable. Thus a girl would go out and polish floors while in training for a hospital nurse, but would have shrunk from helping to nurse her sick mother or an aged aunt. Rather than teach her own little brothers and sisters, she would be a kindergarten teacher or take the post of a nursery governess for the sake of getting away from the home she found so irksome. Again, she would become a waitress at a fashionable teashop, but jibbed at helping her mother with a bi-monthly At Home day or a parish festivity. It would have been considered a social lapse to have gone into the kitchen and learned what the cook there could teach her, so that she could have carried on during a domestic crisis in her own home, or later when she was married and left without a cook through illness or some other emergency. But she would go to an expensive cookery school, or study domestic science, and afterwards earn her living as a lecturer or go out to cook for parties at other folk's houses for which she would ask a high fee.

During the war a great many women felt it in their own hearts a terrible degradation to be obliged to do some of their own housework, especially if it became visible, such as opening the front-door to visitors. But although she would try to scramble out of a sensible overall, fearing a morning caller might realise she had been cooking the mid-day meal, she would not mind appearing in another overall far more dirty, and herself more dishevelled, explaining quite cheerfully that she had been gardening or attending to her poultry. But then it was war-time, and everyone was making a point of doing something they had never done before. And after the war was over one found women becoming more apologetic still when diminished funds made it necessary for them to go on opening the door or looking after their own children.

During the course of advancing civilisation the home fell into increasing disfavour, although recently there seems to be a tendency to try to revive interest in it. It would be a great pity were it to stay under a cloud for the sake of the girls. There are a large number who have not the type of mind that wants to devote itself to one particular branch of study as well as those who have no outstanding talent for any art or science, who in the variety of jobs necessary for the satisfactory running of a home would find excellent outlets for abilities which most women possess, although they do their best to stifle them at present. They do so because of the two reasons we have suggested, first because these occupations are ranked as degrading and intellectually sterile, and also because they are out of fashion. There is no fun to be derived from the joy of creating things *per se*, unless to sell them.

We hear a good deal about arts and crafts nowadays, but professional arts and professional crafts made to sell to other people to decorate their homes, and for purposes which we shall never see. They do not provide a means of expressing ourselves in our own surroundings, for a particular place and an especial purpose. This may sound dreadfully old-fashioned or exceedingly highbrow and modern, whichever way one likes to take it; but let us get down to simple facts. Why should it be boring to work one's own table-mats rather than make them for a shop and with the proceeds go round to a large store and buy cheap ones that have been imported from Italy? Or it might be considered strange to ask friends round to spend the evening and entertain them with food cooked by oneself, specially chosen to suit the occasion, and the guests invited to partake, rather than ask them to admire one's water-colour sketches or listen to music which we made for them.

This may be an odd perversion of civilisation, but the truth that people do feel that way is assured when we hear them offer an apology for anything to eat cooked or prepared by their own hands.

At the other end of the middle-class scale, that slips into that of the working-classes, we find the adolescent girl joining the ranks of the world's workers during the early days of puberty. Her parents definitely want her to become a wage-earner as soon as possible, to contribute to the family budget, which of course she is expected to do until she gets married. Should we inquire into their conception of the word *Home*, we might in many cases get the same answer as that made by the child who was being taught to sing *Home, Sweet Home* at school. Asked by her teacher what Home meant, she said, "Please, teacher, it's the place where we all eats and sleeps." To the very little girl who goes out to work, taking probably the first chance that offers in order to be able to help at home, whether she likes it or not, adolescence must be a time of many conflicts between wishes and reality. It is not surprising that she is anxious to get away to the cinema, join a girls' club, or even waits anxiously for the day to come round for the appearance of her favourite weekly journal of exciting stories, which supply her, by proxy, with adventures and love-affairs that add a little colour to her otherwise drab existence.

Of course, the Girl Guides Movement and the formation of Settlement Clubs, Ramblers' Societies, and the Athletic Clubs belonging to many of the large stores and factories have filled a great need in the lives of many of these girls, but still more are wanted, and an especially urgent necessity is to find the right women to run them.

This, however, is not easy, because the people who are most willing as a rule to give up their time and energy to this sort of thing, interested as they may be in the welfare of our growing girls, are sometimes rather out of date and sympathy with the modern outlook on life, and may try to hold up to the girls a point of view which the girls themselves will regard as old-fashioned. Even if these adolescents do not feel slightly contemptuous, quite affectionately, however, at times, of these usually middle-aged spinsters, they will miss some of the benefits they would undoubtedly gain otherwise from association with persons who were keener upon present-day opportunities and who understood more of the girl's problems of to-day. In this case they could all look together to the ideals of the future rather than one side of the companionship trying to hark back to a standard that has already slipped a long way into the limbo of the past. This question becomes a vital one when we come to describe the part played by friendships and identifications in the life of the adolescent girl, and so we will leave it for further discussion until then.

The chief drawback provided by the education of the modern girl is to the opinion of some that in pushing forward to a new and wider horizon we may stretch the breach between the girl and her home. In all grades of society we find that the majority of parents are inclined to try to keep home conditions approximating to ideals which obtained when they themselves were young. Relatively speaking, we learn upon inquiry that those who are spiritually capable of making progress and advancing with the times are in the minority, although numerically there are a great many. These, of course, will not try to handicap their children from further development, although we may still notice an occasional tendency to want to keep their young sons and daughters at their own level at the present time. They will wish all to advance together and keep together, regardless of the fact that the young need the society of their own contemporaries, and that adolescence is the time for the home ties to be loosened. The natural tendency of the young folk at this age is to show their inclination to leave the parents and wish to join others of the new generation for work and play.

The parents nevertheless often feel a little hurt, thinking that when they are so ready to join the younger generation in their amusements and help them with their work, they ought to be equally satisfied with their society. But this cannot be. Youth calls to youth, and however much the parents believe themselves to be entering into the spirit of youthful adventure, they cannot help doing so from an entirely different angle. It becomes necessary for them to relax their hold on the old bond.

If this natural tendency is not allowed to find fulfilment, and the younger generation permitted to break away gradually from the home-fixation, it will often become almost impossible for it to take place later on. This will frequently be a cause of trouble in the case of the women who have never been able to complete their adolescence and continue into maturity. They remain so closely attached to the home that they *cannot* gain their freedom from it, actually or metaphorically.

Very often, especially in former days, the girl would continue to live at home, and have no friends and few interests outside it. Except, perhaps, she might work in the parish where her home was situated, she went about with her parents, helped in the house, entertained their friends, visited them and her relations. She would never stay away from home, except at the houses of old friends and relations. She had very little opportunity ever to get away from her home or the intimate home circle. She was not allowed to make friends of her own, to know anyone whose family was not on the parents' visiting-list. Thus she never had a chance to get a glimpse of the world outside, to see the inside of a home belonging to a different set of people from those associated with her family. Should she try to do so, she would be severely reprimanded or her feelings appealed to with the reproach: were not her home and her parents' friends good enough for her that she wanted to find others for herself?

For such reasons her world was exceedingly narrow. If by chance marriage took her into a rather different social environment, she was uncomfortable and shy with her new relations, always making comparisons, which were often none too favourable, between her own home and family and those of her husband.

But the girl who is too much of the home-bird and the parents' stand-by seldom marries. She lives with them, their shadow and reflection until they die and the home is broken up. What happens then? Often there is not very much money left for her to live upon. Her parents have cherished a vain hope that of course *some day* she would get married, but not until they were dead and gone. Somebody would look after her, without doubt!

Still, the results were tragic. Her income is inadequate as a means of existence. Perhaps it had been reduced almost to vanishing-point by a long and costly illness of the last surviving parent. Investments which may have brought in a fairly considerable sum years ago when they were first made have dwindled or become entirely worthless. We find before us a woman between forty and fifty, mentally an adolescent, physically middle-aged, who is under the serious and immediate obligation of earning her living, but without assets that will be useful to her in the present-day employment market.

She will tell you that she is a good housekeeper. This means she used to look after her parents' house and keep them in comfort. Yet her ability will not now stand her in very good stead should she try to take a post as housekeeper in a large private house, nor in an institution. She knows nothing about the science and art of catering on a large scale, household management, organising the work of a staff of maids, arranging meals for large numbers attractively or economically. She tells you she can do some fancy-work, and was always in request to make *little things* for bazaars

or sweet stalls, so perhaps she could do something like this?
One looks at her piteous, childlike face full of trust that
something can be found for her to do that won't be too
difficult. One tries as kindly as possible to suggest that the
making of fancy articles is easier than marketing them. As a
last resource, she hints that she was the parish right hand.
Is there nothing she could do in that way—perhaps as a
paid social worker? Vainly does one do one's best to convey
to her that most of the paid work of this kind is now done
by those who have been trained for the work, and that it is
practically impossible these days to earn a living by picking-
up the way. The competition provided by the keen young
folk who have trained for their jobs is far too great.

She may suggest then that she could learn typing, or
perhaps take hair-dressing lessons and become a beauty
specialist. She has heard that there are good openings in that
now. It is pitiful to see the fate of these good home-keeping
daughters after their parents have no further use for them.
And it is this terrible wastage of human beings which makes
one feel resentful when one comes across the view expressed
that it is wrong to bring girls up to some trade or profession
as though they were boys. It may create some economic
congestion, it is true. It may make some parents annoyed
that they can no longer without hesitation keep their
daughters at home to look after them until they need their
services no more, and then turn them adrift into the world
to starve, because they have not any means whereby they
can earn a living.

The urge of the adolescent to rebel against home and to
wish gradually to detach herself from it to make new friends
and to see the world from other points of view is at root a
natural and healthy one. The rebellion need not be a too
sudden or violent one; that it is so is usually the result of
too much pressure being exerted by the home influence. We
are familiar with the same action when applied to the nature

M

of gases. If adequate safety-valves and harmless outlets are supplied, all is well; they can be used to serve excellent purposes. But should we allow no outlets or use for the energy created, supply no safety-valves, and exert undue pressure, the consequence is bound to be a pretty thorough explosion sooner or later.

The conjecture that something of the kind must have occurred is usually correct when we are told a sad tale of woe and home mutiny by a troubled parent, about the sins of the modern young people. They do not realise that it is not a workable hypothesis that what was enough freedom for their own young day ought to be sufficient for the children who are growing up now. One does not know who is most to be pitied—the parent or the daughter. Both seem so utterly incapable of grasping that the other's point of view is honest or genuine. The child thinks that the parents are being wilfully unkind or that they are maliciously denying the chance of doing interesting things, just because they did not do them, nor want to do them when they were young, and the parents believe that the daughter is perverse and purposely wants to do *these impossible things* just for the sake of being tiresome, rebellious, and in the fashion.

Well, perhaps she does. It is an honest sign of growth and development that she should be. The parents, if we could get them to realise it, were probably equally anxious to exceed family rules and regulations when they were the same age. But they have generally forgotten these events, and the *rows* that took place in their families over very much the same sort of thing, if not, of course, the identical occurrences, although the similarity might have been surprisingly close. Each succeeding generation, once it has settled down to feel its own way the right way, begins to think the one before it old-fashioned and the one that is following hard upon its heels as thoroughly abandoned and wanting in moral stability. Yet one generation as it follows another carries on somehow, and manages to acquit itself fairly creditably, in spite of the head-shakings of the last and the amused contempt of the next. In this way the young folk of the Edwardian era used to ridicule what they called Early Victorian ways and manners. But nowadays bright young Georgians find endless amusement over the habits and pleasures of the Edwardian age.

Although so many adolescents will be dissatisfied with their homes and may look forward to marriage as a means of having one of their own to escape that of their parents, which is still fairly frequent, in spite of the moan of the pessimist, who declares a complete absence of all maternal or home-making instinct in modern young females, *vagrancy* is comparatively rare among girls. It ranks numerically high, however, among the misdemeanours that bring adolescent *boys* into trouble with authorities. It would be interesting to know exactly why this should be the case, whether fundamentally the girl does cling more to the home and its symbolic protection than her brother, although it is actually no more happy or comfortable than to him.

We find, should we examine the supposed causes for many boys running away from home, that a second marriage and a stepfather or mother, who has treated the children badly, and given the preference to the other or second family, have been given as the main cause of the trouble. This we will notice is the traditional reason why the young folks in the fairy-tale set out from home to seek their fortunes. But whereas the girl in the fairy-tale did so, too, in an attempt to find something better, and the present-day girl may copy her to the extent of constructing her phantasies upon these lines, it would seem that an unhappy home and an unsympathetic stepmother or father does not prevail upon her to try to put the phantasy into practice. Does she gain sufficient consolation from her day-dream, we may ask, to enable her to endure reality, or does she obtain enough compensation from the reality through her masochistic instinct that derives so much strange pleasure from suffering?

We have now considered briefly the adolescent girl who is anxious to break away from her childish ties with home, and the one who is kept there because of her parents' efforts to do so; but what of the third type, the one who has grown up incapable of going away even for a short time, because the old fixation shackles her so tightly—the home-sick girl? The fact that a girl is suffering from this troublesome state of affairs often does not become evident until, or in some cases if she has been educated at home or at a day-school; until she undertakes some work or training which necessitates her living away from her people; or perhaps she gets married.

She will be desperately unhappy about the separation. Sometimes the mere anticipation of it will make her so reluctant to face the ordeal that the project is abandoned. If she pursues it, what do we usually notice among the symptoms of this form of psychological trouble? She will be shy and frightened during the day, finding it difficult to adapt herself to new conditions and fresh surroundings. She does not make friends easily with any of the other people around her, neither with her contemporaries nor those older than herself. She seems unable to give her attention to what is going on around her; and we may remark that she suffers from headaches, some form of gastric trouble, or severe pain during her periods. She will often cry herself to sleep at night, or have her sleep diminished by anxiety dreams, or she will only be able to get to sleep for a few hours. She will creep about as though trying all the time to hide or remain unnoticed, white-faced and miserable, so that everyone can see she is unhappy or ill. Usually these acute symptoms wear off or abate after a few days, but one occasionally hears that it has been necessary to send the girl home from boarding-school, because the medical adviser there thought it would be unwise to keep her in case the continuance of the symptoms, which showed no sign of diminution, undermined her health permanently.

Should one come to inquire into the home conditions which existed during the years preceding this extreme home-sickness, it is usual to find that she has never left her home nor the family before. In one case that came to our notice the girl in question had never before leaving for school slept one night in her life out of her mother's room, where they had actually shared the same bed for many years, the girl being now about fourteen or fifteen. Why this should have been the case was not known. The family were in good circumstances; it was no instance of shortage of accommodation, but it suggests that the presence of the child must also have satisfied some emotional need on the part of the mother, which had left its dire stamp upon the girl in this form.

The relationship between mothers and daughters during adolescence as well as in childhood gives us material for many most interesting observations. One finds that the time will be of the utmost importance to both. It will often happen that the mother, who is separated for the first time from her daughter, when the latter goes to boarding-school for the last few years of her education, suffers quite as much as the daughter. In point of fact, for some mothers each stepping-stone in life, which leads to the widening of the separation between mother and daughter, offers a risk to her, as well as to the girl, of grave psychological or nervous breakdown, as it is popularly termed. We may occasionally notice each point in succession—birth, weaning, going to school, marriage—will be marked by some disturbance of a more or less serious description, which leads us to suppose that the tie between the mother and daughter may, after all, be as strong in its own way as that between mother and son.

We may remember the old couplet related to this idea:

My son's my son 'till he gets him a wife,
My daughter's my daughter all the days of her life.

CHAPTER V

ADOLESCENT GIRL'S CONFLICTS WITH HER PARENTS

THE GIRL AND HER MOTHER

Let us first consider the problems connected with the adolescent girl and her mother, because should we think of these as revivals of old struggles of early childhood we must then reflect that they took place consequently with the mother at an earlier age than with the father.

The small baby very soon comes into conflict with the mother, as soon as she begins to restrict her little daughter's absolute freedom and liberty in any respect, as well as over the question of the child's sole possession of her. We see, of course, these same causes of strife appearing between the mother and daughter as she grows up. Some of the most vigorous disputes that arise in the household will concern the same question—the liberty of the girl. It will be argued, to what extent she should still obey her mother's wishes without question, should they run counter to her own, whether she can do as she thinks fit herself, or should defer to her mother's judgment in all things.

Baby troubles used to arise over dressing and undressing, going to bed, food, and the like, which we will find repeated in the girl's adolescence, as well as in the family battles over when the girl should leave off her play in the evenings and how much sleep she needs. The mother often, quite oblivious of the passage of time, sometimes tries to treat her now growing-up daughter like a small child, and pursues the same tactics as in the past, which now as then further inflames the quarrel. The fact, of course, that these are repetitions of old disputes will make them doubly difficult subjects, and both the mother and daughter will be prone to repeat their own behaviour upon the original occasions without being aware of it.

Once the process has started it runs upon the same old track, without either of the contestants having the power to check the conflict in mid-career. What do we see happen next? Sometimes we may find the father going to the rescue and acting peacemaker, as in the past. Sometimes the girl will let the struggle go on until it ends in mutual sulks, again following an old pattern, or the difficulty, which may have had a duration of several days, will suddenly end in an outburst of violent temper upon one side or the other. The girl may be threatened or punished in some way, and then, appearing content with having brought affairs to a climax, makes it up with tears, says that she is sorry, and becomes once more her mother's good little girl.

It is interesting to see how closely these reactions keep to the old models, without anyone in the family remembering the fact, as a rule. We may often notice, too, the two-sided masochistic and sadistic tendencies, and the strange fact that quarrels may take on the colour of love-scenes. This becomes especially clear from the affectionate termination they so frequently have, and it forms an additional motive for some of these household conflicts between mother and daughter, or father and daughter, beyond the other side of the story, that of the girl's hatred and jealousy of the mother where the father is concerned, or because she thought the mother preferred some other brother or sister. Thus the quarrel and its tender sequel, the reconciliation, will serve to prove to the girl that, after all, she does possess a large part of the mother's love. For a time all will go smoothly, until the girl finds it necessary to make another demonstration about getting her own way, or to prove how much her mother loves her. Sometimes it will even be motivated for the purpose of trying to wound the mother's affection through acting the part of rebellious child. This will often show us one of the ways in which the girl's sadistic instinct tries to work itself out upon the mother.

The adolescent girl may love her mother very tenderly, or she may, at this age especially, hate her very much indeed. The two can be almost inseparable, or the girl sometimes takes the greatest pains to avoid her mother, feeling that she is trying to prevent her growing up. The actions of both need examining with the greatest care, because the attitude of the mother to the father as well as to her daughter is of extreme significance. It is just as possible for the mother to be fixated to her daughter as the bond to be most tightly fastened from the girl's side. Usually we notice, in cases where there is a keen hatred between them, that there are not only psychological mechanisms at work from both sides, but they have been of long standing, which partly accounts for their strength.

In every instance, however, we should pay detailed attention to the attitude of the parents towards one another, because it is of no frequent occurrence to find that when a mother and daughter are more than usually attached to one another, and the girl plays the part of her constant companion and confidante, the mother's love for the father has not been very great. She may never have cared for him, but consented to the marriage because she wanted children of her own, and particularly hoped for a daughter. In this case the advent of the baby girl supplied all her needs, and the whole of her love and attention was concentrated upon the child, who remained the only one.

The little daughter responded to her mother's love with similar exclusiveness, adopted her views about the father, and learned actively to dislike him, quite successfully in many instances usurping his place and sparing no pains to show him that he was not wanted in the house. This feeling and behaviour towards the father will later on colour her thoughts about men in general. We observe that she grows up with the idea that all men are unpleasant persons, always in the way, so that one is better off without them. Usually she does not marry, unless she follows her mother's example and allows herself to consent to taking a husband in the hope of obtaining thus a daughter companion. Frequently she will continue to live with her mother, preferring women friends, and then after the death of the mother not uncommonly finds a new mother-substitute, with whom she lives, sharing a house, or travels about with her.

This *mother-daughter complex*, as we may call it, is an exceedingly interesting one, because we find it appearing in several guises during the world's history. Scientists tell us that in most countries there have been mother deities before there were patriarchal gods; that they were served by priestesses, consecrated at adolescence to service in her temple, such as the maidens of Diana, who in one of their ritual dances wore masks or bears' heads upon their shoulders, representing an old legend connected with that goddess. They were usually under a vow of virginity, but in some places undertook the position of temple prostitutes, therefore married to no one husband, and attached to no other home but that of the mother, her temple.

It would seem that we may discover a revival of a similar survival of an ancient cult during the Middle Ages, which continued throughout Central Europe in the seventeenth and eighteenth centuries, to cause the greatest agitation in that curious phenomenon in which women were most implicated, namely, the witch-cult. In the three principal countries where it was most prevalent—France, Scotland, and England—we learn that it was a frequent custom for mothers to dedicate their daughters to this service from infancy, and that they would be initiated at adolescence, if not before. Mother and daughter would go off together to the regular weekly meetings of the local Coven, while the father was left at home to get on the best he could without them, or in bed asleep with a bundle of rags or the broomstick to represent his wife.

From details of family history, which were disclosed in the evidence given by these neglected men during famous witch-trials, it would seem that the union had never been a happy one, the husband and wife had not much love for one another. This attempt of the wife and daughter to procure excitement and interest outside the home was merely another instance of what we have described among the homes of to-day of the too intimate mothers and daughters.

We have already mentioned, on the other hand, that the estrangement which may exist between mother and daughter, that often increases at puberty, may sometimes have the result of preventing the girl seeking assistance and explanations from her mother, when she needs consolation so much at her first menstruation. Why should this be? There are many roots of it implanted deeply in the past, which account for the girl's reluctance. Some of them will be typical repetitions of past events, because the facts of the first period revive in the girl's mind incidents with childish lapses from nursery training in cleanliness, for which she used to get into trouble years ago. The stained clothing; the dampness of the bed, should the first traces have occurred during the night, may repeat experiences connected with urination—that is, bed-wetting—for which the child was scolded and punished. Although an association between the two may not be immediately clear to the girl, her guilt flashes out and prevents her in the first place wanting to admit to her mother that something similar has taken place. The close resemblance often makes the girl feel that menstruation is a particularly defiling and shameful process. Again, there is another connection with those far-off days which adds to the general discomfort experienced at this time. We usually find that the mother taught her little daughter the first principles of self-control in relation to these bodily functions.

The child may first have rebelled fiercely against the interference with her liberty, but afterwards adopted the mother's standard as her own, and took great pride in the exercise of mental or bodily self-control, making it one of the main strands of her self-confidence. This flow, therefore, over which she can exert no conscious control, is an intense shock to her pride and self-confidence as well.

We have already shown that the girl's rapidly awakening emotions often put severe strain upon her self-control from the psychological standpoint, and she may experience intense difficulty always to restrain her impulses rather than give immediate discharge to her feelings when something upsets her. For such reasons the adolescent girl will frequently be inclined to nervous outbreaks, which are often classed as hysterical, and it is not considered unusual for a girl of this age to be so. Nevertheless, she will feel resentful of constant reminders from her mother and others that she must learn to control herself better.

Imagine, therefore, the horror of a young girl who may originally in childhood have struggled against and overcome her lack of personal physical or emotional self-control, to find herself once more assailed, first by outbursts of emotionalism, tears, or giggles, which she cannot suppress or control, and then suddenly to become the victim of a new physical function which is altogether out of her control. The flow begins and continues without her slightest volition. It may start when she is quite unprepared, and land her in an awkward predicament. She can do nothing about stopping it or controlling it. She must allow it to take its course and do her best to prevent difficulties arising because of it as best she can. It is a great humiliation to her, this sudden taking away of her own power over the functions of her body, and for this reason, too, she will hesitate to mention it to her mother for fear of what she may say, connected with old difficulties concerning self-control.

Let us at the conclusion of this first section turn for a while to the study of the feelings of the mother with regard to the fact that she has now a daughter old enough to be considered a woman also. For the mother who has valued her good looks and her youthful appearance it will come as a severe shock. Many women do not like to be branded as old enough to have a grown-up daughter. They will resent it, and for this superficial cause as well as others, which are scarcely permitted to come through to consciousness, do their best to deny the girl all the privileges of her approaching maturity. Thus she will refuse to give her any welcome to womanhood, which the daughter would be so grateful to have. She finds it hard also to teach the girl to be her still more powerful rival by encouraging her over the awkward stages of her adolescence, and helping her in the choice of her clothes. It will be the same with her parties: she will not want to initiate her into all the little rituals of entertaining and etiquette, which the girl needs to know. She will leave her to find out for herself, which will take some time, and the daughter no doubt meets with difficulties and unpleasant *contretemps* in the process that might have been decreased or avoided altogether with the help of the mother.

A very attractive daughter is not a pleasant rival. We often remark the father taking a good deal of notice of her, choosing her for his companion and finding reasons why he and his daughter should go out together and leave the mother at home, in case she might be over-tired with their more strenuous undertaking. She is jealous of the daughter, whether she realises it or not, and the fact that the girl is at the threshold of life, while she is drawing nearer the next transition of her life as a woman, that of middle age.

This unconscious jealousy, which cannot help affecting the relationship between mother and daughter, will often be one of the main causes for the girl wishing to find a new mother-substitute during adolescence. In its turn, of course, this may provoke further jealousy on the part of the mother, but in any case the girl needs the counsel and friendship of an older woman at this time, connected with whom there are not so many old and new elements of emotional tension.

Of course it is by no means impossible for a happy state of affairs to exist between mothers and their adolescent daughters. A very great many survive the strain without any particular difficulty. In this case we shall generally find that the mother in question had a happy life herself as a child, girl, wife, and mother. Her love-life with her husband has probably been successful too, and her love has been always shared between husband and children, as well as reciprocated by them. The girl's adolescence always tends to revive memories of the mother's own experiences as a girl, whether they were happy or unhappy. If she went through a difficult time during her adolescence, the experiences of her daughter will reanimate her own emotional stress in the past and cause her once more to live through the sorrows of the past. This, of course, will not tend to make her any more sympathetic with the troubles of her daughter. She will, in the re-staging of the old drama, take the part formerly played by her own mother, and act towards her young daughter as perhaps the mother behaved in the old days, while the girl plays her own part once more.

The Girl and Her Father

The relationship of the girl and her father does not present us with psychological difficulties of the same kind as those which we have been describing, but others which arise from different and opposite causes. The intense element of jealousy, which often accounts for so much of the heightened tension between the mother and the adolescent daughter, is far more probable to occur between the father and his sons, who are approaching early manhood.

Generally we find the father and the daughter upon particularly good terms. If she should happen to be attractive, with a fair share of good looks, and intelligent, too, he will usually take the credit to himself, and point out that she takes after himself. Perhaps she does. She may have been doing her best, since early childhood, to identify herself with him and grow up "just like Daddy." This would lead us to think that she had always been his pet, and had preferred him to her mother, because no doubt she had been able to rely upon his support and to get her own way with him after her mother has said *No!*

Once again, in situations of this kind, it is wise to investigate the intimate relations between father and mother, and to discover if we can whether they are really happy one with the other. It will often happen that the father who says *Yes!* to his little daughter, and encourages her to come to him with her troubles that arise with the mother, shows in this way that all is not well between himself and his wife. The feeling which exists may not be fully conscious, it is true, to the grown-ups, but the child is sufficiently in touch with her own unconscious mind to be able to realise these things in her parents, and is equally quick to take full advantage of them in her own interests.

This taking sides with one parent or the other is of the utmost formative value in the development of the daughter's psychology, as we have already tried to show in the case of the mother and daughter, who combine to exclude the father. It is the normal state of affairs, however, for the little girl to become her father's favourite and the mother to find hers among her sons. But it is by no means uncommon to notice the reversed situation, when the father himself has always had something of the woman about him, and the mother decided masculine traits. In this case the father may be most attracted by his sons, while the mother chooses her favourite in the family from among the daughters. Or, we will observe a different quality in the father's love for the daughter. She may represent to him *what he would have liked to have been* if he could have had his wish. The fact that this wish has in most cases been sternly and rapidly repressed into the unconscious may, nevertheless, sometimes have the effect of making the father jealous of his adolescent daughter and behave in a hostile manner towards her. This is one possibility; the other is more frequent, that which we suggested at the commencement of this section, that he believes her to resemble himself, and often makes the remark that she takes after her father and should have been the boy of the family.

He will make her his close companion, let her share his interests, sports, and amusements, taking an equal share in hers and her friends. He likes to see her have a good time, and does not get seriously jealous of her many social engagements until too many boy friends come upon the scene, and the girl becomes evidently interested in them, so that they begin to rob him entirely or partly of his former companionship. Then acute trouble may arise. He becomes the jealous father in that he fears that one of these attractive young men will some day steal away his daughter. We find him turning the cold shoulder upon them, and, like jealous fathers of a former generation, forbidding young men the house altogether. He does not wish his daughter to leave him and marry. At least not until he has departed this life, and so does not need her any longer.

And what of the girl who is so devotedly fond of her father, even from childhood? Do we not sometimes notice her doing her best, deliberately, or apparently by accident, as the case may be, trying to insinuate herself between her parents? She proves to him that she is far more interested in his pursuits than her mother, who often makes a point of not taking much notice of his hobbies. She may say that she considers them a waste of time or money, and complains that they make a great deal of noise and mess about the house, if they should take the form of carpentry, collecting, or one of the dozens of things men like to do in their spare time. A practical wife cannot see the use of them, while the daddy's girl joins in the fun with all her heart and soul.

The little girl is often never quite so happy as when the mother goes away and she is allowed to come downstairs and pour out her father's coffee for breakfast. Sometimes she may actually put her thoughts into words by suggesting that they should write to tell mummy there is no hurry for her to come back—everything is going on quite nicely. But the mother does come back. She often reproaches the father that he has spoilt his little daughter, letting her sit up too late and eat all sorts of unwholesome things for dinner with him. The child is sent back to the nursery, sulky and disconsolate, and the mother feels rather hurt because she does not show greater pleasure at her return.

It is an interesting version of this sort of trouble in the house when the mother becomes an invalid, possibly through some illness of a psychological origin, and actually does surrender her post as housekeeper and father's companion to the young daughter. It used often to happen in the past, when it was not thought the right thing for the married woman to continue to lead an active life, at any rate outside the home, and would often at middle age retire to her sofa, leaving the burden of household affairs to her daughter or daughters. But then it was only a half-and-half measure. She still kept the reins of government in her hands, and often it was a particularly tight rein too, which could always be shortened by the plea, "Remember, my darlings, that I am an invalid, and we cannot entertain or have so many noisy parties because of my health." And the girls and boys were made to feel that they had been terribly heartless and inconsiderate.

This was a favourite theme for books written for young girls in the latter half of the last century, especially of those by Charlotte M. Yonge, such as *The Daisy Chain* or *The Heir of Redcliffe*—books which, by the way, found immense popularity amongst the girls of that time, because they dealt with this phantasy of taking the mother's place, no doubt.

We may sometimes be surprised to see a change take place rather suddenly in the young girl's attitude to her father during adolescence. Heretofore they have been the best of friends. Then suddenly she appears not to want to have anything to do with him. She will not kiss him any more, and avoids being kissed by him. Nothing has occurred between them as far as the family knows, and when questioned the girl may be equally at a loss to explain matters— or she says she is. What has happened that has caused this strange alteration in the girl's behaviour?

The girl might be able to account for it if she cared to do so, or she might really have no understanding of her own reactions. The superficial cause may possibly have been that she had a dream which frightened her, of being in love with her father, perhaps of having a child by him, and she is terrified that it could happen. She may have gained some information of the sexual life, not wisely imparted, of the procreation of infants and of cohabitation. She has been repulsed by the idea, becomes afraid and horrified at the idea that men *do that to women*, and has alarming phantasies about her father in this connection. Sometimes, having gained most inadequate sex information, or perhaps having heard something not intended for her ears, or witnessed something of sexual intercourse in a lane or casually when walking through the woods or fields, she imagines that there are other ways in which babies may be conceived. She may think that living in the same house with a man is sufficient *to make it happen,* and that a kiss will provide the necessary stimulus, or perhaps some man may have made advances to her, or may have exposed himself. What she feels first in relation to some other man, a stranger or to men in general, will become transferred to her father, and thus accounts for her sudden hostile attitude to him, just as later on she frequently passes over to strangers her former relationship with her father as a child or girl.

Of course we may remember that in a great many cases of very young unmarried girls, adolescents, in fact, who come into the maternity hospitals for their first confinement, they actually do bear the child of their father. This is no isolated occurrence, but one that happens in a very high percentage of cases. If it is not the father it may be an uncle or close relative, or an old friend of the family, whom the girl has regarded in the light of one of the family, as often as a contemporary of her own. In early days of primitive culture the father's first right to his daughters made incest of this kind not held as a criminal offence, comparable with intercourse which took place between mother and son. This is an exceedingly interesting state of affairs with respect to legislation, as well as one that throws further light upon this subject of the father's love for his daughter to-day and his susceptibility to her charms, as well as to the mother's jealousy directed to their daughter.

Unconsciously the daughter, when a little girl, as we have already pointed out, as later during adolescence, might very much like to take her mother's place altogether with the father and have a semi-conscious wish for him to give her a baby, so that she might have one too, instead of the mother keeping the privilege all to herself. The adolescent dislike of the father will thus often be an unconscious incest barrier, or develop from the fear that the father may become too fond of her and want her in this way.

This particular theme is to be found in a few fairy-tales,

in its direct form, but in very few. We discover it both in legend, phantasy, and reality, however, in the indirect form of the girl marrying a father-substitute. It may be an old friend of his, someone who reminds her of him, because he is old and lonely, or under a curse like the Flying Dutchman; maybe in order to save the father from some financial or other embarrassment. This will appear again in the theme of the father promising his daughter to almost certain destruction in order to save himself from a predicament in a fairy-tale or legend, or as the result of a rash vow. It occurs in the Bible story of Jephthah's daughter, as well as in that of Iphigenia and in countless fairy-tales of the Beauty and the Beast type.

It also presents in the latter the idea of marriage to the girl as that of the sacrifice and death of the maiden, the end of her virginity and childhood. This is true enough, but it puts us into touch with the time when the daughters of the household were family assets, of which the father made as much use as possible and disposed of when convenient. We have an example of this in the beautiful Russian fairy-tale of the *Frost*, where the father takes the girl out with him in his sleigh and abandons her to wait for her bridegroom, King Frost, by the roadside, in order to have one mouth less to feed in time of famine. The daughters have always been thought of in the light of household assets more than the sons, especially in the countries where marriage by purchase was in vogue; whereas the provision of a dowry made it very inconvenient to have too many daughters.

Still, in later times the daughters of the family were always supposed to be ready to stay at home to look after aged or invalid parents, when the same duty would never have been expected or imposed upon the sons. It was always understood, too, that daughters who were earning money out at service, or in other ways, would continue to contribute to the financial resources of the old home long after the boys had married and had homes of their own, which made it impossible for them to do so. The daughters, therefore, were expected to shoulder the burden of supporting the old parents to a greater extent than the sons, and it was taken for granted that they would be glad of this privilege being assigned to them.

One further problem before the end of the chapter, which is the familiar figure of the fairy-tale once more. It is the man who marries again after the death of his first wife, and who has a daughter by his first marriage, and another family by the second. Over and over again history repeats itself, and the man takes up the same helpless attitude of not being able to do anything about it except to sympathise with the girl rather furtively. Of course a very great deal of the adolescent's resentment to her stepmother comes from her conscious and unconscious wish to have taken the dead mother's place with her father, and her great disappointment at not being allowed to do so, especially if she feels grown up enough—and there is really not much difference in age between the two. The fact that this should be the case and the father marries a very young woman points to the fact that his unconscious wish is probably like the fairy-tales we have mentioned in an earlier chapter—to have married his daughter as she only can be the image of the first wife. The jealousy between the two is intense, usually upon both sides, and the husband and father seems powerless to know what to think and do in the matter. Once again he is weak, surrendering utterly to the second wife. Why he does this we cannot say, unless it is connected with some deep daughter-fixation and an unconscious incest barrier upon his side also. But it shows us a strange problem, nevertheless, that bitterly as the girl generally hates the stepmother she does not, as a rule, resent the intrusion of a stepfather as much, except under exceptional circumstances, even when she has been much attached to her own father.

CHAPTER VI

A. THE ONLY CHILD OR ONLY GIRL

When we come to analyse the lives and life-problems of adolescent girls, what difference do we find by examining those who have gone through these important years as the only child in the family or as one with numerous brothers and sisters? The particular class of society to which the girl belongs should also be taken into consideration, for reasons which have been already given in part. The girl from a working-class home, however, is obliged to find some employment almost at the commencement of her adolescence; the daughter who comes from one where it is the custom for the girls not to begin the more serious stages of their education often goes on to a university or starts training for a career when this section of life is almost at an end.

And yet, if we leave the externals of family opportunities out of our reckoning in comparison with the influence exerted upon the girl by her psychological tendencies, it is doubtful whether we will discover very great differences in the essential factors at all. We notice, whatever the home conditions, the girl will suffer from similar emotional conflicts, will be swayed by the same revivals of hatred and love for her parents, wishing to rebel against the one and cling to the other with implicit and childlike obedience. If one should be in a position to be consulted upon family complications by the parents as well as the adolescent daughters themselves, and hear more of their mutual troubles and misunderstandings from both sides, one is compelled to come to this decision, that radically they are of the same quality in whatever social circle they occur, and the variations that are visible are those of accent and detail.

The girl who is still living at home with her family finds

the situation much the same, whatever the size of the house. They all live together at closer quarters, it is true, and quarrels when they arise may be rather more devastating in a small house or a couple of rooms than in a spacious mansion. But, nevertheless, this particular girl has probably always lived under these same conditions, and so does not feel the strain of never being alone, any more than one who constantly shares her bedroom with one sister for whom she has no particular affection and with whom she has few interests in common. Certainly the absence of solitude, often so ardently longed for by one type of adolescent, may be terribly irksome to one who has to share a school dormitory with many others, friends or enemies, when from childhood she has always been used to her own room at home. What is the fundamental difference, after all?

We may suggest that the home difficulties of the adolescent girl, who is hurried out to work at a very early age because her father may be out of work and her mother's health is breaking down from the strain of keeping the home together and providing for the entire household, will find these additions to her own physical and psychological disturbances worrying. But, as a matter of fact, is it really a greater condition of tension than that in another home, where the father, a professional man, finds his work dwindle alarmingly, his health fail, or he reaches the age at which he is bound to retire from his position just when the younger members of the family need expensive education and the older ones, which he has been trying to launch upon professional careers, cannot yet earn sufficient to provide for their own needs? It would seem doubtful. Of the two, one might suggest that the all-round tension in the last-described home would be the more severe, because of the attempt to keep the difficulties hidden. In the first instance there would be no disguise of the financial worry. There would not be any necessity to try to keep up appearances where the outside world was concerned.

The proletarian daughter who was allowed to go out to business straight away and do her share to help the home, and to enjoy herself after the work was done, probably would not suffer so much *psychologically* as the young girl of good family who, sensitive as adolescents always are to externals, has to go to school not so well dressed as her friends, with clothes evidently made over from last year, or her mother's, and with less pocket-money than they. She would not be able to come back from the holidays with adventures to tell of exciting visits to seaside resorts or the Continent, nor be able to invite them to parties similar to those they give, which she shares without being able to return the hospitality.

The relations of the girl to her parents remain the same, whatever their social class, concerning the problems of being the only one, or growing up among a party of brothers and sisters. The family life varies according to the psychological make-up of the members of it, and does not depend, except in a limited, comparative way, upon the large bank balance, or the small one, or whether there be none at all, and the weekly earnings of the father or the family jointly have to be made to carry on until the next supply arrives.

One observation, however, might be in place here, and it will be given for what it is worth. It is not the theory of the writer of this book only, but has been remarked by various persons who have made a study of the subject from the angle of their own different professions. It is this: that parents in middle-class homes, who have not had very much education themselves, seem now to be suffering from the snobbishness that formerly was supposed to be the hall-mark of the class above them. They are trying to bring up their girls too strictly, to limit their activities, and to force them into old-fashioned standards of exaggerated gentility which have otherwise vanished into the past and have been replaced by more natural and youthful sincerity.

This seems to apply most particularly to the parents of an only girl. The pressure is exerted not only by the mother, but also by the father. Both are determined that their girl shall be brought up to be that stilted figure which they believe is *a lady*, and the result only causes a great deal of unhappiness for the girl and disappointment for the parents. The girl misses opportunities for healthful exercise and enjoyment because she is not allowed to mix with other girls, whom her parents do not consider her social equals. Eventually it may undermine her health psychologically by the effort she makes to conform to the parental standards against her own wishes, and what she feels is the custom of the day. Should she adopt their impossible standard, however, she will finally suffer the additional misery of being forced to look down upon her own parents. She struggles and contrives always to pretend to be something different from what she is, and to keep the grim and uncomfortable secret from her new friends—the history of her former more humble antecedents.

Let us now consider the position of the only girl in the household, irrespective of what her father does to keep the home going, and look at her as a unit within the family circle, be it large or small.

The remarks we have already made in the last chapter about the conflicts which arise between the girl and her parents often become intensified, in some respects, when this daughter is the only child, diminished in others, for reasons that must be obvious enough. She may perhaps feel lonely sometimes, and long for a sister with whom she can share her pleasures and disappointments, with whom she can have adventures and share confidences. But frequently she will congratulate herself that she reigns supreme in the home, and thus keeps her parents' love and attention all to herself.

She grows up usually rather a solitary person, often not too fond of the company of friends who are her own age, preferring those older than herself, who treat her with more consideration than contemporaries are in the habit of doing.

It is scarcely necessary to mention that she will be much older for her age, and enjoys more mature interests—having been the companion of her parents—than the girl who has always lived with other girls and boys about her own age or even younger, unless, being the eldest in a large family, she has been made responsible for them almost from her own childhood. Her life consists mainly of her thoughts about herself, her attitude towards her father and mother, which we have already described, her relationships to sisters and brothers, and what will be explained later in the last section of the book, her feelings and experiences at school and in the wider circle of the world with her friends and strangers.

The only girl among a family of brothers, or the adolescent with one brother, either older or younger than she, offers a wide selection of problems, so important and so intricate that it is difficult to give to all of them the attention they merit. The girl with one brother or more is brought up against the problem of her sex more acutely than the girl alone in the house, and it will depend largely what her parents' attitude may be to the comparative estimation of the two sexes how her life will be shaped. Let us suppose, first, a family consisting of one brother and one sister, the girl being the elder, which so often happens in reality.

The girl has reigned supreme for the number of years which lie between them. Then comes the little brother, and usually she finds then, for some reason she cannot fathom, he becomes the favourite with both the parents, and she is constantly forced to give in to him, because, they tell her, he is the boy, the son of the house. Why should there be this distinction, she wonders? She is still older than he; she can do more than he can; she is still stronger than he; perhaps she feels more attractive from these points of view, and yet she notices that the parents and friends who come to the house always put him first. Is it merely because he is the baby that he must be taken such care of? It would appear not, because as he grows older this early preference does not vanish, but grows still stronger. Immense care is taken over his education and what he is going to be when he grows up. Yet the same question in relation to herself seems scarcely mentioned.

Can we be surprised that the little girl, who began to feel jealous of this brother in his babyhood, experiences hostility towards him which reaches a climax when both are growing up. She is going through the stress of adolescence, made to feel rather an outcast and unwanted, as though reaching womanhood were a thing to be ashamed of, and her brother gains applause everywhere because of his approaching manhood? His attention towards her will be perceptibly changing too. Term by term, when the holidays arrive, she feels that he is less willing to play with her, to go about with her, share in her interests, or to allow her a part in his. He shows plainly enough that he considers girls an inferior sort of human beings, and prefers his own boy friends. He may tease her, laugh at her, but he avoids her for the most part. Often, should there be several brothers in the family, this attitude becomes still more emphatic. The boys gather courage through the support of numbers to make their feelings about their sister yet more plain.

The girl's psychological difficulties will be considerably less, we find occasionally, when he is the elder of the two, for she then seems to take his superiority as part of the general advantages of being the elder, and accept the fact. Unless, of course, it will appear to her that it is all part of the evidence of the parents' initial favouritism that the son is the first-born, and envies him doubly upon both accounts.

It would appear that this preference is not quite so marked in America as in England, and that the sons and daughters are treated with more equality, the advantage, if any, falling to the share of the girls rather than the boys. This is what one is told from the conscious opinions of one's informants; but yet, all the same, when one has had the chance to observe the deeper currents of unconscious feelings concerning the old family situation, it is just as possible to find that the girl brought up in an American home some time ago and now feels that it is an advantage to be a boy, and that the luck is all upon the side of the brothers.

This is the dark side of the picture, and an unpleasant one, but it is nevertheless true in the generality of cases. We may sometimes, however, see a brother and sister growing up in the closest friendship, so that the difficulty which arises from this state of affairs does not represent any jealousy or feelings of rivalry between them, but one of exclusiveness and supreme content with one another. This will lead to grave trouble when the time comes, when normally the brother and sister should be transferring their affections outside the family circle and seeking a life companionship elsewhere. It reminds us of the fairy-tales of the little brother and sister who wander away from home, happy and content with each other's company, their only desire to escape from the cruelty of the stepmother or the parents until enchantment separates them. But even then this is never successful, and they come together again in spite of the greatest difficulties and hardships.

It may also have the unfortunate results of influencing both to identify with each other, the boy taking over a great many characteristics, which are generally supposed to be attributes of the girl, and cause the girl to become as masculine as she can. However, there is always a tendency for this to happen whenever the girl notices that the boy is pre-eminently the favourite. The same thought will also occur to the boy, nevertheless, and he may equally feel that the sister has more advantages than he. That either state of affairs should be present in an exaggerated form is, of course, the doing of the parents, and the result of their unconscious wishes. If they show so clearly that they think either the girl or the boy, usually the latter, is the superior, the other will naturally become dissatisfied with the sex that nature has decreed, and seek to emulate the other, feeling that all of the advantages lie in the direction of the opposite sex.

In families where the girl has several brothers we often find that she singles out one of them as her companion, which friendship may survive adolescence, strengthening rather than decreasing with time, with some of the characteristics of the companionship of an only brother and sister.

We see many other conflicts arising in the mind of the only adolescent girl concerning her home that offer complicated problems, which in a way are increasing at the present day. In the past it was, of course, taken for granted that an *only* girl should remain at home to carry out her *duties* towards her parents as well as her obligations, however much her talents and inclinations urged her to seek a wider sphere of satisfaction and interest. Nowadays the individualist group of young persons would say that this is an entirely exploded theory, and that it is quite absurd even to mention it as a problem for a modern girl. But still, one constantly finds it occupying such a place in the girl's thoughts, and therefore we feel it cannot be omitted. It does cause her a great deal of mental worry until she squares it with her conscience as best she can, according to her instincts and tendencies as well as her unconscious wishes. What all these may be and what part her conscience plays cannot be explained in this brief summary, but it is well for us to remember that the conscience, or super-ego of the adolescent girl, is characteristically strong at this time, and will augment her conflicts upon an ethical question of this kind almost intolerably.

B. THE ADOLESCENT GIRL AMONG BROTHERS AND SISTERS

Having thus briefly touched upon some of the most outstanding difficulties and problems of adolescence in the case of the only girl in the family, with or without brothers, we must now turn our attention for a little while to the one who is part of a family, which includes *sisters* as well as brothers. All the complications that arise from the ages and grouping of these boys and girls might well occupy one whole volume before the complete story were told, rather than having one half-chapter in which to unfold the difficulties arising from the adolescent girl's position among others.

Naturally enough the component instincts of Love and Hate, with jealousy never far away, between the interaction of the two, provide it with the major portion of the stresses. A large part of this jealousy will be stimulated by the preferences of the parents for their various children. On the other hand the children themselves will show marked favouritism for one parent or the other, and struggle hard for pledges of love from the one they prefer, sometimes quite independently of any signs their elders will give of favouring the children or the reverse. Of course the parents always say they have *no* favourites, and they may think it is true. They may also believe the fallacy that, even should they prefer one child to another, they are clever enough not to let the children suspect it. But this is impossible.

One may gain some information on this subject from the children in the family themselves very often, and find that it is remarkably accurate, and will frequently repeat almost word for word what one or other of the parents may have said a few days or weeks before. Their reasons will be given, too, and prove sound enough.

It is exceedingly hard to keep secrets from children or adolescents who live in the same house. And their elders would often be amused or shocked to hear what is discussed after the young people have gone to bed, or when they are in their own quarters, and they believe no adults are within earshot. Usually they will not show any signs of knowing before their parents, unless some outburst, which has been brought about by most exceptional circumstances, unlock the sealed lips and allow their real thoughts to escape. They are not deceitful in this, scarcely secretive, but just as the parents do their best to reserve their secrets from the children, so do they, the children and adolescents, believe that it is not done to tell all one thinks and feels to one's elders. *"It is not done!"* is one of the strongest rules and reasons for controlling one's actions at this time, and connected with it one often finds the strangest as well as the most binding prohibitions existing among young people. These conditions, of course, will generally, if not always, be imposed by themselves, and are frequently conditions peculiar to one family only.

A different complexity of difficulties will beset the adolescent girl, whether she is the eldest, middle, or youngest member of the family, whether her next in age be a boy or a girl. But we generally find that broadly speaking the great step of puberty, making the commencement of adolescence, severs her from her next in age below herself, and tends to unite her closely to an elder one, especially if this should be a sister. They have suddenly found great interests in common. The younger needs the information that the elder can impart, and the older girl is flattered at being able to show her superior knowledge to her younger sister. She will also realise that it is nice to have someone in the house with whom she can discuss the intimate details of adolescent interests in a way that she has never been able to do with her mother, although she will probably have very much wanted to do so.

For this reason the second sister of the family, who attains adolescence, has a more advantageous position than the elder. Her crossing of the boundary-line achieves her distinction, it is true, but isolation. We usually find her especially wishing for her mother's confidence more than the younger ones, who gain this satisfaction from her when the time comes. The younger girls, too, will probably resent at the time the sudden aloofness which commonly descends upon the adolescent girl with younger sisters when puberty commences, although they may not know exactly how to account for this change in her attitude towards them. It is almost unbelievable that the eldest sister of a family can reach puberty, sometimes continuing to share the same bedroom with younger sisters, although it is more usual for her to be given a room of her own at this time, and for the juniors not to have any idea that she has reached a physical stage farther on than themselves, and what this step means and comprises. But still we find quite often that it does occur. Naturally it is the consequence of considerable repression and very strict teaching that puberty and especially menstruation are subjects that are quite unmentionable, and that they should be hidden from everybody with the greatest care, which is not altogether to be recommended.

The younger ones may be inclined to dislike her for this alteration in her bearing towards them, her frequent assumption of additional responsibility towards them, the increase in extent and power of her conscience, perhaps a greater interest in herself, her own appearance and affairs. They tease and laugh at her for playing what they call *the grown-up young lady*, and accuse her of putting on airs, and want to know whether she has dates with her boy friends when she goes out to parties to which they are not invited too. She may become still more remote with them in consequence of this jesting, or she will become annoyed and turn to do battle with them, physically or verbally. Sometimes, then, with the uncertainty of emotional control typical of adolescence, her tears betray her irritation and perhaps the truth of their jibes, and she feels herself humiliated. She will dash out of the room, away from the teasing brothers and sisters, and make for the sanctuary of her own room, furious with them as well as herself for having broken down like this, when she most wanted to preserve her dignity *in front of the children.*

As we have already hinted, the second girl in the family to reach adolescence usually has a happier time than the first, because she finds a companion already awaiting her, and she derives the benefit of the experience of one who has already trodden that path, and thus can tell her what she wants to know. It is the third daughter, perhaps, who may once more feel isolated, especially if the two elder ones are great allies and her own nearest in age younger, maybe a brother. The adolescent girl always feels herself most sadly bereft of her former companion and playmate when this has been a brother. Suddenly a gulf of unimagined immensity yawns at her feet. She believes that their friendship will never be quite the same again. In almost every case she holds the opinion that men and boys know nothing about this, unless perhaps married men like her father. To tell her brother anything about it she certainly would never do, come what may, and she never suspects that they see through her wildest excuses and most improbable headaches which she goes on inventing with the ingenuity of Eve and every other feminine ancestress should the day come when some strenuous expedition or a bathing party has been arranged and she either did not feel up to the exertion of it or did not feel she wanted to bathe.

Most boys, nevertheless, by the time they reach their own

adolescence have found out something about it, although the information which passes from one to the other at school on the subject of "woman and her peculiarities," usually considered by them as *a disease*, is strange almost beyond belief and totally inadequate. They realise enough, however, to know that the girl is fibbing when she makes transparent excuses of this sort, and never mentions the subject either frankly to his sisters, however intimate they may be. It would seem that a little more openness between the two sexes about the trials and tribulations of adolescence would clear away a good many of their difficulties and lead to a far better understanding of one another instead of the endless subterfuges which are kept up, although all parties concerned realise the disguise which thus provokes these useless lies.

Perhaps the middle girl in the family may now claim a few moments' notice, because of especial difficulties in her position. The chief cause of interest is that in the half-way situation it always shows the tendency to shift and fluctuate so that the girl never knows quite what to expect. She never knows where her place is to be for this reason. Sometimes, should one more be wanted to make up even numbers, or should one of the elder sisters fall out suddenly, not being well, she will be admitted to the older group, although otherwise rather younger than the rest. Then, when she is enjoying herself tremendously, feeling quite grown up, something will happen, and equally suddenly she will be sent upstairs to become one of the younger set again, should it be more convenient that day to put her in that group or someone were wanted to amuse the little ones. She drifts hither and thither, or tries to push herself from one sphere into another, which may not want her, or not always.

The indefinite position has another quality, too, that leads to difficulties later on. She may form the habit of always trying to find consolation among those who are very much her junior, deriving considerable pleasure from being among those to whom she can play *big sister*. She likes to feel superior as a balm to her pride at being refused the companionship of her seniors, and likes to feel wanted and welcome whenever she goes up to the nursery. But, because of her tendency to arrive upstairs upon these occasions in anything but a gracious mood, thoroughly disappointed at not being allowed to join in something that seemed especially attractive because forbidden, they may not appear pleased to see her. They may have learned that she will probably interfere with what they are doing when she feels like this, laugh at their games, and make out that they are silly and childish, and therefore make boring companions.

Whenever it is possible she will go off to mope by herself. She will long for the time to come when she will definitely reach the happy state of always and by right being included in the grown-up parties, and cheers herself meanwhile with Cinderella phantasies or others equally consoling, which help to take the sting out of the present.

It is just as possible for an adolescent girl to be very lonely when she is one of a large family as when she is an only child. Probably more so, if she does not readily fall within any of the various groups into which a large family divides, or form one of a pair of companions who are inseparable. Should a girl be the only child, she generally finds some sort of companionship in one of the parents, or she will have some friend outside the family with whom she is on intimate terms. But it is more than likely that the members of large families do not make friends from the outside sources quite so readily as those belonging to small ones. They frequently show a tendency to become rather exclusive and absorbed in their own affairs, so that companions from the outside world are not so eagerly sought. In this case, suggested above, it may never be suspected that one of the family will be lonely because of the age or sex grouping of the others, and it will be thought instead that she keeps to herself merely because she is the odd-man-out, rather different from the rest, or since she is possessed of a sulky disposition.

Perhaps the friendships which have been growing up around her since her birth or from early childhood will have been the cause of this isolation, or the result of an almost congenital solitariness; but whatever the cause it will have a marked influence upon her subsequent development of character and her choice of occupations. It will also affect her selection of some outlet for her emotions, when their adolescent heaping-up drives her on to find some way of expressing herself and her desires. But these are questions that may be left for later chapters, such as those in which we shall discuss adolescent friendships and the choice of emotional outlets to provide the girl with the means of realising herself and proving her capacity of discovering a form of self-expression suitable to her impulses.

The youngest girl in the family will often reveal a double-sided attitude respecting her adolescence, both in its anticipation as well as during its experience. She may welcome its advent exceedingly, because she may have felt a certain amount of inferiority at being the one daughter left who was not grown up or nearly so. But on the other hand, she may feel her position of youngest in the family so privileged that she does not want to forgo it and be merely one among the rest, having surrendered her unique position.

It is curious that during this period of adolescence we so frequently observe that the girl wants two opposite conditions at practically the same time. It will produce a sensation of confusion and bewilderment in herself as much as to those who may be watching her. When she realises it, she is forced to admit to herself that she does not really know what she does want most. Sometimes she feels definitely that she needs one thing above all others, at others the reverse just as urgently; then again another day she has to face the fact that she would prefer both, as neither seems fit to be relinquished. Then again her feelings will swing round once more; both of the old alternatives are equally repugnant, and she wants to reach out for something entirely new that she has scarcely even formulated to herself. These changes in her wishes lead to her feelings of unutterable depression and longing which are so characteristic of the young adolescent girl.

Adults may become annoyed with her for this indecision and changeableness. She herself will often be exasperated by it, and the impossibility of explaining herself to others so that they can understand when it is all so vague to herself. For the time, however, she is powerless to grapple with the alternations of feelings and wishes. For example, to take but one instance of the changes, she wants the company of her family and feels lonely and uncomfortable with strangers. Then later her only wish seems to be to avoid the family with their teasing ways and their perpetual criticism, and to get away among those who have not known her as a child, so that the newly expanding self is free to try its wings without the possibility of a brother or sister giving a humorous sketch of her behaviour at a party when they all return from it.

PART III
SCHOOLDAYS AND LATER

CHAPTER I

ADOLESCENTS' CONFLICTS AT SCHOOL

Having studied some of the most urgent problems of the adolescent girl at home, let us now follow her to school and see for ourselves what is the state of affairs there. We must be prepared to find that in all cases she may not be exactly the same person at home as at school. For instance, an unruly girl at home may be happy and a model of propriety at school, where she receives better understanding and has plenty to do which interests her. On the other hand, one who is always contented and interested in her home-life may become a school rebel and one who is always in trouble. What the reasons may be for these changes we will attempt to show by a summary of some of her difficulties and conflicts at school in relationship to her early home environment.

In the first place, one of the most important factors which provide an alteration in the girl's behaviour at school will be, on the one hand, her liking or dislike for the companionship of the other girls; on the other, whether she can be happy away from her old surroundings—that is, the home of her childhood, which signifies the protection and security that is so precious to her. We must also notice whether she can make a transference of some of her former feelings towards her mother and father to other people in the persons of her teachers. Each of these elements will take its place as reason for change in the girl's feelings and behaviour away from home.

We will find that some girls, as those to whom we have already referred as suffering from severe homesickness, have not yet mentally grown up and developed far enough to be able to face this step of breaking away from the original home situation. It may even have appeared originally as a difficulty in connection with first going to a day-school for a few hours only. We sometimes come across children who become mentally upset, or contract some physical illness, when the time comes for them to leave home for the short time which their visit to a kindergarten or infant school entails. This may be overcome in time, and yet may revive when the second step towards moving away from the parents is made to go to a boarding-school, or even a day-school, which is some distance from home, so that the midday meal will be partaken of there to save the double journey to and fro.

If the girl's fixation to home and parents is not too strong she will, of course, be able to transfer the old feelings to the new situation and start satisfactorily upon the fresh phase under her different surroundings, and find a second home in the school. The teachers will become substitute parents and the other girls take up the position of sisters—that is, if she should have had them before; if not, they become useful sister-substitutes, through which the loves, hatred, and jealousy of the sister-relationship may be worked out by proxy. This enables the only girl to gain most valuable experiences for the construction of her later life that otherwise she might have missed altogether.

It is interesting to observe how closely these old attitudes will be repeated in this second phase. The girl who has been very fond of her mother and has had no particular difficulty in carrying out her wishes and learning what she had to teach her, will pass on this same happy relationship to the head mistress or to her special teacher. Contrarily, should the girl have been a rebel at home, regarding rules as things to be broken as soon and as completely as possible, she usually continues this behaviour at school, finding it additionally satisfactorily to herself, that she is regarded as a heroine by the other girls who, although they may have had the same inclination, have neither the courage nor initiative to put them into practice.

She immediately establishes herself as a leader of the opposition, enjoying herself thoroughly, since this position gratifies a great many of her primitive impulses at one and the same time. The typical aggressive tendency of the young adolescent who wishes to be a boy will have free rein. She will enthusiastically buy boys' school stories, and do her best to copy their escapades, which are described in each chapter. If she attracts a great deal of admiration from her school-mates, as she is almost certain to do, so much the more gratification for her, because she will be delighted to feel her power over them, and appreciate the fact that she is a leader and as such more notorious than she could be through her legitimate school work. Frequently she is not clever in the usual application of the term.

The attention which her doings provoke, moreover, from the side of the teaching staff is also important. She may be popular with some of them, in spite of the disturbance she causes. This type of girl is generally quick and intelligent, if not brilliant, and they realise her excellent abilities and fund of initiative. But they will often mourn to themselves, among each other, or occasionally to the girl herself, that it is a pity she does not direct her talent for leadership to more constructive ends. This, however, in all probability would not give her the same satisfaction, for these reasons: the *raison d'être* of her leadership is to head a rebellion. Her power is derived from her desire to overthrow discipline, and to prove herself one too many for the authorities. In other words, it signifies her conquest over her parents by proxy, and her victory over the home. This will occur in cases where the girl has been a known rebel at home and also when she has been the dutiful daughter there, and until she went to school had not the opportunity to put her unconscious wishes into action.

She becomes a school problem. They do not want to expel her for her misdemeanours, except in some very old-fashioned schools, where they have no room for any but the most tractable of children. The chief reason for this, they say, is that the *parents* would not like them to associate with any others unless they were of the same stamp. They are afraid that these parents would most likely remove their own meek little daughters, were any of these adventures to reach their ears. The authorities are frankly often at a loss what to do to induce her to mend her ways, and to turn her capabilities into more useful channels. They try in all ways to influence her. But the more notice of this sort she gets the more she triumphs over them, realising that they are helpless to deal with her rebellion.

If they resort to punishments they will gratify that other important wish of the adolescent—*to be a suffering heroine*, the martyr for her cause. The girl becomes firmly convinced they have a grudge against her (sometimes a fore-shadowing of a persecution mania in later life), that they are trying to penalise her for something which, skilfully handled, makes a still more potent bond to unite her followers to her. It will also make her doubly anxious to keep their applause to compensate for the ill-treatment which she feels she is receiving from the hands of the authorities. Once again she seeks the proofs of her power. And to her it appears so much more powerful, as well as being more dramatic, to succeed as leader of the opposition, and work for the destruction of law and order, than to reverse the object and the aim by carrying out her leadership in the interests of the school, under the guidance of authorities, towards construction. This to her would appear very tame, because the necessary element, the overcoming of resistance, would be therefore reduced to a minimum.

Should we go back to examine the root cause of this urge we may find it to be another attempt to procure proofs of her power over others, arising from an exaggerated and often repressed inferiority complex. These school rebels will quite frequently be only children, or sometimes the inconspicuous second or middle daughter in a family of girls. They may believe they ought to have been the boy in the family, but that some regrettable accident arranged otherwise. Perhaps it has always been said in the family, but most unwisely, that a boy was expected when they were born, or that they resemble some male member of the family, perhaps a youthful uncle or cousin. They have never forgiven nor forgotten it, and do their best to try to prove themselves a boy's equal, or even superior, as consolation for the mistake.

They feel consequently that to obey, to be amiable and docile, is playing the part of the good little girl, and therefore shun this type of behaviour to adopt that of the rebel, which is more in accordance with their conception of being masculine. The main struggle in the home used to be with the mother, and therefore it will be passed on to those teachers who most nearly approximate to the mother-type. Should there be any visiting masters attending the school, they would probably find little difficulty in managing her, and consider that she was a model pupil, wondering why the others should give her such a bad name or find her troublesome and lazy.

Yet beneath this confident, daring exterior we would seldom guess that it is the unconscious inferiority, the feeling that no one loves her but everyone is against her, which causes her response of the *don't-care attitude* towards the world, by which she tries to keep the balance and show that she is not afraid or overawed by the hostility she feels around her.

On the one hand, taking as little notice as possible of her lack of discipline and her leadership of the school rebels is the best way to deal with this difficult problem. It is impossible to keep up an exchange of hostilities when there is no response from the other side. The stimulus being lessened, the feud dies of itself of inanition. If it should happen that somebody can make a contact with the girl without giving her the least suspicion of adverse criticism, gain her confidence, and gradually lead her to talk of her doings, guiding her to appreciate her reasons for adopting this course of action, but so gradually that she does not feel she is being preached at or influenced, much benefit will grow out of it. She will come to realise that there are other and better ways of gaining what she wants; she may also in course of time identify herself with this older woman, whom she regards in the light of a true friend, whom she actually needs very much, and so gain what she has lacked through her former strained relationship with her own mother, whom she has not looked upon as a possible ideal, for many reasons.

It was probable that she had never been on particularly good terms with her mother, and thus was never able to take advantage of identification possibilities developing where she was concerned. They have always been upon the side of the father or the male relative she was supposed to resemble. Nor has she ever felt any great love for her mother, unless it may have been when she was quite a baby—that is, before something happened which re-directed her former affection for the mother to the person of the father. The girl needs this mother-figure, especially during adolescence, for the purpose of helping her to develop into a woman; and, among other things, she may not be able to find her present ideal in the mother because of the very early transference to her. She and her love are associated with the days of early childhood. Therefore, as the child-self is vanishing into the past, the old mother-ideal cannot be revived in one and the same person because of the old link. A new ideal is wanted of a more progressive mother who can be imitated, and therefore the person who can become the representative of the new ideal must make her appearance out of the mists of the future and point the way towards a fresh goal. She must of necessity be someone to whom the girl feels she can grow and reach up to, not one who pulls her back to the past. She feels ready to cut herself adrift from the past to a certain extent. This is one of the reasons why the adolescent girl so eagerly seeks in her phantasies, if she is too shy to do so in reality, a substitute mother-image, the foster-mother or lost mother of the fairy-tale phantasy, to whom she can confide her troubles and ideals without running the risk of being laughed at.

It is this longing for a new mother which will often be one of the foundations of that difficult state of affairs which we recognise frequently among many of the older girls at school in relation to their teachers, commonly known as *the crush* or *G.P.* The girls, because of their age, are only too ready to fall headlong into it; many of the mistresses, too, because of their age or temperament, are just as willing to receive the devotion of the girls as they are to give it. Both gain a great deal of emotional gratification from the exchange, but whether it is a healthy outlet for either in the long run we must leave for further discussion in the next chapter, when we examine the causes and effects of adolescent friendships.

The girl's most significant conflicts connected with her schooldays naturally fall into several groups, besides those which we have already mentioned. We will have to consider all of them among the three main groups of *the social, the educational,* and *the emotional* aspects. But it should be realised that we cannot always keep these three strictly apart; they will cross and recross in their causes, manifestations, and results many times. Among the former we must place those with which we began this chapter; her attitude to the school as a replacement of the home; her relationships with the girls as the substitutes of her sisters, and to the teachers, who reflect her former attitude to her mother. In the educational group we must ascertain what the girl herself wishes to gain from the many years which she spends getting what is called *her education*. We need to discover what she intends to do with it when she has it? Does it represent to her merely a space of time which has to be dragged out in some way to fill the gap between childhood and taking her place in the world as a grown-up person? Or has she a definite love of study and learning, arising from the wish to gratify her impulse of curiosity? Again, does she like school because it supplies her with a gratification from games and other interests carried out in the company of others that she could not gain otherwise, which includes modern school enterprises such as orchestras, theatricals, arts and crafts classes, domestic science lectures and practice?

When we come to consider the emotional conflicts of school-life we shall find there a repetition of many that have been previously dealt with in these pages of emotional situations first found in the home, with her parents and sisters; if the school be a co-educational one, then with her brothers as well. We may expect to find that the old preferences attached to one parent or the other will be revived; her former jealousy experiences on account of a sister, whom she believed to be her mother's favourite, will be rediscovered in the person of a school-fellow, whom she imagines to be singled out for preferential treatment by one of the teachers, of whom also she is exceptionally fond. All that has been said consequently in the foregoing chapters concerning the conflict at home will be equally applicable to this world of school; in additional ways we will find others of importance finding a place in subsequent chapters. A few others, however, seem to be necessary to describe later on in this chapter, because they are peculiarly associated with the gratification that may be attained emotionally from the acquisition of knowledge, connected with the instinct Curiosity, the inhibition of this instinct and ways in which the girl tries during schooldays to counteract her feelings of inferiority relative to her lack of knowledge and a curious aspect of the phantasy, serving the purpose of adding to her own superiority through getting her schoolmates to believe what she tells them, which she knows at first is not true, even though she may come to believe it, or almost believe it, in course of time.

We can only answer all these important questions concerning the girl's school-life and solve its problems by examining the tendencies and interests of individual girls. We can then compute what use she will make of her education. We may also be able to predict whether she is likely to thrive most when under the direction of a leader, when she is working with others at a set subject, at a given time, having her entire life mapped out for her, or after schooldays are over, when she has the time and the opportunity to continue working at her favourite subjects, when and how she likes. This will depend, of course, not only upon her own dependence or independence of character, but also the aim she has in view.

Our general experience is, however, that unless it is necessary for her to do special work, because she is intending to try to earn her own living by this means, or at least to increase her pocket-money that way, the girl at home does not often continue her studies when she has not the stimulus of working with the other girls and under the guidance of a teacher, except in quite rare instances, driven on by the urge of some unconscious wish, connected with the gratification of the instinct of curiosity.

This may cause us to wonder whether we have a greater or less advantage in the fact that the school does cultivate the time-table and the set task. Whether it has been found that the girl does not work without it. If she would give up definite study in any case as soon as there was no need for her to continue it, or if it is the outcome of working under the direction of another for so long which causes her to be helpless when left to her own initiative. It will be interesting to know whether girls educated under the Dalton System are better able to go on with definite study after they have left school; but even then it has been found necessary to keep up the standard of work and the interest of the pupils from flagging by the issue of assignments and constant test papers to be written upon each section of the work which is to be accomplished.

Usually, however, we find that the ordinary school time-table system leaves girls unable to occupy their time when they are without its help. They are inclined to wander about rather aimlessly, doing nothing particular all day, unless they have a definite arrangement for games or an occupation that they are going to share with friends. The girl who has been brought up all her life at a boarding-school or a day-school where she has so much homework to do in the evening that she has very little time in which she is free to find her own occupations or to do them, does not grow up capable of arranging her own day afterwards, nor of knowing what she wants to do or how to do it unless she has been taught or shown.

This cultivated faculty for following the direction of others, which may be due to the mass-production system of large schools, may extend still farther and injuriously into the intellectual life. The perfect schoolgirl even waits to be told what *to think* about books, music, art, because she has lessons upon these subjects, not only upon the theory of their production and the works themselves, but what is called appreciation, that is what to think about them, and the estimation of another person, which she has to accept rather than to learn to know enough about them to form her own taste. Hence she is not taught to think for herself any more than she is encouraged to act for herself, because it is impossible to learn this together with a large number of others.

An institution where the close proximity of many others reduces each individual to the representation of an average, like the wearing of a school uniform that is the outward and visible sign of mass-production in education, gives us also the average mentality represented by the inculcation of school traditions, as their supposed inward and spiritual grace. However, the wholesale adoption of these stereotyped opinions, without discrimination, may often lead to a girl collecting a many-headed hydra of snobbish prejudices.

The adolescent girl, not sure in many instances of what she is and what she wants, is often only too ready to seize on any suggestion of the moment which seems to offer her an easy solution of her problem. Just as many girls of this age, nevertheless, are equally afraid of losing their independence and individuality if they once conform to any rules, they imagine it to be the thin end of the wedge to being swamped by them.

Girls may be found reacting in countless ways according to their own particular type, and their types are legion. Therefore it is necessary to remind readers from time to time that while certain manifestations are pointed out that may be seen among a large number of adolescents, this does not mean that all will behave in this way and in no other. The fluctuations and modifications even within the type-grouping are very extensive. And when we show that a certain sort of behaviour may arise from one kind of home environment, we do not mean that this home situation cannot produce another result, nor that the reaction under discussion has never been known to come from circumstances which appear to the onlooker as completely different. The human being is no automatic machine which can be calculated to produce one type of goods in the shape of a psychological reaction in return for the coin—the stimulus—that we put into the slot.

The slightest stimulus during the years of adolescence may have a profound effect upon a sensitive girl, whom we may not have considered to be impressionable because she has always been so careful to encase herself in impenetrable armour in order to preserve her secrets and her easily wounded pride. While tremendous catastrophes, which the onlooker expects to have a quite shattering result upon another, may serve to stabilise her, because they give her something definite and external to contend with instead of continuing her concentration upon her internal conflicts.

It is exactly this variability to be found among adolescents which makes it so difficult to arrange a suitable scheme of education and a curriculum for them from the point of view of their psychological development. It is impossible, as well as inadvisable, to give each girl there such a thorough psychological investigation that it can be determined what is necessary to provide for her, in order that she may gain all she requires to fulfil her instinctual needs. She will be better satisfied should she find some of these for herself, being given a choice of various opportunities, and allowed to select for herself from among them. To turn all of them into the right channel, and to be sure that none of them are deriving an unwelcome influence from any of the sources we have mentioned throughout this book, would mean we should have to furnish each with a trained psychologist and a special curriculum. In any case, it would not be sufficient to carry this out only at her entrance to the school; it would have to be a continuous process. The adolescent changes so rapidly that it would be necessary to keep a psychological finger on the pulse of her emotions and reactions all the time, and change her school-work as often, to be able to accomplish what we should set out to do in this case, which would entirely paralyse the requirements of school-leaving examination or matriculation needs, which are now almost considered essentials for girls to carry away from school when they leave, as the girl of several generations ago took her sampler to hang upon the wall as a proof of her skill.

By this it must not be inferred that one would advocate throwing all children into a rough sea to teach them to swim, and only have a competent person at hand to render artificial respiration in case they should be almost drowned. The analogy one would wish to make would be rather that if you have a collection of healthy young saplings it is unnecessary to keep on pulling them up by the roots to see whether they are growing. The afforestation expert can see that by walking through, and it is time enough to examine them from the roots upwards when they are obviously wilting and the cause cannot be determined in any other fashion.

The school, it would seem, must of necessity provide for the average girl, and in order to make up its mind what is necessary for girls of various ages, should draw their conclusions from a sufficiently large number of different types of girls, giving them always the choice from a few alternatives, which will both fit in with the arrangements of the school and the capacities of the staff. But at the same time it is well to keep clearly in the forefront of our minds, so that it is readily available for practice and not left among our collection of theories only, that we cannot arrange the preferences or needs of girls by the date which appears upon their birth certificates. Because we have found a good many girls of, say, thirteen are interested in handicrafts, it is not wise to make it compulsory that all those of this age should spend all their free time in this way, for by so doing we may be afflicting a large number with the torture of the damned. At the same time a girl of twelve may long to join the class, but is not considered old enough to do so, and another of fifteen is told she is too old; she should have got beyond that stage, and she should now have developed other interests.

If it were only possible to establish an ideal education for every girl, we should, of course, endeavour to follow the line of her development and not lead her along a set path of what we feel is good for her. This path of our making, and the conviction that this is the right one, frequently arises from our own wishes and preferences at that age. Or perhaps some psychological specialist has laid down a law that the girl of such and such age needs precisely this element to develop her mind or her body at this time. Some may, but others may not. The chronological age, as we have hinted before, is very little to go by, as those industrious folks who spend a deal of time making neat statistics of the results of intelligence tests will also assure us in theory, and yet go on to make pronouncements which seem as though they forget it.

A characteristic of many of the modern schools seems to have developed this scheme of things into a fetish, where the idea of liberty and freedom in education is concerned, and in it once more we may see theory and practice at variance. In many cases it appears that they have merely set up one educational idol in place of one they have pulled down. They have exchanged old lamps for new ones, which have the same faults as the old. They have established a new order of things, the name of which sounds ideal, but which upon investigation seems to possess quite as much rigidity as the old one. It assumes that all the girls who go to that school shall now be equally interested in cutting lino-stencils, in dramatising their history lessons, in writing poetry as a method of learning English, but that to learn simple mechanics or chemistry would be bad for them, as it would encourage the mechanistic tendency of the age, which is already too strong, although some girls are far more interested in it, or them, than art. They decree that it is good for their development for all to learn to play some musical instrument and take part in the school orchestra, because that is a speciality of the school; learn domestic science or home nursing, or join the Girl Guides, because the head of that school is particularly interested in these things herself, and feels that in this direction only lies the salvation of the flock entrusted to her care. In other instances, of course, there is another accent to the fetishism. It may be that the whole school must live upon a vegetarian diet, or be brought up in the ethics of Christian Science or Theosophy.

Many of these matters apply equally or especially to the use of the children's *free time*. This is as much planned and arranged as their school work. They shall all keep pets. It gives them so much interest in life to study animals and learn how to look after them. On one free afternoon it is decreed that all the girls shall cultivate the plots of ground that have been allotted to them. On another afternoon they shall play basket- or net-ball. On Saturday morning they attend a cooking lesson. All is according to schedule, and if one should question the plan, for which one girl got herself into serious trouble, it will not give her teachers five minutes' thought upon the subject:

"Don't we ever have a half-holiday?"
"Why yes, practically every afternoon. We do all our work in the morning here."
"But there is something arranged for every afternoon. When do we have any free time to do as we like in?"
"But all your afternoons are free. Don't you understand?"
"No, not quite. I mean time to do anything one likes, when one likes to, or do nothing if one wants."

That is the secret of liberty for her development which the adolescent needs. She does urgently require some time during the day to do what she likes in, with absence of all criticism concerning her use of it. That will give her the true recreation that she wants to carry her through the busily planned hard-working day. It is essential for her to have some real relaxation time during the day that she can call her own, just as she needs some place to call her own, if this can possibly be managed, so that eventually she may be able to call her soul her own.

We seldom allow the girl enough freedom for those requirements. We are too busy educating her and influencing her in this most impressionable time of her life. But do we consider even for a fleeting moment that it is possible for her to pick up impressions from our arrangements or behaviour which we may not have anticipated, thought no concern of hers, or believed could be overlooked because the rest were so important? We have to watch for the possible disadvantages of our methods as well as stressing their advantages, and honestly weigh them up one against the other before we can be sure that we are upon the right track.

Among the various emotional conflicts which trouble the adolescent girl we must mention especially in this chapter those which are connected in different ways with her desire for the gratification of the instinct of curiosity, or those which are derived from the inhibition of the instinct. A great many of the emotional disturbances related with other factors of her home- or school-life may sap her energy, so that little interest or attention is available for her actual school work. For instance, troubles at home, or an erotic attachment to some other girl or one of the mistresses will often account for her apparent *stupidity* or *laziness*, about which she will get into trouble with the authorities.

Another frequent cause for her inability to learn is still more definitely connected with her wish for knowledge and the early refusal to gratify her curiosity. She cannot learn now because in the past, as well as perhaps in the present, she was denied a great deal of information she required. It is not uncommon for children to put many unconscious symbolic values upon this subject of Knowledge as a sign of superiority. Their own comparative ignorance respecting the things their parents know and they do not is a proof in their eyes of their own inferiority. These things will generally be such problems as whence do babies come and details of the love-life of the parents. These matters, in which they feel they are kept in ignorance, give rise to many educational difficulties in years to come. They try to deal with the subject in several ways, the inability, i.e. the unconscious refusal to learn because they have been denied information, may lead them to show an intense eagerness to acquire all sorts of knowledge in order to cancel the inequality in the original direction, to make them possessed of more knowledge than their contemporaries or others. In this way they go on to seek proofs for their own comfort, and to demonstrate to others their great knowledge, by passing examinations with the highest possible marks, or general knowledge competitions of all kinds.

Another means is what we might call the *bluff method*. The girl always wants to give the impression that she knows everything, and more about everything than other people. Her one reply is, "Yes, I know"; although when questioned as to the exact details of what she knows, she is often at a loss to make good her assumption of superior knowledge of previous information, or obviously invents her answer from the inspiration of the moment.

This leads us to another manifestation of the same trend, the desire to be better informed carries over to the wish to have more exciting experiences to relate to her school friends than other girls in her class. She wants to tell them things that she has done, which they will believe and wonder at, but which are quite untrue. She wants to gain their admiration or applause in this way once more to prove her superiority. It shows us once again, also, one of the ways in which the phantasy may be used in her daily life. Here we find it breaking through its secrecy and repressions to be narrated to others for a certain purpose. We shall notice the girl telling her companions things which are not true, but that represent her dearest wishes, in order to improve her position in some fashion.

The subjects chosen for this Pseudologia Phantastica, as it is called, or, more simply, Pathological Lying, may concern the wealth or importance of parents or family, or her own doings and experiences. They may be tales of the daring-adventure type of exploits during the holidays or at a former school, but in the adolescent girl they frequently take the form of romantic, highly coloured love-stories. A phantasy boy friend or more mature lover (the father-image) will be invented. He is given a distinguished name, his appearance described in full detail. He is supposed to take her out, and together they will visit theatres, movies, and restaurants. She may write herself letters, signed with his name, show photographs with devoted inscriptions that are supposed to be his, buy herself flowers and chocolates which she has sent to herself in his name, for the edification of her school friends. They, naturally enough, regard her as a most enviable person, and never suspect that the accounts she gives are not actual facts. This fabrication may continue for years, before it comes to an end in some way, either because it is found out or because she herself gets tired of it for some reason. The principal causes for the girl dropping this phantasy of her own accord will be that she may really fall in love with someone, and so does not need the substitute, or she wearies of its unsatisfactoriness as a substitute for the real thing, or it loses its emotional gratification through long repetition. Then she may either cease to speak of it or finish it off in what she considers an artistic fashion. She will arrange for him to jilt her, or he will meet with some accident or death by illness. Perhaps her parents will interfere according to her phantasy, and she will become the object of intense sympathy and additional thrills of romance as the girl who is suffering from a secret sorrow, bereaved of the person she has loved. After much vivid description she sometimes almost believes these narratives of her own to be true, but very seldom.

Should this habit of hers come to the knowledge of her parents or the school authorities there may be grave trouble in store for the girl. It may be regarded as an attempt to deceive them that is quite unwarrantable, and her lifelike phantasy love-story is described by them as a tissue of lies. Psychologists regard it as one of the familiar expressions of adolescent wishes for romance as well as the girl's attempt to find consolation for something she feels she is missing from reality, or her striving to counter a feeling of inferiority in comparison with her school companions who, she feels, have more exciting lives than she. But it will frequently cause a great deal of annoyance and misunderstanding on the part of those who have never heard of it as one of the psychological symptoms which are frequent during adolescence.

Many of her other emotional conflicts typical of school-life will be described in the remaining chapters of the section, and so we must leave this interesting subject for the present to deal with other important topics which present the girl with difficulties that arise from her environment.

It is a great handicap to the average adolescent girl that she should so frequently change her school or method of education just at this time. Entering new surroundings and having to adjust herself to fresh conditions usually increase her mental strain, when her physical and psychological development and the stress provided by them are at their height—that is, between twelve and sixteen. The attitude that one finds in many schools to-day is that the physical changes of puberty, being a perfectly natural and normal state in the life of the girl, should not cause her either physical pain or mental conflict. Therefore the best way to cope with the situation is to ignore it, and encourage the girl to carry on exactly the same, however she may feel, or in any case urge that she should pretend she does not feel any fluctuation in health or feelings during the month. But a large number of persons are beginning to feel that this is a mistaken view, and may lead to most unsatisfactory results.

We may suspect that it is derived, as we have suggested earlier in this book, from some of the complexes of the teachers or the medical women who advocate it. But there are other roots besides the conscious or unconscious masculinity complexes of these women. It has also been put forward that the treatment of girls during their schooldays will resemble in many ways the ancient puberty and initiation rites of the primitives. Let us see in further detail how this may be. It certainly provides the girl with the training and education she needs for her life in the future, more or less adequately, we must admit. But we must also take into our consideration that whereas the primitive races had only one possible future to contemplate for their girls, therefore it was so much the more simple to prepare them for it. In our own days there are numberless opportunities for the girl, once her schooldays are ended.

For the primitive girl there were practically no alternatives, although some modification in her training might occur should she belong to the royal household or be the daughter of a powerful chief, unless it were decided that she should be initiated to the service of a local goddess or consider being trained as a medicine woman. For our girls there are now so many possibilities. Life was simpler, too, because we imagine that the people who undertook her training were likewise educated all on the same plan, which would exclude some of the strange complications which may arise at the present.

It will probably be an unpopular subject to bring forward for discussion, but it is unavoidable nevertheless. The special training received by the teachers, their original methods and motives concerned with getting away from their own homes and surroundings, and why they should have taken up this profession when so many others were before them for selection, will of necessity have some important bearing upon their behaviour as well as their treatment of the girls. We may find that a great many teachers of the past had homes with which they were not satisfied in many respects, and did their best to get away from by this means. Large numbers of them have been scholarship girls who, in their struggle to gain their education, also strove hard to rise from simple homes and achieve a higher social status. We may often notice that this may provide some unconscious jealousy of the girls whom they teach, who have not had a similar struggle. On the contrary, however, these antecedents may cause some not to be particularly kind or sympathetic to other scholarship girls, who find their way into schools where most of the other pupils are drawn from a different class, and who pay fees in the ordinary way. This attitude of making a difference in their treatment between them may be the outcome of the hostility provided by unconscious inferiority, the feeling that they have climbed the ladder successfully, but they do not want too many others to do so. Or again—a very important factor—because they do not want anyone to accuse them of favouritism shown to these girls, since this might lead others to suspect it came from a social kinship. A good deal of bullying arises from causes such as these, and because of the likes and dislikes of the teachers, springing from these as well as other causes derived from the component instinct *sadism*. This subject will be referred to again in the next chapter, because it so often happens that the relationships of girls and their teachers will be influenced thus. In this connection we shall find the manifestations of impulses of love and hate, the curious love requirements that are to be found showing sadistic or masochistic components as outlets for increasing emotional tension.

Should we be in a position to gain some insight into the early home-life of these teachers of adolescent girls, their own relationships with their mothers and sisters, older or younger than themselves, we would be better able to understand their reasons for behaviour which so often may puzzle us, and realise that they derive some means of satisfying or compensating old deprivations or inferiority by their treatment of the girls in their care.

Curious treatment of special girls often takes place so insidiously and secretly in a school that only the girls themselves know about it, and they are the least likely to mention it at home or elsewhere, for one reason alone— because they feel that somehow the blame would be pushed back upon themselves. Also from the ideal of loyalty, which is instilled so early and thoroughly into the young in relation to the doings of their elders.

In passing it may also be as well to mention that we often find extremely harmful results arising from a girl being sent to a school where the other girls are of a different social class to themselves, and especially should this be one of the changes which happen during adolescence. Whether through financial losses at home or the death of a parent, the girl goes to a new school, where the girls are from less cultured homes, or if she through winning a scholarship or the supreme efforts of her family will be sent to one where the girls are all far better-off than herself, there are many difficulties awaiting her. She feels different to the rest of her school-mates, feels that they do not like her for this reason, and finds it difficult to settle down in these new surroundings. It may be true, because we often find that both schoolgirls and schools can be exceedingly snobbish in both directions up or down.

We may, in fact, often see connected with these difficulties which we have just been describing that conflicts will arise upon both sides between the home and the school, the parents and the teachers, the girls becoming the unfortunate recipients of them from each side. The parents may, and frequently do, become jealous of the strong influence of the teachers, and they in turn will strive to separate the daughters from their parents by showing them directly or indirectly that they are old-fashioned, or inferior in some way to the ideals put forward by themselves as members of the staff of that particular school. The girls often do not need much encouragement to adopt this attitude of intense criticism of the parents and the home, especially when it is supported by the opinion of their teachers and school authorities. Consequently the parents will feel annoyed and injured, considering that their authority is being undermined.

It is a difficult and complex problem. On the one side one wishes for advance and development from one generation to another, but it would often seem that too sudden and violent steps towards progress will have a dangerous effect upon the psychological health of the young girls by forcing them along at a pace for which they are not yet prepared. Their elders do not notice the strain that may be caused by a rapid introduction to entirely new ideas, and give too many at once. They do not seem to realise that mental exertion or physical exercise which they can easily accomplish may be too much for the immature strength of the adolescent, who at this time is bound to use up much of her energy for internal readjustments. This being the case, she has not so much to spare for the assimilation of fresh external stimuli which call for efforts she can scarcely sustain without risking too great a drain upon her reserves at command, which are not very great then. During adolescence it is not possible for reserves to collect because the girl is drawing heavily upon her stock of energy daily, although mentally she is eager enough to seize everything she can get. Often the inertia or lethargy of the adolescent girl may be a warning to us that nature is putting up a defence against overstrain, or they will be a sign that it has already taken place, and we should let her take things easily until she recuperates.

We older people should keep all these facts in mind when we have young folks to deal with, and not take undue advantage of their willingness or delight in pressing forward after new experiences. We should constantly keep in mind that we can injuriously increase the adolescent strain by urging them on to keep pace with us mentally or physically when it may be beyond their capacity at present.

FRIENDSHIPS AND IDENTIFICATIONS

When we come seriously to consider the friendships of the adolescent girl, it may strike us that there are many most significant qualities about them which are not so prominent in those of either younger or older persons as a rule. We shall notice that they are more highly charged with emotions of various kinds then than at other times, and they undergo modifications and changes with greater swiftness. They will come into being, increase until they reach a climax, when one or both of the friends can scarcely bear to be separated from the other for any length of time, and turn into the most mordant hatred—all within the space of a few days. Occasionally reconciliation occurs equally rapidly, or vacillation between the two stages takes place several times in as many days, weeks, or months. Then they may suddenly cease to be, almost as quickly as they arose. On the other hand we often find some friendships existing during adolescence, which ripened out of companionships of childhood, and continue throughout life, although after a time they may take on that quality of habit or custom that comes over friendships of long standing.

Frequently adolescent friendships will be the result of proximity or expediency, and because the girls have something of importance in common. They may be the only two new girls going to school on the same day, and share a railway carriage or a bedroom. The strangeness of the experience brings them together, and they make common cause over their mutual loneliness, so becoming fast friends. Again, we may see friendships arise between pairs of opposites, part, apparently, of the attraction founded upon the fact that the one serves as an excellent foil to the other.

Thus a brilliantly clever girl and a rather dull one become close friends. The clever girl likes to have her stupid companion at hand, so that she may appear even more clever by contrast. The dull one almost worships her gifted friend because she is flattered at being in her company or known as her friend. We will often see the same thing occur in the case of another pair of girls, the one being tall and good-looking and the other plain and quite unattractive.

There is another frequent cause for the foundations of such friendships which may not always be apparent from surface observation. This is that both supply something that the other admires but knows she lacks, some quality of mind or body; or each will represent a person of the particular *age*, which the other believes to be an ideal; therefore she is the personification of her ideal self. This ideal age is of great interest, as it may represent variously a time when the girl was particularly happy herself—in the past, of course—when we shall find the chosen friend is younger than the girl by several years. Or, contrarily, when she was intensely unhappy, in which case, by trying to make the other girl happy, she may gain what she herself missed at that age by proxy as it were. Perhaps the ideal age will be in the far future, which will apply to a friendship with an older woman, who then represents something to which the girl looks forward. It does not take much guessing to realise that this will be the mother-figure, or even a portrait of a grandmother, known as quite a young child, who seemed then all that was most lovable and to be desired.

We may find another bond of friendship which is fairly common, yet is seldom understood at its true value. This is a pair of girls who seem to be constantly quarrelling. One will bully or tease the other without mercy. Here, naturally, it will be the sadistic impulse at work, gaining its direct gratification upon another person, who is equally satisfied to derive her emotional outlet through suffering. Without doubt, she is powerfully attracted by her persecutor, and instead of trying to escape from this apparently unkind treatment, is constantly putting herself in the way of it and provoking it.

The typical adolescent friendships of the *crush*, *pash*, or *G.P.* varieties, as they are popularly known at school, are usually of the simple, effusive, direct-love type. The two are devoted to one another. They go about together as much as possible, put their arms round each other's necks or waists, kiss each other, do everything together, and feel that this friendship will endure to the end of time. These girls will generally be quite simple souls, whose psychological quality will be that of the hysteric. They are easily given to tears if anything disturbs the friendship from the outside, quickly excited to jealousy, or angry and reproachful should the friend prove unkind or show any diminution of her love. Usually reconciliation takes place rapidly without much difficulty, and they kiss again with tears. All goes well until the next recurrence, or another cause for jealousy interferes with their love idyll.

The adolescent girl is commonly extremely jealous of her friends. They must not swerve in their allegiance for a moment to the right hand or to the left. They allow their best-beloved no latitude. No one else must be shown any attention, or there is trouble, hurt feelings, and probably the injured party goes off to nurse her wounded pride in silence and the sulks, until the friend comes after her to find out what is the matter. In fact, they behave very much the same as the majority of older, heterosexual lovers. But then we must consider this point. It is not so much that the girls are imitating the more adult men and women, but *they* who are repeating their own former adolescent behaviour when they fall in love later; because a great deal of the play and amusements of love-making is a direct repetition of childish or adolescent manifestations. We can see it at all its stages if only we take the trouble to watch those who come within our range of observation.

The depth or amount of emotion which will be discharged in these adolescent friendships depends upon a great many different factors. In place of first importance as a determinant of the amount or quality of the emotion which will be expended must be reckoned the fact if the girl has been very much repressed and inhibited in the past in the expression of her love towards another person, probably a mother or sister; whether this manages to break loose upon this new love-object found during adolescence, or is still unable to free itself and find direct satisfaction, also how much stimulus will be provided from the other partner of the friendship, or again, whether these ardent, emotional love-relationships have been continuous throughout life in a long series of repetitions, uninhibited and unrepressed.

All of these are extremely important points when we come to consider adolescent friendships between persons of any age, or either sex for the matter of that, although until now we have been thinking chiefly of those in connection with members of the girl's own sex. Let us take first a few instances when the girl's love has never been able to gain free expression to her own mother. This may happen through loss of the mother in early infancy, followed by absence of transference of affection at the time to a mother-substitute. A second cause can be that all her love becomes turned to hated or repressed and stifled because of some early trauma connected with the mother. We may see the child's love sometimes in these cases turn inwards towards itself, or outwards, but projected upon inanimate objects, such as animals, dolls, or other toys rather than a person. Subsequently, should the adolescent manage to find an ideal woman friend, who will take the place of the long-lost mother, or a second self in the person of a contemporary, we may expect the friendship which develops to be highly charged with emotion because of the previous deprivation. This, however, is not so likely to occur between those whose love-life has been satisfied in the normal way during childhood, nor in the case of those who are still suffering even from a partial inhibition, which prevents them giving free expression to the love they feel.

Among all the many varieties of adolescent friendships, the girls who can be classed in this last-mentioned group suffer most. They suffer especially because they are often not fully aware of what they are striving for. They will want to throw their affections at the feet of someone who attracts them, but frequently will not be able to do this in a way which proves acceptable or even at times recognisable to the beloved woman. They will be more than usually gauche with that person; inarticulate, even rude, and frequently get laughed at for their trouble; ignored, or thought a bore. *They* may be aware that it is love which is disturbing them, but it may disguise itself at source as the opposite feeling, dislike or hatred, and avoidance of the very person who, were they but a little less inhibited, ought to be the vehicle of this pent-up affection.

We will be ready to admit that girls who are absorbed in the stress of a violent adolescent friendship, either with a girl of the same age, a little older, or with a mature woman, find it difficult to carry on the ordinary affairs of their daily life. Their school work deteriorates. They are unable to concentrate upon their former outside interests. They will cease to care for their old friends or relations. Everything else fades out, or is pushed into the background until the blaze of this fierce passion has burnt itself out. Often the girl suffers extremely from her failure to gain the response she desires. Yet it can be so exacting as to be impossible to attain, or to be long continued. The girl, then, feeling bitterly disappointed and disillusioned, breaks off the friendship in anger. She may often fall into a severe depression for some time, with a nervous breakdown of some kind terminating the episode.

How far these relationships go, and what actual expressions of love gratification the participants allow themselves, naturally varies according to the degree of freedom possessed by each for deriving satisfaction from different forms of sexual requirements and love-play connected with the several component instincts. They may only want to kiss each other, look at each other's bodies, or to be looked at, touch one another, tickle or stroke each other. They may indulge in various ways of causing one another pain, following the dictates of the sadistic impulse, or may procure pleasure from various more direct forms of mutual or one-sided masturbatory acts. This question of type of gratification chosen will depend upon the particular wishes of one or both of the individuals concerned.

Occasionally we shall find these friendships taking place among groups of several girls, friends, or school-mates, who share schooldays or holidays, and remain warmly attached throughout life. They may often continue this close friendship so that no other outside attachment manages to break through the union, and all the members of the little group avoid or refuse marriage, preferring their own, or rather one another's company, to any that men's society can offer them.

It is very rare that we find girl friends wandering away from home with one another, as boys will do, although an interesting case of this occurred a few years ago and attracted a good deal of attention until they were found. A young nursemaid disappeared with a little girl in her charge, and were missing for several days, after which they arrived at the home of the elder girl. Suicide may very seldom occur as the result of an unrequited love of a girl for another, but it is rare, and it has been thought that occasionally cases have been found of suicide pacts between adolescent girl friends; but this does not happen nearly so often among pairs of girl friends as when the companionship is a mixed one, consisting of an adolescent girl and boy.

What of the friendships which take place between girls and boys to-day, with their freedom and happiness, liberty and danger, that is seen in them, according to the point of view of the onlooker, or the results of the particular sort of friendship it may turn out to be?

Upon this question of friendships between boys and girls there is both much to be said and little to be said, because it is a topic which has been worked almost threadbare from many angles. There is little new that can be written about it, perhaps, from the standpoint of outside observation; yet it may be as well to call attention to some of the less obvious internal elements of the friendships which attract notice, as well as to show some of the chief reasons why they should take place, apart from the primary one. This is, of course, that they represent a typical, emotional outlet of preliminary love-making on the part of the boy and girl, who rather pre-cociously derive this gratification for their impulses in a normal fashion, although at an earlier age, than that which is supposed to be necessary or wise. They may also in other cases represent the equally typical present-day, unemotional, pally companionship between a girl and a boy, or a group of young persons of both sexes, who enjoy one another's society and take pleasure in the same amusements, with or without the admixture of some love-play that is recognisable as such, which may increase until it resembles that usually associated with *necking* or *petting parties*.

We may often notice that friendships of this unemotional type are likely to occur between girls and their brothers' friends, which seem to indicate a transference of the love for the brother one step farther off, outside the family. These friendships may sometimes develop and end in a marriage partnership among young folks who are inclined to be somewhat tied to the home and who dare not venture too far afield in their friendships or love-relationships. The stay-at-home girl will attach herself to the familiar boy whom she has known practically always, or who is almost part of the home circle. The companionship gathers weight during adolescence in some cases, still taking place within the intimate circle of the home. It may remain practically unnoticed, and therefore the girl escapes the usual comments and teasing which many shy girls find so intolerable, that in many instances might prevent them being able to have a boy friend at all otherwise.

This brings us to the interesting point which often shows itself among adolescent friendships. This is, that it may be an extremely important condition for the girl that to be thoroughly enjoyable the friendship must be a secret, because it will increase the romantic element arising from the attraction of doing the forbidden, daring thing. This same condition may also be an essential in friendships of all kinds, with boys, other girls, or older women. In this instance, the girl will frequently choose her friend from well outside the home circle, or away from the friends of her parents; often deliberately selecting someone of whom she knows that her parents will not approve, or from a family not on good terms with her own, like the typical adolescent love-affair of Romeo and Juliet. In this case it will become all the more exciting and steeped with romance, in addition to having the thrill of wondering what might happen should it be discovered. For her friendship subsequently to win the sanction of her parents would cause it quickly to come to an end. Parents often forget this factor when, in order to separate their young daughter from a rather undesirable friend of either sex or any age, they strictly forbid the girl to have anything to do with the chosen companion. This will not merely strengthen the attachment, but supply the girl with the feeling of martyrdom, feeling that she is suffering persecution for the sake of her faithful devotion to a person whom she loves.

We have now briefly examined a good many of the determining causes for adolescent friendships, and must seriously begin to investigate those in which identification of some kind plays an especially prominent part. It is to be found in a great number of cases, one or two of which have already been pointed out, and it has been hinted that they will have a remarkable effect upon the girl's future development. We will often find that it is one of the main roots of many girl and boy attractions too. The girl, who would have liked to be a boy herself, chooses a boy friend, whom she feels is exactly what she would have liked to be. She goes about with him, does as he does, copies his manners, speech, ideas. She becomes like him as closely as she can, and in this way finds a compensation for not having been a boy after all. The boy himself, in this case, may frequently be repeating the same manœuvre, for we often discover that boys or men who are fond of women's society may like their companionship because they feel that they have so much in common. At one time they may have had a wish to have been a girl, because of some advantages they believe them to possess. In a great many instances, however, this wish was swiftly repressed deep into their unconscious mind, whence it causes them to prefer the company of women, but from a very different point of view from that of the purely masculine preference for the society of the opposite sex.

We have already suggested two other varieties of identification friendships, which are to be noticed as occurring in the adolescent girl, those for the younger child, who resembles herself when a child, or some tiny brother or sister, and the friend felt to be so similar to the self at the present as to be almost a double, resembling the friendship occurring between twins or even sisters if a family of several girls.

But some of the most important friendships of adolescence, which provide very serious problems, are those which arise between the young girl and the older one, or again with the mature woman. On the one hand, it will represent an elder sister identification; on the other, the ideal mother, who is not the mother of childhood, connected in the girl's mind with memories of early threats and punishments, loves, hatreds, and jealousies.

Very rarely is it a one-sided affair, although it is possible that some strange phenomena of the girl's masochism might cause a necessary condition of her love to be that it is offered to someone who does not show the slightest return of it, and who obviously does not want it. This might happen in order to give the girl the opportunity to feel herself once again unwanted, and utterly unloved or unlovable. But the most constructive as well as the most destructive of the adolescent friendships are those which provide a strong emotional outlet on both sides. Let us examine both aspects of the friendship and try to gain a clearer view of how and why they can be either so formative or dangerous for the character-development of the young girl.

The adolescent finds some woman attracts her because of her appearance, intellect, manners, or general *savoir-faire*. She seems to be so sure of herself. She has arrived where the girl hopes to come some day. Other people admire her too, and show themselves equally anxious to be with her, because of some quality she possesses. She has had what the girl envies most of all—experience of life. She has read books, seen things and places; has numbered among her friends interesting people who sound so exciting when she tells the girl about them. She seems to have, in short, all that the girl feels she lacks, but wishes so ardently to have. Some girls may become jealous and hate her for this superiority to themselves in this wealth of attainment, but others fall under her spell and love her for it instead, only really happy when they can be near her. They will seek to do little services for her, take her small presents, often costing much more than they can actually afford, offerings of flowers and the like, and do their best to model themselves upon the same pattern.

Now, what the ultimate results of this infatuation will be depends upon what sort of woman she is to whom the girl has attached herself, and what she wants from this unequal friendship. We will frequently notice that she is a type exactly opposite to that of the girl's own mother. Sometimes she will be a younger sister of hers, the aunt, who fills the place, but in this case a sister of whom the mother is rather doubtful herself and not particularly fond, often because of this wide difference between them. The girl's mother may have been the eldest of the family, brought up like *her* mother upon rather old-fashioned lines. Her youngest sister, on the other hand, may have broken away from family tradition and be far more in sympathy with modern views, and has always kept herself abreast with modern ideas and ideals.

Any woman who is sufficiently unlike the family will serve to fascinate an adolescent girl, because of the attraction offered by novelty and variety. She will resemble a bracing gust of fresh air, that she breathes in eagerly. This beloved woman may on the one hand be of the adventuress type, of advanced views and corresponding morals, which offers the peculiar attraction of something forbidden and therefore daring to the girl, or on the other a social worker, an intellectual, an artist, musician, any type of woman, in fact. One can never predict who will occupy this position of the adolescent girl's woman friend. Her parents may approve or disapprove, encourage the friendship or forbid the relationship. The girl's response may be any of the varieties which we have hinted at before.

But whatever the type of woman, the identification usually takes place for better or for worse. Even when the two may be separated in course of time, because one of them might move out of the neighbourhood of the other, or for any of the other reasons for the separation of friends, we find that the identification produces a stratum in the girl's character development which is virtually indelible. She first adopts the characteristic which originally attracted her, whether it were an external one or a psychological one. She will model her appearance upon that of her friend, copying her dress, her mannerisms, voice, mode of speech, behaviour. She imitates her handwriting, too, to mention but a few of the externals of the identification, which will serve to show us upon whom the pattern has been constructed. Intellectually she will also take as much colour from the older woman as she possibly can, through the incorporation of her ideals, her outlook on life, her artistic taste and preferences, her choice of books and reading, her hobbies, even her politics or ethics—anything which she believes to be characteristic of the woman upon whom she has set her immature affections.

Because of the depth and permanence of this identification we are quite rightly anxious about the influence of these older women, with whom our daughters come in contact, at home, school, or in the houses of friends and elsewhere. This friendship, naturally enough, should the woman chosen offer a desirable model for the girls to copy, may provide them with the richest materials for a happy and satisfactory life in the future, but they may prove disastrous. Just as they can teach her valuable things by the easiest way—imitation—things that could never be derived from books or from a formal education, they may show her things which it is better for her to leave for several years before she comes in contact with them, and her mind is better able to discriminate about their worth.

The mind that will sometimes fascinate that of the adolescent may not be stored with materials of any particular worth. It may be brilliant and scintillating, it is true, but valueless, nevertheless, intellectually, giving the girl a piteous or cynical view of human nature and life, but which endures like the rest. It may be mean and paltry, seeking what it can get for itself out of this friendship, and not what it can give to the girl. Yet, at present, she will not have gathered enough discrimination to realise to what extent her youthful affection and generous love are being merely exploited to serve the selfish ends of her friend. What these may be let us now inquire.

We have mentioned before that there is a frequent tendency among human beings to be attracted to others of similar age or type as well as by the opposite. Why, then, should we find some woman glad to gather one girl or a group of them into her most intimate circle? Firstly, she may do it because of what she can give to them, and, secondly, what she may get from it. The conditions of the friendship must be reckoned in terms of the older woman's instinctual demands for gratification or to fill some psychological lack in her own development.

Primarily, let us consider the instance of the giving woman. She may be married or not; she may have had daughters of her own or not; she may have had sisters or not. Hence the girl may supply the need of a daughter-substitute to take the place of one she may have had and lost, or one she would have loved to have had but never obtained, or a little sister to whom she was tenderly attached. Again, she may be a picture of herself during her own adolescence to whom she is now giving what she would have liked but could never find—the friendship of an older woman as an ideal mother.

That covers a good deal of ground for a start. It will rest upon the amount of deprivation or love gratification, which the woman has already attained during her life, whether she is out to get as well as give, or if the main condition of her requirements should be that she gives the girl all and gains nothing but the pleasure of giving as her return. Among the possible gains, however, that she does desire may be that of putting the girl under an extreme obligation, winning her utterly for herself, so that she will always come first, and be cut off from her own family and other friends. In this case we may discover or suspect that the woman had already carried out something of this same sort of strategy of winning the affections of a younger sister and alienating her from their mother. Formerly, in gaining the child through her love, she obtained a kind of revenge upon the mother for having had the child in the first place, because she may have been jealous of the mother always having the babies and not she.

This coming between the adolescent girl and her mother seems to offer a peculiar and irresistible attraction to a great many women with such an early history. It will usually have the desired effect likewise of producing in the girl's mother a considerable amount of hostility and jealousy towards the woman friend, which will also through the repetition provide an additional satisfaction to the friend.

This particular manifestation and sequence of events will have frequent opportunity for occurrence in the girl's school, where it is carried out with all its factors showing complete fulfilment. The teacher, who in this case is the girl's woman friend, gains complete satisfaction all round for each of these conditions. She wins the girl for herself entirely; severs her utterly from the influence of her mother and home by coming between them; gives the girl the feeling of intense obligation; establishes herself in the place of the mother, and arouses in her extreme jealousy, as a rule, for having done so.

Another variety of seeking personal gratification in the girl's friendship will be noticed when the affair satisfies some repressed and perverted sexual desire on the part of the older woman. A great number of women, and not always those who have never been married, teachers and others, because of inhibitions of various kinds, have never been able to derive any normal gratification for their sexual impulses. We may see them continually, only able to gain satisfaction from contacts of different sorts with other women in their girlhood, in training-school days, and later on in the schools where they teach. Sometimes they will be most attracted by women older than themselves, some other teacher, or the Head; at others by a younger member of the staff or one of the pupils, an adolescent girl in their charge, or quite a young child.

These affairs appear in countless forms. Occasionally they will be so repressed, disguised, or hidden that onlookers or even the women themselves do not realise what is taking place, nor the secret spring whence comes this devotion to the girls, or to the women in authority over them. It may be reckoned as one of the greatest points in their favour. But such emotional friendships usually have a disastrous result upon the object of their affections, and because the extreme tension produced by their repressed, unsatisfied emotion arouses in the younger partner an intensity of emotion which she has not yet sufficient mature development to assimilate or to withstand. Should these advances on the part of an older woman be resisted entirely or in part by the child or adolescent, it will naturally lead to the keenest animosity in her, which will augur ill for the rest of that girl's happiness or peace in the neighbourhood of the one whom she has rejected. This will often be the real cause of the failure of a younger member of the staff to gain preferment in the school where she is working. The cause will not generally be known, but it is a frequent occurrence nevertheless.

It is usual to find that these women, who are only capable of obtaining gratification of their love-impulses in connection with other women or girls, frequently cherish a good deal of hostility towards men, either consciously or unconsciously. Their attitude will generally become transferred to the girls who come under their influence, by example or precept, which will not be advantageous for their future happy or healthy development.

These devotions or pashes, which take place between older women and girls at school, that are not very wisely handled by the senior partner, will lead to endless trouble, as crippling the girl for the time of their continuance in her school work, unless an exception be made connected with special subjects taken by the beloved teacher. But in any case the interest which is thus stimulated in these subjects does not help her much ultimately, because the energy expended over them will be tinged with emotion that of necessity drains off too much of the reserve strength that the girl needs for so many other purposes, which will not make such a heavy demand upon it. We must also take into consideration that should she meet with very great success owing to the influence of this woman friend, it may even then, in spite of the immediate good results, lead to the disadvantage of the girl becoming so much under the influence of the older woman that she will not be able to work afterwards independently, and therefore stops short in her subsequent achievements, if their lives should take separate ways in the future.

For these reasons we require to be extremely cautious with whom our girls come in contact, because of the possibilities of over-emotional friendships and the identifications arising out of them; and especially careful in our selection of the schools and teachers under whose influence we place them. We will do well to be aware of these eventualities, and not be too ready to join in the chorus of praise of the woman who attracts violent transferences from all the young girls who come into her environment, unless we happen to know of what quality they may be. They may so often be extremely dangerous people, although popular opinion regards them as such a valuable asset to a girls' school, especially should the woman in question be in authority, such as a head mistress of a school or head of a special department. We may often hear it said of them, "Yes, Miss So-and-So is a wonderful woman. All the girls are quite devoted to her. She can do anything with the most troublesome of them. She has a most remarkable influence over them, in fact."

That is the time to pause and think again, and if possible make some inquiries of the kind of influence it may be, also whence it may spring, before we can be sure that the girls in her radius will be safe from some injurious strand in this remarkable influence.

CHAPTER III

ADOLESCENCE FORESHADOWS THE FUTURE

It is always interesting to watch children growing up and developing through adolescence to maturity. It is so gradual, and yet some of the alterations come about with a suddenness which is startling. A change takes place in features, in expression, in new knowledge assimilated by the girl, which we realise was not there yesterday, and now will be there for ever. Still, at the same time, although the features of her face may change and her expression alter, we can always trace plainly enough at one and the same time the child she was and the woman who is to be. The sudden changes, which happen so rapidly so that we may observe them occurring from day to day, whether they are of the body or the mind, remind us of the wonderful unfolding of a bud into a flower. They gather shape and colour that delight us while we watch. But sometimes we may see the reverse. The promise of beauty withers and the girl seems to shrink farther and farther away from reality, or contacts which ought now to be establishing themselves with the outside world, into silence and unhappiness, where she has only her phantasies for consolation and company.

Watching the girl during the beginnings of adolescence we see a very subtle change creeping into all her ways, and in her games especially. She may find excuses for them, will seem to offer apologies for taking out old toys and perhaps playing with younger children, games of which she used to be particularly fond. She will play, too, but with two important differences. She seems self-conscious about playing as she used both to play and enjoy them long ago, but now she is aware that she is playing. She does not give herself to the games wholeheartedly as before, feeling in all seriousness that it is reality and that she is a living part of it. She is *pretending* to play. She has become self-conscious, too, about these old forms of make-believe, hence her apologies. She used not to do that. She never left off when a grown-up person came upon the scene a year or so ago. But she does now. She leaves off suddenly as soon as she notices an audience, and appears to be doing nothing at all, or if she has a little companion to give an excuse for the game, makes this her reason for playing, and tells the child they will go on presently, meaning when they are alone, of course.

If she plays or pretends to be a child in the presence of adults, as she does sometimes, she exaggerates her childishness so much that they usually become annoyed at the travesty and often tell her sharply not to be so silly and babyish. Does that stop her? Not a bit. She goes on with further wild exaggerations. She likes them to tell her not to act like a child, because it will reassure her that they think she is now too old for this kind of thing. They, too, are realising she is growing up.

There is a transformation appearing also in her attitude towards her elders. Vanished or disappearing fast is her childish trust of them; coming into view the typical adolescent suspicion. What will they think of her? Will they accept her as one of themselves or not? She becomes afraid of showing them her real self. That is why the adolescent girl is frequently so shy and artificial with strangers, showing them a stilted, strange manner which is her carefully thought out disguise, until she has had time to watch them a little and to make up her mind what they are like. When she has decided that important step, she will know better how to proceed.

She is very anxious to disguise herself from her parents. She is fond of all ways in which she can have secrets and keep secrets from them. We can notice this in the intense joy that adolescents take in the making and use of secret languages, or codes in which they send each other messages. Not that the average adolescent girl has anything particular to say in them that others should not hear, but just in order that they can speak to each other in the presence of adults in a language of their own which cannot be understood. The method is effective, too, from the point of view of the adolescent, since the grown-ups usually become extremely annoyed at not being able to understand the children, but they never show any signs of trying to understand what the children say. This, in itself, is extremely interesting, because in all probability when they were young they did precisely the same thing with the same result, irritated their elders by this means and enjoyed it.

We may gain so much information from these secret code languages of adolescence that it may be as well to give a little space to their explanation. They reflect quite a number of the adolescent's various ways of trying to turn the tables upon the grown-ups. And they manage it very well in their choice of methods upon which their codes are formed. In the past it was not uncommon for the children to have suffered from their parents talking secrets before them, but in such a way that they could not understand, either because they spoke too fast or used long words, which the young folks did not know, or because they made use of a foreign language. The children were annoyed. They realised that directly their elders started to speak in this way something interesting was being discussed, some secret, either about themselves or the adults, which in itself would be equally intriguing, if not more so, could they only find out what was being said. They were annoyed, too, about that, and from both these things deduced that they might be able to produce the same effect by similar means. Which they do. The adults are still so much children at heart that they react in the same way to the old stimulus, although they call the children childish, however.

But why should it be that the adults cannot remember the old methods and answer the adolescents in the same language? They refrain because they must. They have forgotten them. They have put these old languages out of their memory with the rest of their childhood's paraphernalia. Again, why do they not pay enough attention to the children when they talk, to pick them up, as they would if they wanted to learn some foreign tongue? They pretend that it would not be worth while. But they are so simple, these secret codes, when all is said and done. A few moments' careful attention is usually all that is necessary to grasp their construction, and the rest—proficiency in talking—comes with practice. But the adult refuses to recognise them, and certainly will not learn them, for deep, psychological reasons, no doubt, that would be extremely interesting to ascertain.

The very methods upon which some of the simplest of them are constructed show us their origin as childish comments based upon their listening to the adults in the past. One of the most frequent is to say everything backwards, or to reverse the meaning with the addition of negatives or their withdrawal. Thus either the last syllable of the word is put first and the remainder stay as they are, or negation takes the place of affirmation all the time. A very conscientious and clever young person, possibly one who may also be troubled with compulsions, may take the pains to transpose from back to front every syllable and sometimes each letter. But this is complicated in the treatment of long words, and is not very practicable for rapid transmission of thoughts. It has also the additional disadvantage that it is not readily understood by the receiver of the message, who may ask for an explanation or start to argue whether it has been done correctly, which often gives away the secret to listeners. But the principle is clear enough. This is that the first shall be last and the last first. Everything changes places, and becomes the other way round, typifying, amongst other things, the wish of the child and adolescent to change places with the grown-ups, and to make the adult listen helplessly, unable to understand when the young folk talk secrets.

Another of the chief methods is equally built up on the experiences of the past. To the child, the adult using a foreign language or even long words in the mother tongue is unintelligible. The words sound twice as long, extra complicated. And once again the adolescent secret code makes a caricature of adult language heard by the child who cannot understand. Every word will consequently be made extravagantly long; sometimes the prolongation is accomplished by the repetition of one or more of its inside syllables, sometimes by the addition of some special prefix or affix to each word, or one may be incorporated near the accented syllable of the word. By some of the most used additional syllables the words will be given quite a foreign sound and have a misleading effect, until one has caught the knack of speaking in this way too, and of understanding what the other says with a fair amount of ease. There are many other ways of inventing languages of this sort, and various adolescents proceed differently in regard to them.

Some will prefer to make their own. Others adopt one ready-made from a special friend, girl or boy, but both conditions occur, for reasons of individualism or identification, such as we described in the last chapter.

This love of secrecy or disguise is usually particularly strong in the adolescent girl. We have already mentioned it once or twice connected with the attraction of a secret friend. It appears once more in the prevalent interest taken by the young girl in dressing-up and acting, which, after all, is but the disguising oneself as another. We often find that when acting a girl becomes far less inhibited and is able to accomplish much that she would never be able to carry through without the disguise and the borrowed personality.

It takes away her self-consciousness, because she has for the time being lost that self in whom she has so little confidence, and she takes over that of the other person whom she represents by means of identification with the part. For this reason the girl should derive a great deal of valuable help as well as enjoyment from theatricals or dramatic work, unless she is too much inhibited to do so, or lacks imagination to such an extent that she is quite unable to feel herself into the character of another.

This subject is closely associated with the secret life which the girl leads in the world of her phantasies. This will of course vary in degree from the occasional use of them to supply her need for romance and consolation, when the gratification of her impulse requirements derived from reality is more threadbare than she can tolerate, to almost complete turning away from the world of reality into one of her own making. This may happen fairly frequently during adolescence; but although it often begins then, or perhaps even shows traces in childhood, it usually only reaches a stage at which it becomes recognised later on, when adolescence should rightly be terminating and giving place to maturity. The condition is one of extreme gravity, and calls for expert medical advice as soon as the least suspicion should cross the mind of those who are accustomed to the phenomena of adolescence that all is not well with the girl. Some other related signs will be that she seeks her own society more profoundly than she used to do, showing intense irritability when she is disturbed, sleeps more than usually heavily, and turns away from all her old interests connected with the environment and friends, spending her days wandering aimlessly about the house or garden, or sitting quietly and silently gazing into space.

If we were able to discover what thoughts were occupying her mind meanwhile, they might be altogether vague and nebulous, or centre round the idea that she was a princess or a queen, living upon a solitary enchanted island, in a cave of impenetrable darkness or in some far-off fairyland, where few things happened to disturb her unruffled peace. These are the beginnings or early symptoms of adolescent insanity or *dementia præcox*, which offers little hope of cure unless it is treated immediately and very carefully.

From this warning, however, one does not mean that alarm should be felt for the mental health of every adolescent who seeks the compensation of weaving phantasies at some time or other during these troublous years. Should this be so, our whole girl population would be in the most serious danger. It is a perfectly normal pastime, in moderation, and one that may often act as a safety-valve to protect the girl from too great deprivations. The phantasies will frequently furnish her also with emotional outlets which her impulses need to form strong and healthy transitions from childhood to maturity.

Phantasies may well be called food for the soul of the adolescent girl. It is only when she indulges in too much, and in those of a mentally indigestible kind, without the steadying effects of some compensations streaming in upon her from the side of reality, that they are harmful or cause an impoverishment of her mental welfare. We might say the same thing in relation to her diet. Everyone would agree that the adolescent girl needs food of all kinds rightly and adequately to nourish every part of her body and build up all her tissues as well as her brain. She does not only require the good plain fare of the old-fashioned nursery to nourish her body. That was totally devoid of interest or variety. She needs both variety and interest supplied by different ways of serving her viands in order to stimulate her appetite, which will serve to increase her digestive action, and so add to the nutritive values of the food she consumes, so benefiting mind and body as well.

So with her phantasies, which represent real nourish-

ment for her mind during the strain of adolescent development, just as their products take the same place during the
years to come. What purposes, we may ask, can the phantasy
serve besides providing her with a refuge in times of distress,
with consolation and the discharge for her emotions and
impulses? Running the risk, perhaps, of emulating Mrs.
Markham, let us try to give an answer to this important
question. They will, in many instances, point out the way
the girl's ambition will take in the future, because she will
often try to put her phantasy into reality. They will, should
she allow them to escape from the early secrecy with which
she has disguised them, probably because of some guilty
feeling attached to the subject of her phantasy, make them
the theme upon which she may construct some artistic,
creative work. Out of the early or adolescent phantasy
frequently come books, plays, or other works of art, released
from their private hiding-places, and turned once again to
the service of the public for their enjoyment and interest,
instead of being only the preoccupation of a solitary child
or adolescent.

Dr. Hanns Sachs gives us a vivid account of the apotheosis of the phantasy in his most interesting book, *Gemeinsame Tagträume.* He tells us how we may trace the path
of the phantasy through various, often clearly defined
stages. In childhood it will appear as a game or as a story
which the children love to hear told to them over and over
again, and afterwards act for all to see. They are not in the
least self-conscious about it then, and will not try to hide
it. All may share in it and enjoy it, without being apparently
aware that it contains any element connected with things
forbidden or guilty. But as the child grows older, we notice
there is a tendency to limit the number of persons taking
part in the game. It will no longer be free to all comers; those
who participate will be a small and chosen group of close
friends, perhaps only two or three.

The suggestion of something that is not suitable to share with everybody begins to creep in. There will be clearer indications that the game is providing some gratification for the primary impulses of those who take part in it. We find love and hate, jealousy and death represented. Great victories over the rival take place, and heroic actions are performed by the chief character who will be the leader of the group, be it boy or girl; and the idea gathers weight that were a grown-up person to see it the game would call forth their derision or prohibition.

Time goes on, and when next the phantasy comes to our notice a great change in the themes and their representation will probably have taken place. We rediscover it as a solitary day-dream of the adolescent, kept secret unless told to a special friend after the lights are out at bedtime, or brought forth written in an exercise-book, where it has been copied out laboriously on half-holidays, or in spare moments during an especially dull lesson. Here it is beginning to turn outwards to the world again, finding an outlet in a rudimentary literary form, seeking an audience of one or a few whom, it may be assumed, will understand what it hopes to express, because it is felt or known that this other human being has experienced feelings of a similar kind. This is the essence of artistic creation; the rendering into a communicative form of some phantasy of human experience or emotion. It passes its early stages in secrecy, and later comes to birth *sometimes* as a work of art.

We should recall in this connection that special type of phantasy mentioned in the last chapter as *Pseudologia Phantastica*, where the girl weaves a tale of adventure or romance, that she passes on to her school-friends as the truth in order to win their admiration or as compensation for great unhappiness, as well as a sense of inferiority.

What may be its fate if it should not find some expression of this kind, because not every adolescent who is the weaver of day-dreams and a maker of phantasies achieves fame as creator of works of art in any form, although very few have not tried to do something of this sort during this surging period of development?

It will determine the owner's preference for books, plays and pictures, or the artistic efforts of others, causing them to feel more interest in one subject than another, in whatever form it may be found. Artistic appreciation is the outcome of the phantasy as well as achievement. The choice of a business or profession, the seeking out of a satisfactory method of living one's life, will be as much the result and outcome of the phantasy as those which we have already described.

Crime or delinquency will be other methods, not so satis- factory, of trying to put the phantasy into reality. They will be the expression of different forms of the component instincts once again, because practically all crime and misdemeanours, especially those for which our adolescents get themselves into trouble with the law and authorities, are an attempt to find outlets for their component instincts, that succeed in doing so in an asocial form. How this comes about is frequently a matter of individual deprivations and an individual selection of a form of gratification forced into reality, or an attempt to do so, rather than allowing it to be discharged in phantasy. This, therefore, being the case, in order to spare our adolescents the need of having to seek outlets for their emotions in reality through crime, and what is technically known as delinquency, we should strive, with all the opportunities of which organisations dealing with the young are capable, to offer them similar instinctual gratifications, but in a socially accepted form. They require substitute ways of gaining their compensation through phantasy externalised in forms of artistic creations, drama, literary efforts or reading, in games or in any other ways that will serve as channels to drain off the surplus energy of active adolescent emotions, so that tension caused by repressions, which allow of no discharge, do not accumulate until they become so intense, so pent up, that they have no other course than to seek the fulfilment of their needs in asocial ways.

One of the greatest stimuli for the production of phantasies during adolescence is sudden deprivation of other normal outlets of emotion. The human being always tries to attain natural compensation whenever possible, either in connection with physical deprivation or weakness, or a psychological one that is related to the emotions. In this way it—the human organism—tries to regain its physical balance by means of assimilation, the conquest of the invading danger, or the healing of an internal injury. Given the opportunity or the strength to do so, it will usually be accomplished in course of time, provided the threatening danger or actual injury is not too great, the time available for re-establishment not too short, or the counteracting handicaps too great.

The phantasy will provide many ways of assimilating psychological dangers or injuries to living human beings. The dangers that may be presented at the critical time of adolescence may be sudden changes in the home-life, such as those caused by the death, serious illness, or divorce of one or other of the parents. They cause great alterations in the home conditions to which the girl has previously been used: personal illness, grief, or disappointment. We will frequently notice that such shocks, which occur during the adolescent years, leave a far greater impression than those which happen either in the later years of childhood or when adolescence is past and the personality has a greater stability with which it may cope with difficulties impinging upon her from without, because by this time the internal conflicts which have been troubling her heretofore, ought to have reached some sort of satisfactory resolution.

One of the most serious troubles that can happen to the

girl of this age is certainly the disintegration of her home. She is, of course, already preparing psychologically to loosen her hold upon it, and her need of its protection is gradually lessening in normal cases. We have mentioned that she is often extremely impatient of family rules and regulations, it is true. From these signs we may often imagine that freedom from the old home might be welcomed by her growing wishes for independence and liberty. Yet when her chance comes, and the opportunity is forced upon her, we usually do not see her making the most of it. It shows her now the other side of the picture, makes her feel her extreme need for the help and protection of home, and its value as a background, to which she can always return at times of difficulty, when her growing wings do not feel quite strong enough to battle alone against the pressure of circumstance.

The death of one of the parents, or heavy financial losses, which may mean that the home of her childhood has to be broken up and her plans for the future changed, often seem seriously to threaten her psychological stability. She wishes to grow away from her home, but to be able to do it gradually and of her own accord, not to be forced out into the world because there is no longer a home to shelter her. She finds it difficult to settle down to the new plans which become necessary for her future, and life shows itself doubly grim and disconsolate. She may have to go to a new school, where the fees are not so high, and will often react to the change as though it were some indication of personal disgrace. She hates her new surroundings in consequence, the teachers and the girls, remaining aloof from them and unhappy, quite unable to feel herself part of the fresh atmosphere. Mentally she fails to assimilate the altered conditions because they are repugnant to her, and she spends her time longing to return to the time when her life seemed so easy and comfortable.

In retrospect, the old state of affairs seems happy and

ideal, although when these conditions were her daily life she was always wishing to escape from them. Should she be given her choice of making her new plans, we often find her at a loss what to do next. Given the opportunity of setting out to make her own way with what help her relations or friends can offer her under these straightened circumstances, she does not know what to do, in spite of the fact that before she may always have been weaving phantasies of what she would prefer if only she was free to do as she liked. Now the time has come to make her choice she cannot do so.

This may be partly owing to the inherent difficulty for the average girl to bring herself to make important decisions respecting her affairs, for reasons we have already shown, and partly also due to the effect which the shock has had upon her. Whatever the catastrophe has been, it has gravely disturbed her emotional ties to her parents, and her former love or hatred of them makes it increasingly difficult for her to accommodate herself to the new stage of life, now to be lived without one parent who may have been especially dear to her, and maybe act as the companion of the one whom she may never have liked. She may, in fact, have actively hated the one who is left. But even should the tragedy be the other way round, that the parent for whom she has always entertained feelings of rivalry and hatred is the one who has died, she can often not enjoy being now left in sole possession of her favourite, as we might have imagined would have been the case. Her old feelings of rivalry and hatred will nearly always awaken her guilt, with the realisation that her wishes have come true. She has, indeed, now become free of this parent whom she has so often wished out of her way, but the consequent guilt derived from these conscious or unconscious death-wishes will prevent her being able peacefully to enjoy what she has so ardently longed for, perhaps all her life.

There is another family tragedy which may occasionally

come upon the adolescent girl. This is the divorce or separation of her parents. It is always a grave problem, especially from the aspect of the effect it may have upon the children of this marriage. The strained relationship between the parents, however, which probably existed before this step was taken, was not for many reasons a satisfactory or happy atmosphere for the psychological development of children of any age; but adolescents will perhaps feel the conditions still more acutely, since they are better able to understand what is going on around them. It is impossible for them not to realise what is the situation at home. The mother is most likely to tell her growing daughter something of her difficulties, even if she does not take her completely into her confidence, occasionally working off her feelings of grievance towards her husband extensively, to draw her over to her side, and alienate her from the father, should the girl have always been his favourite.

This naturally puts the girl into an extremely difficult position, and plunges her into an emotional conflict about having to side with one or the other. She is brought up suddenly against problems of the rights and wrongs of the situation between her parents, which becomes inevitably tangled up with her personal feelings and preferences. This causes her in itself the greatest sorrow and anxiety, because she may have loved both of her parents in various ways. The actual separation of the parents, the arrangements which are made concerning herself, will all increase her difficulties. Where or with whom she will live in the future becomes a question that may assume even more acute conflict than that which will arise in the case of the death of one parent. Will she be allotted to the father or the mother, which will give her the presence of the one she loves best or the one she dislikes, may be the same trouble as in the former case, but now it has an element of choice about it that instead of helping hinders, because even if the choice in some cases should rest with her she finds it hard openly to choose to live with one parent and to renounce the other, while an arrangement to spend half the time with the one and half with the other offers complexities from the point of view of her feelings of loyalty respecting both.

We may often see that an unhappy marriage finds its chief battle-ground where the affections and possession of the children are concerned. The parents' reactions and their treatment of the sons and daughters will depend largely upon their feelings, either temporarily or permanently disturbed, where the adolescent is concerned. They may each struggle to capture the affections of the children, either concentrating upon a few or all. If some only, it will be sometimes that the main attempt is made to divert love that is being given already to the other parent, or to adopt affection which seems to be going begging. But in any case, this attitude in the home is disastrous for the welfare of the children or adolescents. We may see also the element of revenge among the various other reactions. One parent will try to be avenged upon the other by unkindness or special harsh treatment of the favourites of the other, and so on.

The adolescent daughter cannot but feel insecure in such an atmosphere, and we will find that it gradually undermines her psychological health. She needs the greatest exterior stability around her, during the time when her own transitional conflicts give her so much internal instability to contend with.

This temperamental wave of insecurity which sweeps over the girl and often arouses quite unfounded feelings of uncertainty concerning her home and the relationships of her parents, and even doubts about her parentage, which have no foundation whatever, frequently revives phantasies which she may have had as a child concerning her birth, related to the foster-child phantasies which we have described. It is a no uncommon discovery to make that a very high percentage of children and adolescents suffer acutely from the other side of the day-dream—the fear that they are not the real offspring of their parents or were born out of wedlock. Yet, in considering these fears and anxiety-situations of the adolescent, it is not wise always to take them at their face value. Because we have found in a very great many instances that the *conscious* fear frequently covers an *unconscious* wish. Freud pointed it out to us many years ago now. At the time it was a discovery that caused a mass of stubborn opposition, although many people have proved it for themselves from their experience after the possibility had once been put before them.

The suspicions which the girl finds so disturbing, that she may be an adopted child or born before the marriage of her parents, may be entirely unfounded, but all the same the ideas of the girl often suggest a very deeply repressed hostile or negative attitude to one or other of the parents, if not towards both of them. But upon occasions, of course, these impressions may be partially if not entirely true. Something of the sort may be *quite true*, and there may be some mystery about the birth and parentage of the girl which does not apply to the other children in the household, although they all pass as one family.

Strangely enough, when it gains fairly wide acceptance that the period of adolescence presents difficulties to the girl, it will be decided that now she is growing up it is the time to tell her anything of this sort which may have occurred in the past. Or perhaps she may find it out by accident, or from the casual remark of some friend of the family who has not known that the girl has been brought up entirely ignorant of the state of affairs.

This sudden shattering of her whole conception of her environment usually has the most terrible consequences, although in some cases the girl seems to take the news calmly enough. Various results may follow the realisation

s

of the truth according to the psychological make-up of the girl, as well as her feelings and love-fixations towards these persons, whom she has always regarded as father and mother. Heavy tempests of mixed emotions sweep over her, and she needs help sorely to get her safely to some firm ground upon the other side of her catastrophe.

The manner of telling the girl this terrific truth, or even the apparent casual letting out the secret inadvertently, often seems to have been an act of sadistic revenge upon the part of the person responsible, especially if he or she should decide that this is the time when it should be told, and thinks out carefully the more or less brutal method of doing so which is employed. It is certain that there are few more cruel wounds that could be given to any girl than this, although apparently done thoughtlessly, or again, with the best *conscious* intentions of the teller of the news.

We may be able usually to trace the consequences of the shock throughout her subsequent life. She feels under some cloud from which she finds it impossible to get free. She will feel that everyone will know about it and not want to have anything more to do with her, or that they have always known, and that is why they treated her differently from the rest. She wonders why *she* has been kept in ignorance when everyone else knew her shame. She will probably never forgive her parents unconsciously, although the affair may be patched up between them consciously, and we find it colouring her life in the future in many most profound ways. One of these is usually that it will make it exceptionally difficult for her to make friends with strangers, to continue her old friendships, and to consent to consider anyone as a marriage-partner, because on the one hand she feels that they would spurn her if they knew; she dare not marry without telling her secret, in case it might be found out later with the most awful consequences, and yet she cannot bring herself to disclose her shame and humiliation.

CHAPTER IV

HOW WE MAY HELP OR HINDER THE ADOLESCENT

In this chapter one has to run the risk of repeating what a good many people who have been connected for many years with the problems of adolescent girls feel they know, and yet, when one watches them at work or hears them talking about these girls one realises that in practice they forget what they may know in theory.

One of our greatest difficulties, which presents itself to those whose own adolescence now lies a good way back into the past, is the tendency to let slip the simple fact that where externals are concerned the adolescent of to-day is a totally different being from what we were. Yet we have said that fundamentally she remains the same psychologically. Are we to consider this a mistake or a contradiction? It would seem from the experience of their troubles, or at least a great many of them, that it is neither. The troubles arising from failure to find realisation in the environment for unconscious wishes remain the same to-day as yesterday, as well as those caused by the fact that the girl in whatever age she may live will discover corresponding problems awaiting her, because there is so much to learn about the future from actual experience which she does not know already. This remains the same, comparatively speaking, however much she has in her childhood, which would be actually in advance of what former generations knew.

The prevailing idea that the adolescent has a far more easy time now than she had a few generations ago, because she has more freedom, is erroneous. Her freedom has increased, it is true, but it will give her an increased personal responsibility than when her parents took this entirely upon their own shoulders. In its turn also the responsibility requires a far greater knowledge of the ways of the world and a keener faculty for discriminating between the people who can be trusted and those who may not; the things which may be done safely and those from which it will be wiser to refrain, than in the old days. Then she merely lived her life, carrying out the minute instructions and obeying every wish of her parents.

In many respects one is forced to the conclusion that a large number of these young people we try to help know much more about their own present-day world and its problems than we do. So that when we try to rush in with advice, kindly and well-meant, maybe, from our own experience of some thirty or forty years ago, we may see a gentle smile flit across their faces. They may be tolerant and good-natured about it, but must often feel that we are rather behind the times.

One of the greatest advantages that we can still offer a young girl, however, who is going through this transition, finding life thick with problems which she finds difficult to think out or work through by herself, is to put ourselves and our *ears* at her disposal. To listen to her sympathetically, with interest, and not to offer her unasked-for advice or criticism, will be one of the greatest boons she can have. It will be a help to her in many ways to find someone who does not tell her not to be so introspective or so self-centred when she is struggling to put her complicated thoughts into words. She can see so much more clearly what it is that is troubling her, or what she cannot make up her mind about, when she tells someone else about it, who may be relied upon not to belittle the worry or to tell her what she ought to do. She wants to make up her own mind, not to have it made up for her without being able to reason out the whys and wherefores—if she is worth her salt, that is to say.

It will be a help to her, too, if she feels that we believe her to be a sensible person and capable of reasoning out a problem if she is only given the time and opportunity to do so. This suggestion that she is capable of using her judgment will help her far more than merely giving her a dose of exaggerated sympathy, such as one might to a very small child. Of course there are plenty of adolescent girls who love to play at being the baby still, and appeal to the sentimental element in older women. They will easily find one who is ready to respond to this call for help, and consent to be made an external conscience. The girl then goes to her for advice upon everything, from what she shall put on for a party, what books to read, how a letter shall be answered, to what sort of face cream or powder is the best, and if she is old enough to use a lip-stick. Upon this last matter the girl herself may be more competent to give an answer than the friend, but she knows she will be flattered at being consulted about it.

This is often one of the main roots of the difficulty. The friend is very much flattered by the girl treating her as a confidential adviser upon everything, and plays up to the adolescent at her most *little girl* manifestation, rather than try to help her on towards real maturity by showing her how to make up her mind for herself, and pointing out that she generally knows what to do and what she ought to wear if she thinks about it. But she likes at the same time to save herself some trouble, gain precious reassurance and some pretty compliments as well, through asking questions and listening to the answers to them.

The adolescent girl greatly appreciates being able to come to someone to whom she can talk, with whom she can exchange ideas upon what she is beginning to discover about books, people, plays, and LIFE. The last, above all, thrills her profoundly, and she is grateful to find someone who will listen to her new views without constantly interrupting her with her opinions.

We may help the girl so much by putting opportunities for new experiences in her way and then leaving her to discover them for herself, rather than showing them to her. She will rejoice at being able to cry "Eureka!" and afterwards remember for a long time her feelings when she suddenly came upon this something new, which she has never known, seen, or appreciated before. To be able to realise the value of something *new* outside herself and her own experiences will add much to the breadth of the girl's mental development. With a little thought we can give her this delight of discovery without much trouble to ourselves, and enjoy it once again in her company afterwards.

It is difficult sometimes to go back and remember our excitement when we first discovered something that was quite fresh to us, and how it seemed to open out a new world or at least allowed us to peep over the edge of our former experience, at a further horizon, and to dream of yet another beyond that. When we are young there are so many unknown horizons, but we may not be adventurous enough to explore them without help of some kind. If we once are put in the way of reaching out to them we will never want to leave off exploring, in order to gain one more thrill of discovery. This tends to keep us young much more surely than the ministrations of the most skilful beauty specialist. We grow old when we can no longer assimilate fresh ideas or take an interest in anything we have never known before, once said someone who was wise. It is true, and we visibly start to grow old directly we cease to take any interest in things that are new and strange.

Hence the adolescent's curiosity and keen desire to know and to find out should be encouraged not only in theory but also in practice. We may get weary of her questions sometimes, and want to suggest that she looks up the answers in a book. Her enthusiasm and vitality sometimes exhaust us. Her endless questions annoy us upon occasions, because were we to speak the truth we should have to confess that we do not know the answers. She has thought of questioning something that we have always taken for granted. We have become so familiar with it that we have ceased to wonder about it, and we find it irritating that she has found us out.

We do not like to tell her we do not know. Because it is a well-worn habit to believe that the older one grows the more we know, and that we must of necessity be wiser than others, because we were born so many years ahead of them. We cling to this tradition whenever we can, just as we find so many clutching at the old tradition that one must never tell one's age to the young folks. Why should one not? They would not be so eager to find out this secret if we did not make it such a mystery. And yet it is one of the first questions that some adults ask of adolescents in order to start the conversation, because they tell us they find it so hard to think of anything to say to "girls of this age."

It is a strange thing that so many quite intelligent, pleasant people become afflicted with paralysis of their speech centres and reduced to a condition bordering upon senile insanity should it become necessary for them to converse socially with an adolescent girl for the space of some five minutes or half an hour. They will beforehand, if possible, implore one not to leave them alone with her, or ask helplessly what they should say to her. What can they talk about? But why talk to her any differently from anyone else? She is not a tiny child who, sometimes one does discover to one's chagrin, can only converse in a strange jargon of its own, which it shares with mother or nurse, and that one really does need an interpreter before communication of ideas is possible. But the adolescent girl will probably look upon one with eternal gratitude if one treats her like any other person of our acquaintance, and talks to her about exactly the same things in the same way. She gets so bored with being regarded as something different from the rest of human beings, or a person who must be talked down to. She hates to feel that people are making allowances for her or her age, or assuming that she is peculiar in some way.

We do not want, if possible, to make the adolescent feel more shy and self-conscious because of our attitude to her. In some ways there is always a danger of this happening if we begin to take a good deal of notice of any special circumstance in her daily life. We may magnify her problems, and through the suggestive influence of our solicitude increase the difficulty. For this reason we should try to steer a middle course between thinking that there is no problem at all, where the psychological development of the adolescent girl is concerned, and the extreme opposite view that she is one mass of them.

A book of this description may be misleading for this reason. In calling attention to this, that, and the other difficulty which arises in certain types of adolescent girl, one finds it necessary to point out from time to time that *every girl* does not suffer from *all* the troubles which are described; that there are a great number who luckily escape practically all of them, or we may only find a small amount of one or two affect them in the least. In writing about these questions it would seem more necessary to pay the greatest attention to the troubles than the unclouded happiness, giving suggestions as to their causes and possible ways of avoiding them in the future or trying to counteract the harm that has been done in the past. We may say "Happy the kingdom that has no history." Does the same apply to the girl? Her adolescence is the happier for being uneventful, if it be true that it can ever be.

We cannot go on blindly hoping that, because everyone does what she imagines is for the best, these old ways of educating and helping the adolescent girl are the only ones that can be devised, now and henceforward. All methods need overhauling from time to time to see whether they may not have become superannuated, and if they are still adequate for the work they are intended to perform. We can be too optimistic as well as too pessimistic. The feeling of "All's right with the world" may be a painfully dangerous one if we shut our eyes and believe it will always hold good in spite of the lapse of time. It is not wise to found all our belief upon the theory that things worked well enough in the past, girls managed to grow up into useful women before, and there were always some outstanding ones amongst them without all this fuss and worry. Why should we bother to think about all these newfangled ways of dealing with them now? Some managed well enough in the past, it is true, but what of the others?

Yes, certainly a great many of them grew up to be most excellent women, but how many fell by the wayside and never grew up at all? How many were hindered in their development so that they never achieved anything worth while, not even their own health and happiness, nor those of others around them—who became warped because of their overwhelming difficulties, warping others in their turn, just because something that might have been done was considered unnecessary fuss or was never thought of at all? It was taken for granted in those days that a girl was likely to be rather odd and peculiar, but that she would get over it. But then, in those days, it was also taken for granted that a woman was hysterical just because she *was* a woman, and no one thought her condition could be helped either.

"Vocational Guidance" is a subject which has come to the fore with startling rapidity during the past few years, especially in regard to the placing of adolescents in business or ascertaining what career they are most fitted for. A few specialised tests, a short examination by one or two complete strangers of varying proficiency or ability, and a personality which may or may not contribute helpfully to gain what is wanted, and the girl's fate is sealed. She shall be trained for this or that occupation because of the findings of the psychologist on that particular day and hour; or over a few separate days, should the tests be carried out in sections over a series of days. We know that a great deal *can* be discovered concerning the personality of the girl at a glance, but one would have thought that there was a great deal that should be taken into consideration beyond that which can be discovered in such a brief acquaintanceship, before deciding a weighty problem of this description such as her future career.

One of the requirements which does not seem to find a place in this mental testing is some method of ruling out the variability caused by the personality of the person carrying out the tests in conjunction with that of the examinee. The adolescent girl particularly is inclined to be influenced profoundly by her contacts with others. She wonders all the time what they are thinking of her, and tries to ascertain what this may be. What she feels their attitude to be will greatly influence her performance, and must affect the results of the tests. It is open to question, however, whether this cause of variability or its existence has ever been tested, if it has ever been proved whether all of a large percentage of girls tested by certain persons give results that do not in any way show the effect of the personality or mood of the person testing. Because it may well happen, especially if the psychologists applying the tests be women, that their moods at different times during the month may not have an appreciable result upon the findings. If so, we cannot remember seeing any reference to it in any paper upon mental testing.

Once this question was put to a lecturer upon this subject. Her first reaction was to appear unable to grasp its purport. She replied that no psychologist was allowed to apply tests until she was considered sufficiently trained to be able to do so correctly. By this answer it was evident that it had been assumed that technical skill in giving the tests had been meant, and the psychological influence of the personal quality or temperament of the psychologists must always have been overlooked, because it did not occur at all as a possibility to the lecturer as a point for discussion.

We might, indeed, be able to sum up the psychology of a girl to some extent from any detail of her appearance, for instance, from the apparently insignificant matter of her shoe-laces. It is easy to distinguish the girl always in a hurry, who kicks off her shoes without untying them, so that the laces are always in knots when she comes to put them on next time. There is the girl who has very little energy for any muscular exertion, perhaps because it is completely bestowed upon the invention of day-dreams. She can never tie them firmly enough to ensure them from working loose. They always come undone, so that she runs the risk of tripping over them, and wonders why. We may recognise the over-energetic girl, gaining so much pleasure from the exercise of her muscles that she pulls the strings too tightly and they break. Then they will be knotted together anyhow and tied in a short bow. We know by like signs the meticulously neat girl, the anyhow girl, the artistic girl, the individualistic girl, who tries to find an original way of tying them up, and many more, from the way she deals with this detail of her apparel.

There are countless other rather more complicated characteristics which we may also compute, as well as a still deeper interpretation of them, from any one item of the girl's clothing. It does not need years of study or scientific research to teach us the simple facts about them, although the more intricate ones do require an individual investigation of the matter from materials supplied by the girl herself, both from the conscious layer of her mind as well as being dredged up from her unconscious stores of memories and secret wishes. Some, it is true, can be derived from direct or most rudimentary observation and common sense. But we should always bear in mind that the adolescent girl possesses these faculties as well as we. She is usually also as critical as she is observant, and if we spend a good deal of time and interest in making a careful study of her ways we may be sure that she pays us the return compliment of summing up our failings and peculiarities.

The adolescent girl is, without question, keenly critical of others, especially of her elders, although she may not always be so about herself and her own doings. It is another method of turning the tables, and often shows how much she dislikes the constant criticism of her elders. But of course we must remember that, whereas it is considered to be only right and proper for the adults openly to criticise the girl at all times and in all places, it is an understood rule that the girl should never criticise the grown-ups, at any rate not so that she can hear or know anything about it. That would be considered the height of bad taste on her part.

This will not prevent her exercising her critical faculty upon them, nevertheless, although it may take place in the company of her brothers and sisters, or other friends of a similar age. In this way she derives a certain amount of compensation for their criticism of her, which she finds so painful. It is interesting, however, to notice the effect that her *unspoken criticism* may have upon adults. Without one word being said, her critical attitude will penetrate their complacency and contrive to make them feel rather foolish. They, in their turn, try to hide it by patronising her, and treating her as a child in the attempt to get the balance even. Or they become annoyed and nervous, floundering about hopelessly, going from bad to worse, leaving the critical young girl cool and perfectly self-possessed, feeling that, after all, the grown-ups are not very superior after all.

The girl weighs up her relations and friends in an exacting balance, especially upon points where she receives censure from them, and acts upon the results of her findings. She is usually fairly just, this critical young person of to-day, although inclined to be pitiless in judging adults by the same standards they apply to her. She allows no quarter. Frequently the more she likes people the more critical she will be, and makes a very high demand upon those whom she accepts as her friends and ideals. If she really likes a person, however, she may in some cases be as blind as anyone else to the one she loves, and pass over any number of faults which would damn others completely in her eyes should they have met with her displeasure.

It is interesting to note the adolescent's attitude to any person, a woman especially, who is considerably older than herself, if she feels that she is not adequately filling the post to which she is appointed—that is, if she will be frank with us and tell us her opinion without any concessions to our feelings. For example, a young girl in early adolescence was once asked what she wanted to do when she left school. She thought for a few moments, then said slowly and very carefully: She would not like to be a school-teacher. One would grow so old and uninteresting. One would look so dull and wear ugly clothes. It would be so awful to go on teaching the same thing to different children over and over again, and never get any farther. Directly you had finished with one lot and felt you had taught them something, you went back and started all over again with another. You never did anything else, and never got away from the same little circle. Teachers grew so old, and their minds seemed always to stand still in the same place, just as they went on teaching the same things to children of one age all the time.

This seems rather a wonderful criticism of a teacher of a certain type from one of her pupils, who evidently did not want to use her for the purposes of identification and develop in imitation of her. It was probably perfectly correct, even if a little more merciless than one of her own contemporaries or a senior in her own profession would have dared to have made it. But then it is difficult to see one's faults or those of one's fellows professionally. But all the same one cannot but regret that it should be possible for such an observation to have come from one of the girls who has the opportunity to observe her constantly, to watch her characteristics, and to know that they are quite true of this certain type.

The indictment is serious. A girl does not want to be a teacher because she has identified a type with the profession and is afraid that should she join this profession she will eventually approximate to this type, which she has observed grow more old and unable to move out of one rut than others. She wants to keep her youth and freshness, and therefore does not want to become what we might have considered a leader of youth, who ought essentially through her work to retain her freshness by keeping in touch with so much that was always changing and new, so that she could not get old in the way that this girl described. But if we read the point of view of the teacher, put before us so graphically in *Unwillingly to School*, by Anne Allardice, and can endorse her statements by hearing many teachers of all ages about their work, they do get very tired of their teaching and learn in school to feel very old, especially at the end of term. Compared with the evidence of observation of the girl quoted above, there is not much amiss with her testimony after all.

Here once again we have a different aspect of the great factor of identification as a principle of education, but the reversed form of it, a few hints from the girl about what she does not want in her elders who are there as her patterns for the future. She needs someone from whom she takes her ideal, in the persons of her parents, her teachers, her older friends; someone with whom she can identify, someone who has trodden the path to maturity ahead of her, who can show her the way by letting her follow in her footsteps. This she will do gladly enough if the person attracts her. But she can be easily repelled by an unattractive example, much as she is only too frequently by her elders not adhering to the standards they set up for her. She knows well enough that they cannot really have a high estimation of these precepts they constantly reiterate if they do not adhere to them. What is the use of an elderly slovenly teacher, rather muddled in her views and untidy in her personal appearance, telling her pupils of the virtues of neatness and orderliness in ways and methods of thought. They will only criticise and laugh at her behind her back. Or the elderly spinster giving classes of adolescents instruction in mothercraft, and telling them that motherhood is the most noble calling for women. What *is* the use of it? The girl learns best by example. She wants to see the ideals put before her working out in someone else's life, before she is impressed by ocular demonstration whether they are worth while adopting or not.

This is our most grave responsibility to the coming generation, represented by the adolescent girls with whom we come in contact. They will look to us and sum up what sort of women they want to be or not by the kind of job we have made of it; comparing us with other women they have known, and from the point of view of their own present-day world as they know it. What else have they to go by? They can judge ideals and the possibilities of life through the personalities of those with whom they come in contact, whose lives have gained the experience of other environments.

BIBLIOGRAPHY

ABRAHAM, DR. KARL. Selected Papers on Psycho-analysis. Chapter XXII. Manifestations of the Female Castration Complex, 1920. Hogarth Press. 1926.
Einige Bemerkungen über den Mutterkultus und seine Symbolik in der Individual und Völkerpsychologie. Zentralblatt für Psychoanalyse. Jahrgang I. 1911. Heft 12.
Amenhotep IV. (Echnaton.) Psychoanalytische Beiträge zum Verständnis seiner Persönlichkeit und des monotheistischen Aton-Kultes. Imago. I. 1912, p. 334.
AGUILA, GRACE. Home Influence: A Tale for Mothers and Daughters. Groombridge & Sons. 1865.
AICHHORN, AUGUST. Verwahrloste Jugend. Int. Ps.-A. Verlag. Wien. 1925.
ALCOTT, LOUISA. Little Women and Good Wives.
ALEXANDER, DR. FRANZ. Kriminalogie, Int.Ps.-A. Verlag. Wien. 1930.
ALLARDICE, ANNE. Unwillingly to School. Benn Bros. 1930.
ANDERSEN, HANS. Fairy-tales. Trans. Mrs. H. B. Paul. Frederick Warne & Co. 1894.
ARBUTHNOT, MRS. P. STEWART-MACKENZIE. Queen Mary's Book. George Bell & Sons. 1917.
AUSTEN, JANE. Collected Novels. 5 vols. Oxford University Press. 1931.
BABEES BOOK, or a Little Report of How Young People Should Behave. 1475.
BAZELEY, E. T. Homer Lane and the Little Commonwealth. George Allen & Unwin. 1928.
BERNFELD, DR. SIEGFRIED. Vom Gemeinschaftsleben der Jugend. Int. Ps.-A. Verlag. 1922.
Sisyphos. Int. Ps.-A. Verlag. 1925.
BLANCHARD, PHYLLIS. The Care of the Adolescent Girl. Kegan Paul. 1921.
BLANCHARD, PHYLLIS, and CARLYN MENASSES. New Girls for Old. The Macauley Co. New York. 1930.
BOOTH, MEYRICK, B.Sc., Ph.D. Woman and Society. Longmans, Green & Co. 1929.
BRONNER, AUGUSTA F. The Intelligence of Delinquent Girls. 1914.
The Psychology of Special Abilities and Disabilities. Kegan Paul. 1919.
BROWN, S. CLEMENT. Some Case Studies of Delinquent Girls Described as Leaders. British Journal of Educational Psychology. Vol. I. Part II. 1931.

BRYHER. Civilians. Pool Publications. Territet. 1927.

BURNETT, FRANCES HODGSON. Sarah Crew. 1887.

The One I Loved the Best of All. 1904.

BURNEY, FRANCES. Evelina, or the History of a Young Lady's Entrance into the World. Thomas Lowndes. 1778.

Diary and Letters of Madame d'Arblay. Edited by Muriel Masefield. New edition. 1930.

BURT, CYRIL, M.A., D.Sc. The Young Delinquent. University of London Press. 1925.

CAMPBELL, HARRY, M.D., B.S.(Lond.). Differences in the Nervous Organisation of Man and Woman. H. K. Lewis. 1891.

CANTON, WILLIAM. Child's Book of Saints. Dent & Co. 1898.

CARROLL, LEWIS. Alice in Wonderland, and Alice Through the Looking Glass. Macmillan & Co., 1884.

CHADWICK, MARY. Difficulties in Child Development. George Allen & Unwin. 1928.

Nursing Psychological Patients. George Allen & Unwin. 1931.

Menstruationsangst. Zeitschrift für Psychoanalytische Pädagogik. Mai–Juni, 1931.

Case of Kleptomania in a Girl. J. of Ps.-A. 1926.

CHARLES, MRS. RUNDLE. Chronicle of the Schönberg-Cotta Family. T. Nelson & Sons. 1895.

COKKINIS, A. J. The Reproduction of Life. Baillière, Tindall & Cox. 1926.

COMENIUS. The School of Infancy. 1628.

The School of the Mother's Lap. 1633.

CUFF, HERBERT, and GORDON PUGH. Practical Nursing. Wm. Blackwood & Sons. 1927.

DAVID-NEEL, ALEXANDRA. With Mystics and Magicians in Tibet. John Lane. 1931.

My Journey to Lhasa. William Heinemann. 1927.

DAVIS, KATHARINE BEMENT, Ph.D. Factors in the Sex-Life of Twenty-Two Hundred Women. Harper Bros. 1929.

DEUTSCH, DR. HELENE. Psychoanalyse der Weiblichen Sexualfunctionen. Int. Ps.-A. Verlag. 1925.

Psychoanalyse der Neurose. Int. Ps.-A. Verlag. 1930.

Über die pathologische Lüge. (Pseudologia Phantastica.) Zeitschrift für Psychoanalyse. VIII. pp. 153–67. 1922.

DITCHFIELD, P. H., M.A., F.S.A. Old English Customs. George Redway. 1896.

DOUGLAS, SIR GEORGE. Scottish Fairy and Folk Tales. Walter Scott, Ltd. N.D.

EDGWORTH, MARIA. Early Lessons. Simpkin Marshall. 1801.

The Parent's Assistant. 1796.

Moral Tales. 1801.

EDUCATION, BOARD OF. Report on the Education of the Adolescent. 1926.

ELLIS, HAVELOCK. Studies in the Psychology of Sex. Vols. I–V. F. A. Davis Co. Philadelphia. 1908–15.

Sex in Relation to Society. Vol. VI. 1919.

FEHLINGER, H. Sexual Life of Primitive People. A. & C. Black. Trans. by S. Herbert and Mrs. Herbert. 1921.

FELDMAN, W. M., M.B., B.S.(Lond.). The Jewish Child. Baillière, Tindall & Cox. 1917.

FLÜGEL, J. C., D.Sc. The Psycho-Analytic Study of the Family. Hogarth Press. 1926.

The Psychology of Clothes. Hogarth Press. 1930.

FRAZER, SIR GEORGE. The Golden Bough. Macmillan. 1922.

FREUD, ANNA. Introduction to Psycho-analysis for Teachers. Trans. Barbara Low. George Allen & Unwin. 1931.

FREUD, PROF. SIGMUND. Collected Works. Hogarth Press. 1924.

"A Child is Being Beaten." Vol. II. 1924.

The Psychogenesis of a Case of Homosexuality in a Woman. Vol. II. 1924.

The Passing of the Œdipus-Complex. Vol. II. 1924.

Totem and Taboo. Kegan Paul. 1919.

GEORGE, W. L. The Story of Woman. Chapman & Hall.

GRIMM BROS. Popular Stories. Oxford University Press. 1909.

GROOS, KARL. The Play of Man. William Heinemann. 1901.

HALL, W. CLARKE. Children's Courts. George Allen & Unwin. 1926.

HALL, G. STANLEY, Ph.D., LL.D. Adolescence. Vols. I and II. D. Appleton & Co. 1911.

HAMBLY, W. D., B.Sc. Origins of Education Among Primitive Peoples. Macmillan & Co. 1926.

HARTLAND, EDWIN SIDNEY. English Fairy and Other Fairy Tales.

The Science of Fairy Tales. Walter Scott, Ltd. 1890.

HEALEY, WILLIAM. The Individual Delinquent. 1924.

Mental Conflicts and Misconduct. Little, Brown & Co. Boston. 1917.

HOGG, JAMES. The Poems of James Hogg. Kilmeny. Walter Scott, Ltd. 1887.

HOLLINGSWORTH, L. S. The Psychology of the Adolescent. 1929.

JAMESON, MRS. Legends of the Monastic Orders. Longmans, Green & Co. 1850.

JONES, ERNEST, M.D. Some Problems of Adolescence. British Journal of Psychology. General Section. July 1922.

JONES, ERNEST, M.D., WITH OTHERS. Social Aspects of Psycho-analysis. Williams & Norgate. 1924.

Significance of the Grandfather(mother) for the Fate of the Individual. Papers on Psycho-analysis. 1918.

LANG, ANDREW. The Maid of France. Being the Story of the Life and Death of Jeanne d'Arc. Longmans, Green & Co. 1908.
Blue, Red, Green, Yellow, Pink, Violet, etc. Fairy Books. Longmans, Green & Co.
LANG, MRS. ANDREW. Men, Women and Minxes. Longmans, Green & Co.
LEKKERKERKER, EUGENIA C. Reformatories for Women in the United States. J. B. Wolters. Hague. 1931.
LINDSEY, JUDGE BEN, with WAINWRIGHT EVANS. The Revolt of Modern Youth. Shaylor. 1928.
LOW, BARBARA, B.A. The Unconscious in Action. University of London Press. 1928.
MARETT, R. R., M.A., D.Sc. Psychology and Folklore. Methuen. 1919.
MARRYAT, CAPTAIN. Children of the New Forest. 1847.
MEAD, MARGARET. Coming of Age in Samoa. Jonathan Cape. 1929.
Growing-up in New Guinea. Routledge. 1931.
MENZIES, K. Auto-Erotic Phenomena of Adolescence. H. K. Lewis. 1919.
MICHESON, NAOMI. Cloud Cuckoo Land. Jonathan Cape.
MILLER, NATHAN. The Child in Primitive Society. Kegan Paul. 1928.
MURRAY, MARGARET ALICE. The Witch-cult in Western Europe. Oxford University Press. 1921.
NEWTON, THE LADY. Lyme Letters, 1660–1760. Heinemann. 1925.
The House of Lyme from its Foundation in the Reign of Richard II to the End of the Eighteenth Century.
OAKDEN, ELLEN, and MARY STURT. Growing-up. How One Did it in Different Times and Places. Kegan Paul. 1930.
PAYNE, MURIEL A. Oliver Untwisted. Edward Arnold. 1929.
PFISTER, OSKAR. Love in Children and its Aberrations. George Allen & Unwin. 1924.
RANK, DR. OTTO. The Myth of the Birth of the Hero. Trans. Nervous and Mental Disease Pub. Co. 1914.
RANK, DR. OTTO, with DR. HANNS SACHS. The Significance of Psychoanalysis for the Mental Sciences. Trans. Nervous and Mental Disease Pub. Co. 1916.
RICHMOND, WINIFRED, Ph.D. The Adolescent Girl.
RICKLIN, FRANZ. Wishfulfilment and Symbolism in Fairy-tales. Trans. Nervous and Mental Disease Pub. Co. 1915.
ROWLAND, EDITH. A Pedagogue's Commonplace Book. Dent. 1925.
RUSKIN, JOHN, LL.D. Sesame and Lilies. George Allen. 1901. 1871.
SACHS, DR. HANNS. Gemeinsame Tagträume. Int. Ps.-A. Verlag. 1924.
SACHS, DR. HANNS, with DR. OTTO RANK. The Significance of Psychoanalysis for the Mental Sciences. Trans. Nervous and Mental Disease Pub. Co. New York. 1916.
SANDS, IRVING J., M.D. Nervous and Mental Diseases for Nurses. W. B. Saunders Co. 1928.

BIBLIOGRAPHY 293

SEABROOK, W. B. Jungle Ways. Harrap. 1931.
SHAW, CLIFFORD R. The Jack Roller. University of Chicago Press. 1929.
The Natural History of a Delinquent Career. University of Chicago Press. 1931.
SHERWOOD, MRS. MARY M. The Fairchild Family. 1818.
SLAUGHTER, T. W. The Adolescent. George Allen & Unwin. 1911.
SMITH, HAMBLIN M. Juvenile and Adolescent Delinquency. The Child. July 1923.
SOSKICE, JULIET M. Chapters from Childhood. Selwyn & Blount. 1921.
STAËL, MADAME DE. Letters to Her Daughter.
THOMAS, ADRIENNE. Catherine Joins Up. Trans. Elkin Matthews. 1931.
UNDSET, SIGRID. Kristin Lavransdatter. Trans. pub. by Knopf. 1930.
VERNEY, FRANCES PARTHENOPE and MARGARET. Memoirs of the Verney Family. Vols. I, II, III. Longmans, Green & Co. Third ed. 1925.
VIERECK, GEORGE SYLVESTER, and PAUL ELDRIDGE. Salome, The Wandering Jewess. Duckworth. 1930.
WARNER, SUSAN. The Wide, Wide World (1850), and Queechy (1852).
WHEELER, OLIVE A. Variations in the Emotional Development in Normal Adolescents. British Journal of Educational Psychology. Vol. I. Part I. 1931.
WHITE, JENNINGS H. D. An Application of Mental Tests to University Students. British Journal of Educational Psychology. Vol. I. Part III. 1931.
WOOLEY, HELEN T. Agnes, A Dominant Personality in the Making. Ped. Sem. 1925. XXXII. 569.
WOOLF, VIRGINIA. A Room of One's Own. Hogarth Press. 1930.
The Waves. Hogarth Press. 1931.
YATES, W. B. Irish Fairy and Folk Tales. Walter Scott, Ltd. N.D.
YOUNG GIRL'S DIARY. George Allen & Unwin.

INDEX

Protection, 46, 269
Protector, 62
Protest, 42
Pseudologia Phantastica, or Patholo-
gical lying, 225, 234, 266
Psycho-analysis, 23
Psycho-analysts, 158
Psychologists, 23, 101, 228, 230, 235, 282
Puberty, 41, 100, 111, 117, 119, 126, 128, 132, 145, 153, 173, 187, 207, 208, 236
rites, 27, 29, 30, 33, 37, 41, 42, 52, 133
boys, 37, 38, 39, 133
girls, 37, 39, 45, 133, 236
Publicity, 28, 32
Punishment, 52, 77, 136, 137, 158, 162, 184, 220, 250

Quakers, 61; see also Society of Friends.
Quarrel, 156, 182, 199, 242
Queen, 50, 68, 264
Queen Anne, 87
Queen Elizabeth, 78, 84
Queen Mary's Book, 78
Queen Victoria, 94
Queen's Square, 87
Quest, 63
Questions, 31, 70, 120, 277, 278

Reaction, 41
Reactions, 28, 146
Readjustments, 239
Reality, 72, 80
Reassurance, 155, 277
Rebel, 140, 157, 198, 217, 218, 221
Rebellion, 106, 157, 169, 177, 219, 220
Re-birth phantasy, 27, 42, 46, 47, 134
Reconciliation, 241
Recreation, 232
Red-ridinghood, 53, 59
Relations, 48, 94, 245, 270, 284
Religion, 44, 49, 65, 68, 72, 166, 167
Repetition, 26, 29, 131, 132, 145, 187, 218, 234, 243
atavistic, 29
impulse of, 33
Repressions, 32, 33, 50, 139, 209, 234, 244, 268
Reproduction of Life, 116
Rescue, 59, 60, 72, 184
Rescuer, 59, 61
Resistance, 34, 220
Responsibility, 25, 29, 31, 42, 43, 149, 150, 157, 208, 275, 276, 287
Restlessness, 35
Restoration, 80
Restraints, 41, 43
Revenge, 272, 274
Revolt, 34
Rewards, 52, 54
Richard II, 70
Riddles, 32, 63
Ridicule, 42, 57, 139

Ritual, 27, 41, 47, 122
dances, 42
Rivals, 62, 64, 189, 204, 266
Roedean, 95
Romance, 57, 58, 71, 72, 97, 148, 235, 248, 263, 266
Rome, 70
Romeo and Juliet, 248
Rowland, Edith, 72
Royal Household, 74, 245
Rude or rudeness, 36, 142, 245
Rules, 31, 47

Sachs, Dr. Hanns, 265
Sacred and Legendary Art, 83, 84
Sacrifice, 49, 70, 72
virgin, 61, 196
Sadism, 158, 160, 237, 274
Safety-first, 103
Safety-valves, 27, 34, 178, 264
Salome—the Wandering Jewess, 125
Samoa, 40
Samplers, 90, 229
Sarah Crewe, 97
Savages, 43, 67, 159
Scholarship girls, 108, 237, 238
School of Infancy, 78
School of the Mother's Lap, 78
School-mistress, see Teachers.
Schools, 59, 89, 95, 106, 157, 169, 181, 200, 218, 220, 224, 226, 229, 235, 238, 239, 241, 252, 256, 269
boarding, 87, 119, 122, 218, 226
change of, 118, 235
School-days, 168, 180, 223, 229, 236
School-life, 167, 225, 232, 235
Scotland, 90, 92, 96, 186
Seclusion, 29, 38, 42
of puberty, 38, 40, 47, 48, 71, 123, 133
duration of, 45, 46
Second chance, 26
Secondary sexual characteristics, 114, 115, 116
Secrecy, 38, 234, 248, 262, 265, 266
Segregation, 45
Secretary, 80
Secret languages, 259, 260
Secrets, 48, 122, 141, 201, 207, 228, 248, 259, 260, 262, 274
Self-adornment, 123, 147, 148, 162
Self-confidence, 82, 144, 188
Self-consciousness, 139, 141, 142, 143, 164, 258, 263, 280
Self-control, 187, 188, 209
Self-expression, 28, 33, 79, 150, 163, 167
Seligman, Mrs., 40
Separation, 180, 181, 252
of parents, 269, 270, 271
Settlers, 51
Sex, 138, 154, 155, 156, 157, 202, 205, 244, 248, 249
Sexual desire, 254
feelings, 159, 160, 165, 166
information, 58
intercourse, 49, 50, 117, 194

GEORGE ALLEN & UNWIN LTD
LONDON: 40 MUSEUM STREET, W.C.1
CAPE TOWN: 73 ST. GEORGE'S STREET
SYDNEY, N.S.W.: WYNYARD SQUARE
AUCKLAND, N.Z.: 41 ALBERT STREET
TORONTO: 91 WELLINGTON STREET, WEST

For Product Safety Concerns and Information please contact our EU
representative GPSR@taylorandfrancis.com
Taylor & Francis Verlag GmbH, Kaufingerstraße 24, 80331 München, Germany